C. BUCHWALTER

Fixed
Income
Portfolio
Management

Fixed Income Portfolio Management

H. Gifford Fong
President
Gifford Fong Associates

Frank J. Fabozzi
Walter E. Hanson / Peat, Marwick, Mitchell
Professor of Business and Finance
Lafayette College

1985

DOW JONES-IRWIN
Homewood, Illinois 60430

ISBN 0-87094-245-X

Library of Congress Catalog Card No. 84–71127

Printed in the United States of America

1 2 3 4 5 6 7 8 9 0   K   2 1 0 9 8 7 6 5

HGF's

*To the associates and
clients of Gifford Fong Associates,
who provided the reason why,
and to my wife Vivian and
sons Steven and Timothy,
who provided the inspiration behind
the reason*

FJF's

*To my parents
Alfonso and Josephine Fabozzi,
who gave me the opportunity*

Preface

This book is concerned with describing some of the new approaches to fixed income portfolio management; new in the sense of analytical innovation, but not new in the sense of the conceptual framework generally followed by the practitioner. In other words, the emphasis will be on defining analytical frameworks, drawing on current investment technologies which offer the promise of better decision making. The intent is to describe techniques which are extensions and complements to most traditional practice.

There is a significant evolution going on in fixed income management. While there are some parallels with the changes occurring in the equity area, bond portfolio analysis offers a unique opportunity for fulfilling a number of investor needs. As the diversity of client investment requirements expands, additional strategies responsive to these needs become highly desirable. We will describe a number of approaches which may provide this assistance. It is the blending of the traditional with the modern investment technologies which promises to expand the capability of bond management to serve the investor better. This book is dedicated to contributing to the process.

It should be no surprise to the practitioner who has followed the development of modern portfolio theory that it relies heavily on mathematical and statistical techniques. In our exposition of the principles of the investment technologies presented in this book, we made every effort to spare the reader the intricate mathematics underlying the technique. Instead, we emphasized the rationale and implications of the technique. However, for the reader who desires a more complete treatment of the underlying mathematics, five technical appendixes are provided at the end of the book.

This book is primarily intended for the investment manager currently managing fixed income portfolios, or for those who intend to. Fund managers should find this book useful since they are responsible for setting investment objectives and policy, and then evaluating the investment performance of those who manage their funds. We also believe that this book could be used in MBA and Ph.D. courses on investment management.

We would like to express our appreciation to the staff of Gifford Fong Associates for their assistance. In particular, we would like to give special thanks to Jim Pearson and Mary Fjeldstad, who gave generously of their time to read and comment on the entire manuscript. We wish to thank Mark Pitts for his helpful comments on Chapter 8. Special mention is also made of Oldrich Vasicek, whose contributions to the theory and application of fixed income portfolio management are significant.

H. Gifford Fong
Frank J. Fabozzi

Contents

1

Introduction

The investment management process involves a series of integrated activities. These activities are applicable to the management of any investment portfolio—be it that of an institutional or an individual investor. Although the focus of this book is bond portfolio management—or, more precisely, fixed income portfolio management—an understanding of the investment management process will provide a framework for discussing the techniques we present in this book.

■ Overview of the Investment Management Process

Figure 1–1 provides a diagrammatic representation of the investment management process. The three areas which could be considered the main functional activities of this process are identified—setting investment objectives and policy, portfolio analysis, and asset analysis.

The first major activity is the setting of investment objectives and policy. For example, for a pension fund this involves the identification of the funding needs of the plan and a policy for pursuing and achieving those needs. The objectives are the goals established by the client. They may take the form of some specific return requirement and the acceptable level of risk. Policy setting takes the form of asset allocation among alterna-

Figure 1–1
Investment Management Process

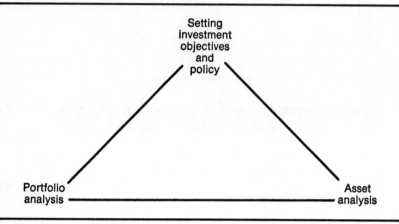

tive asset classes so as to achieve the specified objectives. In establishing an investment policy, constraints may be imposed by the client and/or those that regulate the activities of the client.

Despite the fact that setting an investment policy is one of the key activities from the standpoint of overall investment management, there is evidence that this activity is sometimes neglected in practice. Studies by A. G. Becker and Greenwich Research Associates, for example, found that even though the funding needs of different types of employee benefit plans, such as defined benefit pension funds and profit sharing funds, vary markedly, there was virtually no difference in the basic asset allocations of these funds.[1] Even when employee benefit funds were differentiated by each of the following criteria, the basic asset mix was virtually identical: (1) whether actuarial investment return assumptions were high or low, (2) whether the pension obligations were underfunded or fully funded, (3) the fraction of accrued benefit obligations that were vested, (4) the average age of the affected work force, and (6) the ratio of active versus retired participants.[2]

Under the activity of setting investment objectives and policy we would also include the task of performance measurement and evaluation. The performance of the investment manager should be evaluated in light of the investment policy set by the client. Moreover, when an investment manager claims he or she has a specialized skill that will enhance perform-

---

[1] Charles D. Ellis, "Setting Investment Objectives," Chapter 3 in *The Investment Manager's Handbook*, ed. Sumner Levine (Homewood, Ill.: Dow Jones-Irwin, 1980), p. 62.
[2] Ibid.

ance given the investment policy set, that claim must be measured and evaluated.

Following the setting of investment objectives and policy, the second main activity of the investment management process is portfolio analysis. This is essentially the activity of portfolio management. It is, in very formal terms, the method the investment manager uses to construct an *optimal* or *efficient* portfolio. An optimal or efficient portfolio is one that provides the greatest *expected* return for a given level of risk, or equivalently, the lowest risk for a given *expected* return. Most of the techniques we discuss in this book address issues of portfolio analysis.

Asset analysis is the third main activity of the investment management process. This activity essentially takes the form of individual security analysis that leads to the construction of an optimal portfolio. There are a number of techniques for accomplishing this—bond valuation and term structure analysis, for example. We will discuss these and other state of the art techniques in this book.

■ Overview of Fixed Income Portfolio Management

Given the background we presented in the previous section, let us now look at the area of concern to us in this book—fixed income portfolio management.

Active Management Strategies

The range of active fixed income portfolio management strategies is wide and subject to much variation. As a basis for discussion, we can identify three broad categories. It should be kept in mind, however, that this categorization serves a pedagogical function and in practice will be subject to significant combination and permutation.

The first category includes those strategies seeking to benefit from temporary price disequilibriums. As bonds trade over time, situations may occur where switching from one bond to another will achieve either a price appreciation or increased yield return as the result of the action. One example is where a bond is swapped or exchanged for another which is identical in all respects except for price. In effect, a lower priced bond is acquired by selling off an identical bond having a higher price. Another approach is similar in nature except that instead of exploiting a price discrepancy, differences in yield are sought. More complicated strategies include evaluating the perceived normal spread relationship between two segments of the bond market. When they become distorted, a trade is made in anticipation of a normal spread reappearing. This would result in a capital appreciation as the price of the acquired security conforms to the "correct" spread.

A basic assumption of the foregoing types of analyses is the belief the "correction" in the price or yield will occur before overall market conditions change the underlying relationship. This premise is akin to the stock valuation assumption that the price of the undervalued stock will become properly valued before the overall influence of the market changes the relationships between groups of stocks, thus detracting from the superior return of the undervalued stock. The focus is on the unique characteristics of bonds, particularly those relating to credit worthiness, where individual bond valuation is stressed apart from the expectations of the overall market. The period of time over which the undervaluation is corrected is called the workout time. It is over this horizon that the effect of market influences are assumed to be insignificant. We can call this type of activity the valuation approach to bond analysis.[3]

A second category focuses on the effects of overall changes in the market environment. This takes the form of overall changes in interest rates. The key is to anticipate the direction of interest rates. When rates are projected to drop, the longer maturities are sought to maximize capital appreciation. While maximum enhancement of total return can be achieved, forecasting interest rate movements consistently is extremely difficult to achieve.

The third category is actually a method of evaluating the previous two. To assess fully the impact of unique bond characteristics and the effect of the overall market environment, a sensitivity analysis can be pursued. Bond sensitivity analysis combines the influences of the first two categories such that unique characteristics can be evaluated in the context of overall market movements. To overcome the difficulty in interest rate forecasting, multiscenario projections may be used to test the behavior of securities to alternative outlooks.

Passive Management Strategies

Basic to all passive portfolio management strategies is the minimal expectational input in the process. In fact, this is the distinguishing feature of passive versus active strategies. Minimizing expectational requirements limits the total return potential but enhances the ability to be responsive to other needs of the client. This then recognizes the multiobjective situation where seeking the maximum return is tempered by other client-specified

---

[3] This parallels closely the process of achieving the "alpha" or risk adjusted return in stock valuation terms. This component is sought independent of the effect of overall market movements and has as an emphasis the analysis of individual bonds relative to each other. The problems are in properly timing the swap before market conditions swamp its potential and the need to make a large number of swaps to achieve a meaningful contribution to return.

requisites. As the facility to generate expectational inputs is the key to active management strategies, the qualities for fulfilling alternative investment objectives is the measure for passive approaches. That there may be a diversity in these other objectives suggests a need for a variety of strategies to accommodate the alternatives. Furthermore, as the needs of the client change so will the requirements of passive approaches. Finally, no single strategy is appropriate across the board and the degree of client responsiveness will vary from situation to situation from the same strategy. This may include meeting the unique risk preference of the investor. For example, a fund sponsor may be satisfied with or even require a portion of his portfolio to be committed to long-term, fixed income securities and be satisfied by the rate of return realized by long-term bonds over a long horizon.

There are two types of passive strategies—*buy-and-hold* and *indexing.* A buy-and-hold strategy is the simplest strategy for passive portfolio management. As the term implies, securities are bought and held to maturity. The main considerations are to be assured that there will be no default and to achieve the highest yield to maturity possible. In the face of fluctuating or rising interest rates, a buy-and-hold approach has a potentially severe disadvantage since there will be a tendency to miss opportunities from anticipated changes in interest rates as well as being subject to a lag in yield to maturity as rates rise. Expectational inputs involve credit analysis to minimize default risk. Advantages include low transaction costs, a better resolution of return over near term horizons, and minimal expectational requirements.

The objective of the indexing or index fund strategy is to replicate the performance of the bond market using a proxy which is frequently a designated index. Typically, either the *Salomon Brothers Bond Index* or the *Lehman Brothers Kuhn Loeb Bond Index* is used. Capital market theory suggests that a portfolio containing every outstanding issue held in proportion to its relative market value will be the efficient portfolio. Efficiency is here defined as the least amount of risk assumed for achieving the overall market return. It follows that if one held a portfolio of securities reflecting the same portfolio characteristics as the market (in the form of an "index"), a favorable risk/return trade-off would be achieved. Presumably, it would be very difficult to outperform the index through expectational inputs, and by combining securities in a portfolio with characteristics similar to the market, the efficiency of the market would be captured. A fundamental issue is the identification of the appropriate index.

Immunization and Cash Flow Matching Strategies

These two strategies can be thought of as a hybrid of active and passive portfolio management strategies. At one extreme, they have a similarity to passive strategies in that there is minimal requirement for expectational inputs and there are unique characteristics which allow addressing a number of investment objectives. At the other extreme, many of the same expectational inputs of active management can be integrated to enhance the expected return. Between these extremes there is a range of alternatives providing varying degrees of blend.

Figure 1–2 provides a schematic representation. At one corner can be found active management as exemplified by two specific activities, rate

Figure 1–2
Fixed Income Portfolio Management

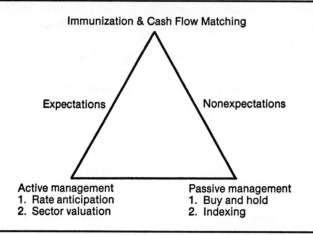

Immunization & Cash Flow Matching

Expectations   Nonexpectations

Active management   Passive management
1. Rate anticipation   1. Buy and hold
2. Sector valuation   2. Indexing

anticipation and sector valuation. At another corner is passive management where risk control is the primary emphasis as exemplified by buy-and-hold and indexing strategies. The basic difference between active and passive management is the use of expectational inputs. Active management derives its returns from expectational inputs and as a consequence also experiences higher expected risk. Passive management, in contrast, emphasizes risk control such that the expected return may be lower but the expected associated risk will also be lower due to the reliance on nonexpectational inputs. Immunization and cash flow matching management can be pursued with either emphasis so that if return maximization is the objective then using expectational inputs would be called for. Alternatively, maximum risk control immunization will make use of nonexpectational inputs.

Immunization can be defined as the process of creating a fixed income portfolio having an assured return for a specified time horizon irrespective of interest rate changes. When a portfolio must be constructed to fund a number of liabilities over time, a hybrid management strategy known as a *dedicated portfolio* strategy is appropriate. A dedicated portfolio is a portfolio with a structure designed to fund a schedule of liabilities from portfolio return and asset value, with the portfolio's value diminishing to zero after payment of the last liability. *Multiperiod immunization* and *cash flow matching* are two approaches for dedicating a portfolio.

■ Overview of the Book

Since investment objectives should be established in terms of required return and risk tolerance levels, in the next chapter we explain how return and risk are measured for individual bonds and portfolios. We also introduce an important characteristic of a bond known as *duration*. This characteristic of a bond plays a key role in many of the strategies we discuss in this book.

There are constraints imposed on a fixed income manager in attempting to achieve a client's objectives. We devote Chapter 3 to a discussion of these constraints—liquidity needs, tax considerations, time horizon, regulatory or legal considerations, and the unique considerations of the client. At the beginning of that chapter, we also provide an overview of the investment manager's fiduciary responsibility to clients.

Given investment objectives and constraints, investment policy must be set. As we noted earlier in this chapter, this involves an asset allocation decision. In Chapter 4, we explain how this decision should be addressed and provide a framework for analyzing risk-return trade-offs in establishing investment policy.

In Chapters 5, 6, and 7 we discuss and illustrate the state of the art strategies of passive, immunization and cash flow matching, and active fixed income portfolio management, respectively. Techniques for measuring and evaluating portfolio performance are discussed in the chapter on active strategies (Chapter 7). The role that interest rate futures and debt options can play in controlling the risk of a fixed income portfolio is discussed in Chapter 8. □

2

Characteristics of Fixed Income Securities and Portfolios

In this chapter we will discuss the characteristics of fixed income securities that affect their return and risk parameters. This will provide a useful background for the portfolio management strategies discussed throughout this book.

Fixed income securities are generally divided into three broad classifications: bonds, mortgages, and preferred stock. Within each category, they may be further classified by certain characteristics, a selected number of which are summarized in Table 2–1.[1] By the proper selection of the appropriate features, the basic ingredients for alternative strategies are determined.

■ Return Characteristics of Fixed Income Securities

The most distinguishing features differentiating fixed income securities from equities are the priority of lien position and, generally, the size and certainty of cash flows. Fixed income securities have specified, contractually guaranteed interest payments during the period to maturity that are

---

[1] For a detailed description of all categories of fixed income instruments, see Chapters 8 through 26 of *The Handbook of Fixed Income Securities*, ed. F. J. Fabozzi and I. M. Pollack (Homewood, Ill.: Dow Jones-Irwin, 1983).

typically larger, in percentage (yield) terms, than the dividends paid on stocks. They also have a defined maturity date as opposed to stocks, which have a perpetual existence. Finally, fixed income securities have relatively large assured cash flows permitting the accommodation of particular objectives, as will be discussed throughout this book.

Sources of Return

There are three sources of fixed income security return. These are coupon (or interest) payments and price (or capital) changes—the usual components of total return—plus reinvestment returns for portfolios where coupon payments are rolled over or invested in succeeding coupon instruments when the original instruments mature or are sold. This last component of total return is often referred to as "interest-on-interest."

The problem with the conventional yield-to-maturity as a measure of the relative attractiveness of a fixed income instrument in a portfolio is that it assumes that the coupon payments can be reinvested at a yield equal to the computed yield-to-maturity. That is, if the yield-to-maturity of a given bond is 12 percent, it is assumed that each coupon payment can be reinvested at a rate of 12 percent. In addition to the problem of realizing a reinvestment rate equal to the yield-to-maturity, this measure also assumes that the entire amount can be reinvested, which is not a plausible assumption for fixed income securities in a portfolio that is subject to income taxes or minimum purchase sizes. Finally, it assumes that the bond will not be redeemed prior to the stated maturity.

Importance of the Interest-on-Interest Component of Total Return

To see the importance of the interest-on-interest component of total return, consider a bond selling at par with seven years remaining to maturity and carrying a 12 percent coupon rate. The total return for this bond consists of two sources: (1) coupon interest of $60 every six months for seven years and (2) interest from the reinvestment of the coupon interest. Since the bond is assumed to be selling at par, there is no capital gain or loss.

The future dollar value generated from the coupon payments and the reinvestment of coupon payments (i.e., interest-on-interest) at 12 percent compounded semiannually is $1,261.[2] The coupon interest is $840 ($60

---

[2] This is found by multiplying the future value of an annuity of $1 by the semiannual coupon interest. For the bond in this illustration, the future value of $1 each six months at 6 percent interest (one half the annual rate) is 21.015. Hence, the future dollar value is $60 times 21.015, or $1,261. (See footnote 4 for the formula to compute the future value of an annuity of $1.)

Table 2–1
Selected Characteristics of Fixed Income Securities

	Bonds	Preferred Stocks	Real Estate Mortgages
Issuers	Federal government Federal agencies Corporations: 　Industrial 　Financial 　Railroads 　Utilities States (provinces) Municipalities Municipal agencies Foreign governments Foreign corporations	Corporations (typically utilities)	Corporations Partnerships Individuals
Security	First mortgage Mortgage-backed pools Collateral trust Equipment trust Debentures Subordinated debentures Income bonds	Unsecured	First mortgage Second mortgage
Income	Fixed coupon rate Variable rate Zero coupon	Fixed dividend rate Variable rate	Fixed interest rate Variable rate

		Perpetual (no maturity)	
Maturity	Fixed date for final principal payment; for mortgage-backed or sinking fund issues, the average life is more important to portfolio managers than the final maturity because of periodic principal repayments	Perpetual (no maturity)	Fixed date for final principal payment, but average life is more important to portfolio managers due to periodic principal repayments
Sinking fund	Retirement of principal on a specified basis with significance dependent on issuer; typically significant for industrials but not for utilities	Some issues have sinking funds	Most mortgage payments include interest and amortization of principal on a monthly, quarterly, or annual basis
Call and/or refunding provision	Utility issuers have the option to retire part or all of the issue after 5 years; industrial issues—typically 10 years; government issues—typically noncallable	Issuer has option to retire part or all of the issue prior to maturity	Mortgagor has option to refinance or pay down the loan after a stipulated period, often five years
Conversion feature	Some corporate issues can be converted into the common stock of the issuer	Some corporate issues can be converted into the common stock of the issuer	Not applicable
Maturity/put option	Many Canadian issues—federal government, provincial, and corporate—provide the holders the option to *retract* the original maturity to an earlier date or *extend* the original maturity to a later date. Some recent U.S. tax-exempt bond issues allow the holder to retract the original maturity to an earlier date. Allowing a holder to retract a bond's maturity date effectively adds a put option to the issue since the holder can redeem or put the bond to the issuer at its par or face value.	Not applicable	Not applicable

times 14). Hence the balance, $421 ($1,261 minus $840), represents the interest-on-interest component of the total return. For this bond, interest-on-interest accounts for 33 percent ($421 divided by $1,261) of the total return.

The importance of the interest-on-interest component becomes greater the longer the maturity. For example, if the 12 percent coupon bond selling at par had a remaining life of 30 years instead of 7 years, the total return would be $31,987. Since coupon interest payments are $3,600 ($60 times 60 semiannual coupon payments), interest-on-interest is $28,387 ($31,987 minus $3,600) or 89 percent of the total return.

For a bond selling at a discount from par, interest-on-interest makes up less of the total return for bonds of equal time remaining to maturity and the same yield-to-maturity. This can be illustrated for a hypothetical 8 percent coupon bond that has seven years remaining to maturity, and has a market price of $814 (rounded to the nearest dollar). The yield-to-maturity for this bond is 12 percent. The total return consists of (1) coupon interest payments of $560, (2) interest-on-interest of $281, and (3) a capital gain of $186 ($1,000 minus $814). The interest-on-interest component accounts for 27 percent of the total return ($281 divided by $1,027). For the 12 percent, seven-year par bonds, the interest-on-interest component makes up 33 percent of the total return.

The interest-on-interest component of a long-term bond selling at a discount would be a substantial portion of the bond's total return, just as in the case of a bond selling at par. In fact the longer the term of the bond, the less important is the capital gain component compared with the other two components. For example, a bond with 30 years remaining to maturity, carrying a coupon rate of 8 percent, and selling at $677 will have a yield-to-maturity of 12 percent. The total return for this bond is $21,648, consisting of: (1) coupon interest payments of $2,400, (2) interest-on-interest of $18,925, and (3) a capital gain of $323. The capital gain component is only 1.5 percent of the total return. For the seven-year bond selling at a discount, the capital gain component represented 18 percent of the total return. The interest-on-interest component for the 30-year bond selling at a discount is about 87 percent, which is approximately the same as in the case of the 30-year bond selling at par.

As would be expected, bonds selling at a premium are more dependent upon the interest-on-interest component of the total return.

Realized Compound Yield as a Measure of Total Return

Because of the importance of the rate that the coupon interest is assumed to be reinvested, a measure of return that can be used for investment decisions must take into account interest-on-interest. Homer and Leibowitz suggest a comprehensive measure that takes into consideration all three sources of a bond's return.[3] The measure they suggest reveals the fully compounded growth rate of an investment under varying reinvestment rates. They call this measure the *realized compound yield.*

The steps to compute the realized compound yield are as follows:

1. Compute the total future dollars that will be received from the investment. This is equal to the sum of the coupon payments, the interest-on-interest from reinvesting the coupon payments at an assumed reinvestment rate, and the redemption value.[4]

2. Divide the amount found in the previous step by the investment. The resulting amount is the future value per dollar invested.

3. Find the interest rate that produces the future value per dollar invested by solving the following equation:

$$(\text{Future value per dollar invested})^{\frac{1}{\text{no. of periods}}} - 1$$

4. Since interest is assumed to be paid semiannually, double the interest rate found in the previous step. The resulting interest rate is the realized compound yield.

The 12 percent, seven-year bond selling at par will be used to demonstrate the computation of the realized compound yield. The reinvestment rate assumed is 10 percent. The steps are as follows:

1. The total future dollars to be received consists of the coupon interest and interest-on-interest of $1,176[5] and the redemption value of $1,000. Hence the total future dollars to be received is $2,176.

---

[3] Sidney Homer and Martin L. Leibowitz, *Inside the Yield Book* (Published jointly: Englewood Cliffs, N.J.: Prentice-Hall, and New York: New York Institute of Finance, 1972).

[4] The future value for the sum of the coupon payments and interest-on-interest from reinvesting the coupon payments is found by multiplying the coupon payment by the future value of an annuity of $1 per period. The formula for the future value of an annuity of $1 per period is

$$\text{FV of an annuity of } \$1 = \frac{(1 + r)^n - 1}{r}$$

where

n = number of payments
r = simple interest rate per period

[5] The future value of an annuity of $1 for 14 periods assuming a 5 percent reinvestment rate (one half of the annual reinvestment rate) is 19.5986 as shown below:

$$\frac{(1.05)^{14} - 1}{.05} = \frac{1.97993 - 1}{.05} = 19.5986$$

The future value of the coupon payments and interest-on-interest by reinvesting the coupon payments is $60 times 19.598, or $1,176.

2. Since the investment is $1,000, the future value per $1 invested is $2.176 ($2,176 divided by $1,000).

3. The interest rate that will produce a future value of $2.176 for a $1 investment made for 14 periods is 5.7 percent.

4. Doubling 5.7 percent we get a realized compound yield of 11.4 percent.

A property of the realized compound yield is that it will be between the yield-to-maturity and the reinvestment rate. Therefore when the reinvestment rate is the same as the yield-to-maturity, the realized compound yield is the same as the yield-to-maturity. When the reinvestment rate is greater than the yield-to-maturity, the realized compound yield will be greater than the yield-to-maturity. The realized compound yield will be less than the yield-to-maturity when the reinvestment rate is less than the latter.

The difference in basis points between the realized compound yield and the yield-to-maturity depends not only on the reinvestment rate but also on the remaining life of the bond and the coupon rate. The longer the term-to-maturity, the more important will be the interest-on-interest component for a given coupon rate and yield-to-maturity. Consequently, the longer the term of a bond, the closer its realized compound yield will be to the reinvestment rate. On the other hand, the shorter the maturity, the closer the realized compound yield will be to the yield-to-maturity.

For a given term-to-maturity and yield-to-maturity, the lower the coupon rate, the less of a bond's total return depends on the interest-on-interest component. Therefore, holding all other factors constant, the realized compound yield will deviate from the yield-to-maturity by less basis points for a given reinvestment rate the lower the coupon rate.

Table 2–2 shows the realized compound yield under different as-

Table 2–2
Realized Compound Yields for 7-Year and 30-Year Bonds with a 12 Percent Yield-to-Maturity: Coupon Rates 12 Percent and 8 Percent

| | Realized Compound Yield* | | | |
| | 7-Year Bonds | | 30-Year Bonds | |
Reinvestment Rate	12 Percent Coupon, Price = 100	8 Percent Coupon, Price = 81.41	12 Percent Coupon, Price = 100	8 Percent Coupon, Price = 677
8%	10.8%	11.1%	9.3%	9.4%
10	11.4	11.6	10.6	10.8
12	12.0	12.0	12.0	12.0
14	12.6	12.5	13.3	13.3
16	13.2	13.0	15.0	14.9

* The yield-to-maturity for each bond is 12 percent.

sumptions for the reinvestment rate for the four bonds discussed in this section. The reader can verify the properties of the realized compound yield stated in the preceding discussion.

Marginal Impact on Returns for Short-Term Investment Horizons

For investment management horizons where time frames are measured in months instead of years, the greatest marginal impact on return is due to price changes, which are caused chiefly by changes in interest rates. If rates rise, then the price of the outstanding bond will fall to reflect the new available yield; conversely, if rates decline, the price of the outstanding bond will increase. As explained later in this chapter, this would occur when bonds are held with a maturity different from the managerial planning horizon.

A popular indicator of changes in interest rates is the yield curve for government securities where the percentage yield is plotted as a function of maturity. Any change in rates across the maturity spectrum will be reflected by comparing the position and shape of the curve at different points in time.

A brief analysis of a simple change in position (level) and shape (slope) of the yield curve is illustrated in Figure 2–1. From this basic illustration, the following three sources of return impact can be identified:

1. The impact of time as the bond moves closer to maturity from point A_1 to point B_3. That is, if there is no change in either the slope or level of

Figure 2–1
Yield Curve Analytical Framework

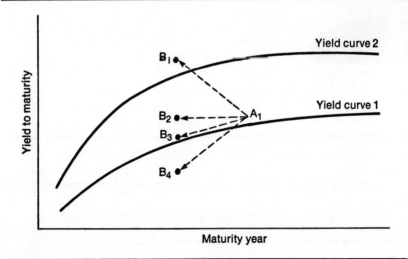

the market yield curve—represented by curve 1—or in the bond's valuation relative to the market, this bond will "ride the yield curve" from A_1 to B_3.

2. The impact of changes in market valuation that can be based on the characteristics of the bond itself. This is illustrated by the movement from A_1 to B_4, as the yield to maturity changes from a premium relative to the market—again represented by curve 1—to a discount with the consequent increase in market value relative to the market. A widening of the yield premium and the consequent lower valuation relative to the market are reflected in the movement from A_1 to B_2.

3. The impact of changes in the slope and/or level of interest rates, such as from curve 1 to curve 2. This is illustrated by the movement from A_1 to B_1.

Both the capital changes and the reinvestment return of fixed income assets will be directly affected by changes in interest rate levels. Interest rate changes can be characterized by various yield curve shifts, as shown in Figure 2–2 and Figure 2–3. Parallel changes are those having equal basis point moves across all maturities (see Figure 2–2); nonparallel changes are exemplified by unequal basis point shifts (see Figure 2–3).

An alternative indicator of interest rate change, *term structure analysis,* which is different from straight yield curve analysis, may be used as described by Fong and Vasicek.[6] The term structure may be defined as the spot rate or yield on a pure discount or zero coupon security for each maturity for a homogeneous universe of bonds. In its most fundamental form the universe would be made up of default-free U.S. Treasury issues. The resulting term structure would consist of a series of spot rates representing the yield on a pure discount or zero coupon default-free security for each maturity in the structure. That is, yields on U.S. Treasuries at any given point in time are adjusted to remove the coupon or tax effect (the effect resulting from different sources of total return—capital change versus coupon income—and their resulting differential tax treatment) and the residual spread between same-maturity Treasury yields that remains even after the coupon/tax effect has been adjusted for. Thus a market-equilibrium, default-free, pure-discount yield curve is, in effect, created.

As shown in Fong and Vasicek, each of the theoretically pure spot rates located on this pure-discount yield curve can be mathematically converted into a set of one-period spot and forward rates based on the *pure expectations theory.*[7] That is, every multiperiod spot rate in the term

---

[6] H. Gifford Fong and Oldrich A. Vasicek, "Term Structure Modelling Using Third Order Exponential Splines," *The Journal of Finance,* May 1982, pp. 339–48.

[7] For a detailed discussion of the expectations theory, as well as other theories of the term structure of interest rates, see Richard W. McEnally, "The Term Structure of Interest Rates," Chapter 46 in *The Handbook of Fixed Income Securities,* ed. F. J. Fabozzi and Irving M. Pollack (Homewood, Ill.: Dow Jones-Irwin, 1983).

Figure 2–2
Parallel Yield Curve Shift

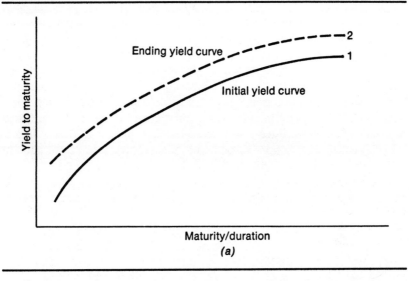

Figure 2–3
Nonparallel Yield Curve Shift

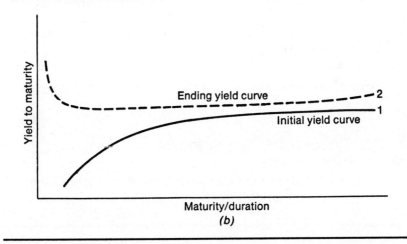

structure is equal to the compound average (nth root) of the current one-period spot rate times all the successive one-period forward rates mathematically implied into the future to the maturity of the multiperiod spot rate. For example, the five-year maturity spot rate would be equal to the compound average (geometric mean) of the current one-year spot rate and each of the four succeeding one-year forward rates, or the 5th root of the product of these five rates.

In effect, each of the spot rates, and, taken together, all of the spot rates in the total term structure, implies a continuum of one-period future reinvestment rates that are expected at each future maturity date *if* the term structure created is assumed to remain constant. When compounded together, this continuum of forward rates or returns on pure discount zero coupon bonds provides the bond investor with a basic market-implicit return *regardless of maturity*—that is, it is the equilibrium-expected compound rate of return for the entire term structure such that no maturities or payment schedules are *ex ante* (before the fact) preferred to any others. Why? Because it encompasses all that the market is currently requiring in the way of return across the entire spectrum of future maturities.

The question then remains of how the market-implicit rate so derived can be most effectively used. Like any other forecast of future interest rates, it has not been an accurate estimator of future rates in an absolute sense. In a relative sense, however, the approach has been shown to be a better prognosticator than recent forecasts by two highly regarded econometric models in a 1982 proprietary study. The prime benefit of market-implicit returns is to provide a most-likely forecast in a probabilistic decision-making framework. This forecast is then bracketed by less probable optimistic and pessimistic rate forecasts to produce a probability distribution of returns. The approach can also be used in simulations where sensitivity analysis is done and the effect of "what if" changes in assumed rates are measured. Hence, this use of the term structure should provide a more comprehensive perspective of potential rate changes and can serve as a basic building block for much further analysis, such as performance analysis as discussed in Chapter 7.

A more thorough discussion of term structure analysis is given in Appendix D.

■ Risk Characteristics of Fixed Income Securities

In general, the holder of a fixed income security is subject to six types of risk: (1) interest-rate risk, (2) reinvestment risk, (3) inflation or purchasing power risk, (4) default risk, (5) call risk, and (6) marketability or liquidity risk. All fixed income securities are subject to interest-rate risk which is the risk that the price of the security will decline if interest rates should rise. The volatility of the price of a bond depends on several factors that will be discussed later.

All coupon bonds are subject to reinvestment risk. As explained earlier in this chapter, interest-on-interest is an important source of total return for some fixed income securities. Reinvestment risk is the risk that coupon payments or repayment of principal will be reinvested at a lower rate than when the instrument was acquired. Of course, zero coupon obligations are not subject to reinvestment risk. As will be seen later in this chapter, interest-rate risk and reinvestment risk are tied together for bonds that are not expected to be held to maturity. As interest rates rise, the price of a bond decreases; however, interest-on-interest increases since coupon payments and other cash flows generated from the issue can be reinvested at a higher rate.

Inflation or purchasing power risk is the risk that the return realized will not be sufficient to offset the loss in purchasing power due to inflation. Default risk, also known as business risk or credit risk, is the risk that the issuer will default in the contractual payment of principal and interest. The ratings of the commercial rating companies are generally used as a benchmark for default risk.

Call risk exists for fixed income securities in which the issuer has the right to call in the issue prior to maturity. The risk that the investor faces is that the issue will be called when interest rates have fallen so much since the issue was originally sold that it is economically beneficial for the issuer to call the issue and refund it at the prevailing lower rate. In such cases, the holder will be forced to reinvest the proceeds received from the issuer at a lower rate. Hence, call risk is tied to reinvestment risk. In addition, there is risk of truncating capital appreciation because of the possibility that the issue will be called as rates drop.

Marketability risk involves the liquidity of a security and the ease with which the issue can be sold at or near prevailing market prices.

Interest-Rate Risk and Bond Price Volatility

Since interest-rate risk is the most important risk faced by holders of fixed income securities and it is a function of the volatility of bond prices, we shall discuss the properties of bond price volatility.

The price of a bond changes in the opposite direction from the change in the yield required by investors. For example, if a 9 percent coupon bond with 20 years remaining to maturity is selling at 100 (par) to yield 9 percent, the price of the bond will decrease to 91.42 if market yields increase by 100 basis points to 10 percent. The increase in market yields decreases the price of the bond by 8.58 percent. If, on the other hand, market yields decline by 100 basis points to 8 percent, the price of the bond will increase by 9.9 percent to 109.90. In addition the change in the price of the bond will be greater the greater the change in the yield required by investors. For example, for the 9 percent coupon, 20-year bond, an increase in market yields from 9 percent to 11 percent (a 200-basis-point increase) will result in a decrease in the price of the bond from 100 to 83.95. Hence, for a 200-basis-point increase in yield, the price of the bond will fall by 16.05 percent compared with 8.58 percent for a 100-basis-point increase in yield.

For a given initial market yield and a given change in basis points, the percentage change in the price of the bond will depend upon certain characteristics of the bond. The relationship between bond price volatility and these characteristics of a bond are illustrated below.[8]

Before proceeding, it is important to understand that the volatility we will be discussing is the change that will result from an *instantaneous* change in market yields. Even if market yields do not change, the price of a bond selling at a premium or discount will change due to the passage of time. For example, consider a bond with a 7 percent coupon rate, 20 years remaining to maturity, and selling at 81.60 to yield 9 percent. If the bond is held for one year and market yields remained at 9 percent, the price of the bond would increase to 81.95, since it would have 19 years remaining to maturity. The increase in price from 81.60 to 81.95 results from an accretion process that will eventually increase the price of the bond to its par value at maturity. For a bond selling at a premium, the price of a bond decreases as it approaches maturity if market yields remain constant. Consider, for example, a bond with a coupon rate of 12 percent, 20 years remaining to maturity, and selling for 127.60 to yield 9 percent. The price of the bond after one year has passed will be 127.07 if market yields do not change. This results from the amortization of the premium. The relationship between the price of a bond and the remaining time to maturity assuming that market yields are unchanged is shown in Figures 2–4 and 2–5.

Bond price volatility and coupon rate. For a given maturity and initial market yield, the volatility of a bond's price increases as the coupon rate decreases. This is illustrated in Table 2–3. The term to maturity is 20 years, and the initial yield is 9 percent. The price of the bond for coupon rates between 5 percent and 12 percent at 1 percent increments for eight hypothetical changes in the market yield are shown in the top panel of the table. In the second panel, the percentage change in the price of the bond is shown.

An implication of this property of price volatility is that bonds selling at a discount are more responsive to changes in market yield, all other factors equal, compared with bonds selling at or above par. Moreover, the deeper the discount resulting from the divergence between the coupon rate and market yield, the greater the responsiveness of the bond's price to changes in market yield. The greatest price response is offered by zero-coupon debt

---

[8] The relationships discussed in this section are mathematically derived in Burton G. Malkiel, "Expectations, Bond Prices, and the Term Structure of Interest Rates," *Quarterly Journal of Economics*, May 1962, pp. 197–218.

Figure 2–4
Time Path of the Value of a 7 Percent Coupon, 20-Year Bond If the Required Yield Begins and Remains at 9 Percent

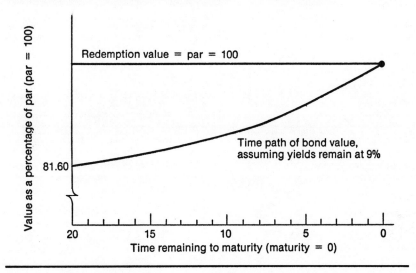

Figure 2–5
Time Path of the Value of a 12 Percent Coupon, 20-Year Bond If the Required Yield Begins and Remains at 9 Percent

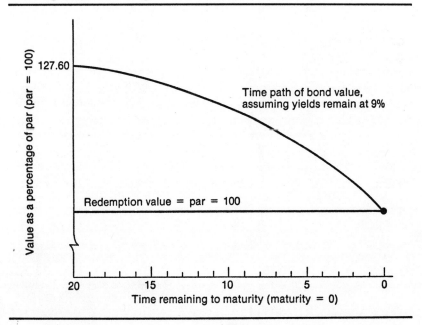

Table 2–3
Bond Price Volatility for Bonds Yielding 9 Percent and 20 Years to Maturity

	Coupon Rate							
	5 Percent $63.20	6 Percent $72.40	7 Percent $81.60	8 Percent $90.80	9 Percent $100.00	10 Percent $109.20	11 Percent $118.40	12 Percent $127.60
Initial price								
Price if yield changes by:								
−200 bp	$78.64	$89.32	$100.00	$110.68	$121.36	$132.03	$142.71	$153.39
−100	70.31	80.21	90.10	100.00	109.90	119.79	129.69	139.59
−50	66.61	76.15	85.69	95.23	104.77	114.31	123.85	133.39
−10	63.86	73.13	82.39	91.66	100.93	110.19	119.46	128.73
+10	62.54	71.68	80.82	89.95	99.09	108.22	117.36	126.49
+50	60.03	68.91	77.80	86.68	95.56	104.44	113.32	122.20
+100	57.10	65.68	74.26	82.84	91.42	100.00	108.58	117.16
+200	51.86	59.88	67.91	75.93	83.95	91.98	100.00	108.02
Percentage change in price if yield changes by:								
−200 bp	+24.43%	+23.37%	+22.55%	+21.89%	+21.36%	+20.91%	+20.53%	+20.21%
−100	+11.25	+10.79	+10.42	+10.13	+9.90	+9.70	+9.54	+9.40

−50	+5.40	+5.18	+5.01	+4.88	+4.77	+4.68	+4.60	+4.54
−10	+1.04	+1.01	+0.97	+0.95	+0.93	+0.91	+0.90	+0.89
+10	−1.04	−0.99	−0.96	−0.94	−0.91	−0.90	−0.88	−0.87
+50	−5.02	−4.82	−4.66	−4.54	−4.44	−4.36	−4.29	−4.23
+100	−9.65	−9.28	−9.00	−8.77	−8.58	−8.42	−8.29	−8.18
+200	−17.94	−17.29	−16.78	−16.38	−16.05	−15.77	−15.54	−15.34

Ratio of percentage price change to
yield movement in basis points if
yield changes by:

−200 bp	−.1222%	−.1169%	−.1128%	−.1095%	−.1068%	−.1046%	−.1027%	−.1011%
−100	−.1125	−.1079	−.1042	−.1013	−.0990	−.0970	−.0954	−.0940
−50	−.1080	−.1036	−.1002	−.0976	−.0954	−.0936	−.0920	−.0908
−10	−.1040	−.1010	−.0970	−.0950	−.0930	−.0910	−.0900	−.0890
+10	−.1040	−.0990	−.0960	−.0940	−.0910	−.0900	−.0880	−.0870
+50	−.1004	−.0964	−.0932	−.0908	−.0888	−.0872	−.0858	−.0846
+100	−.0965	−.0928	−.0900	−.0877	−.0858	−.0842	−.0829	−.0818
+200	−.0897	−.0865	−.0839	−.0819	−.0803	−.0789	−.0777	−.0767

obligations. From a purely capital gain or loss perspective, therefore, investors would avoid bonds selling at a discount if interest rates are expected to rise; however, bonds selling at a discount are attractive if interest rates are anticipated to decline.

Notice in Table 2–3 that the percentage change in the price of a bond is not the same for both an increase and decrease of the same number of basis points. The difference between the percentage change in price increases as the amount of the change in basis points increases. For small changes in basis points, such as 10 basis points, the percentage price change is almost symmetrical. As the coupon rate increases, the difference between the percentage change in price for a given change in basis points decreases.

For analysis purposes, it would be helpful to be able to express the percentage change in price in terms of some fixed volatility factor times the change in yield. Unfortunately, this is not possible because the relationship between the percentage change in the price of a bond is not linear and not symmetrical with respect to yield changes. This can be seen in the third panel in Table 2–3 which shows that the ratio of the percentage price change to the change in yield is not constant.

The change in the price of the bond, however, is only one consideration in evaluating the investment merits of a particular bond issue. Recall that even though interest rates may decline so that the price of the bond increases, the interest-on-interest component of the bond's total return will decrease due to the lower reinvestment rate. It seems that we are missing an important element in assessing the relative attractiveness of a bond issue for a portfolio. That element is the period of time the investor plans to hold the bond. The attractiveness of a bond for a given investment horizon will be explained when we discuss immunization theory in Chapter 6.

Bond price volatility and maturity. The volatility of the price of a bond increases the longer the remaining term to maturity, all other factors constant. For bonds yielding 9 percent and with a coupon rate of 9 percent, this property is illustrated in Table 2–4.[9]

An implication of this property of price volatility is that if interest rates are expected to increase, bond prices will decrease by a greater percentage for long-term bonds compared to short-term bonds, all other factors constant. Therefore, from a purely capital loss perspective, an investor will avoid long-term bonds (holding everything else constant) if interest rates are expected to rise. Conversely, since the percentage change in prices of long-term bonds will increase by a greater percentage than short-term

---

[9] Once again it can be seen that the percentage change in price is not symmetrical for a given change in basis points and a given maturity, except for very small changes. The difference in the percentage change in price decreases as the maturity increases.

bonds, investors will prefer long-term bonds from a purely capital gain perspective when interest rates are projected to fall.

Once again, remember that the capital gain or loss resulting from a change in market yield is only one component of the total return from holding a bond. The immunization strategy discussed in Chapter 6 can be employed to evaluate the relative investment merit of holding a bond over the investor's investment horizon given the investor's projection about the future movement of interest rates.

Bond price volatility and the initial yield level. The two properties of bond price volatility just demonstrated measured the change in yield in terms of basis points. For example, if yields change from 9 percent to 10 percent, the change in yield was measured as 100 basis points. Alternatively, the change in yield can be measured as a percentage change from the initial yield. Using our previous example, the percentage change in yield is 11.11 percent if yields increase to 10 percent from a 9 percent initial yield.

Regardless of whether the movement in yields is measured by the change in basis points or as a percentage of the initial yield, the two properties of bond price volatility discussed above hold. An additional property of bond price volatility when the movement is based upon the expected percentage change from an initial yield level is that for a given percentage change in yield, bond price volatility increases the higher the initial yield level, all other factors constant. This property is illustrated in Table 2–5.

It is not difficult to understand why this occurs. The higher the initial yield, the greater the change in the number of basis points for a given percentage change in yield. Therefore, since bond price volatility depends upon the magnitude of the change in basis points, the higher the initial yield level, the greater the bond's price volatility for a given percentage change in yield. An implication of this property is that as yields rise, bond price volatility increases.

Duration

A pitfall with using the maturity of a bond as a measure of the timing of its cash flow is that it only takes into consideration the final payment. To overcome this shortcoming, Professor Frederick R. Macaulay in 1938 suggested using a measure that would account for all cash flows expected.[10]

---

[10] Frederick R. Macaulay, *Some Theoretical Problems Suggested by the Movement of Interest Rates, Bond Yields, and Stock Prices in the United States Since 1865* (New York: National Bureau of Economic Research, 1938).

Table 2-4
Bond Price Volatility for 9 Percent Coupon Bonds Selling at Par

				Years to Maturity				
	1	5	10	15	20	25	30
Initial price	$100.00	$100.00	$100.00	$100.00	$100.00	$100.00	$100.00
Price if yield changes by:							
−200 bp	$101.90	$108.32	$114.21	$118.39	$121.36	$123.46	$124.94
−100	100.94	104.06	106.80	108.65	109.90	110.74	111.31
−50	100.47	102.00	103.32	104.19	104.77	105.15	105.40
−10	100.09	100.40	100.65	100.82	100.93	101.00	101.04
+10	99.91	99.61	99.35	99.19	99.09	99.02	98.98
+50	99.53	98.05	96.82	96.04	95.56	95.25	95.06
+100	99.07	96.14	93.77	92.31	91.42	90.87	90.54
+200	98.15	92.46	88.05	85.47	83.95	83.07	82.55
Percentage change if yield changes by:							
−200 bp	+1.90%	+8.32%	+14.21%	+18.39%	+21.36%	+23.46%	+24.94%
−100	+0.94	+4.06	+6.80	+8.65	+9.90	+10.74	+11.31

-50	+0.47	+2.00	+3.32	+4.19	+4.77	+5.15	+5.40
-10	+0.09	+0.40	+0.65	+0.82	+0.93	+1.00	+1.04
+10	-0.09	-0.39	-0.65	-0.81	-0.91	-0.98	-1.02
+50	-0.47	-1.95	-3.18	-3.96	-4.44	-4.75	-4.94
+100	-0.93	-3.86	-6.23	-7.69	-8.58	-9.13	-9.46
+200	-1.85	-7.54	-11.95	-14.53	-16.05	-16.93	-17.45

Ratio of percentage price change to yield movement in
basis points if yield changes by:

-200 bp	-.0095%	-.0416%	-.0711%	-.0920%	-.1068%	-.1173%	-.1247%
-100	-.0094	-.0406	-.0680	-.0865	-.0990	-.1074	-.1131
-50	-.0094	-.0400	-.0664	-.0838	-.0954	-.1030	-.1080
-10	-.0090	-.0400	-.0650	-.0820	-.0930	-.1000	-.1040
+10	-.0090	-.0390	-.0650	-.0810	-.0910	-.0980	-.1020
+50	-.0094	-.0390	-.0636	-.0792	-.0888	-.0950	-.0988
+100	-.0093	-.0386	-.0623	-.0769	-.0858	-.0913	-.0946
+200	-.0093	-.0377	-.0598	-.0727	-.0803	-.0847	-.0873

Table 2–5
Bond Price Volatility for a 9 Percent Coupon, 20 Year Bond for a 25 Percent Increase in Market Yield

Initial Yield	New Yield after 25 Percent Increase	Change in Basis Points	Initial Price	New Price	Percentage Change in Price
4.00%	5.00%	100 bp	168.39	150.21	−10.80%
6.00	7.50	150	134.67	115.41	−14.30
8.00	10.00	200	109.90	91.42	−16.82
10.00	12.50	250	91.42	74.48	−18.53
14.00	17.50	350	66.67	53.12	−20.32

The measure he suggested, known as *duration*, is a weighted average term-to-maturity where the cash flows are in terms of their present value.

Duration defined. Mathematically, duration is measured as follows:

$$\text{Duration} = \frac{PVCF_1 \,(1)}{PVTCF} + \frac{PVCF_2 \,(2)}{PVTCF} + \frac{PVCF_3 \,(3)}{PVTCF} + \cdots + \frac{PVCF_n \,(n)}{PVTCF}$$

where

$PVCF_t$ = the present value of the cash flow in period t discounted at the prevailing yield-to-maturity

t = the period when the cash flow is expected to be received

n = remaining number of periods until maturity

$PVTCF$ = total present value of the cash flow from the bond where the present value is determined using the prevailing yield-to-maturity

For a bond in which there are no sinking-fund or call effects and in which interest is paid semiannually, the cash flow for periods 1 to $n - 1$ is just one half of the annual coupon interest. The cash flow in period n is the semiannual coupon interest plus the redemption value. The discount rate is one half the prevailing yield-to-maturity. The resulting value is in half years when semiannual interest payments are used in the computation. To obtain duration in terms of years, duration in half years is divided by two.[11] Since the price of a bond is equal to its cash flow discounted at the prevailing yield-to-maturity, $PVTCF$ is nothing more than the current market price *including accrued interest.*

---

[11] In general, if there are m coupon payments per year, then duration in years is computed by dividing the duration based upon m payments per year by m.

Table 2–6
**Worksheet for Computation of the Duration of a 9 Percent
Coupon Bond with 10 Years to Maturity Selling at par ($1,000) to
Yield 9 Percent (*semiannual interest payments assumed*)**

Period	Cash Flow	PV at 4.5 Percent	PVCF	PVCF × Period
1	$ 45	.9569	43.0605	43.0605
2	45	.9157	41.2065	82.4130
3	45	.8763	39.4335	118.3005
4	45	.8386	37.7370	150.9480
5	45	.8025	36.1125	180.5625
6	45	.7679	34.5555	207.3330
7	45	.7348	33.0666	231.4620
8	45	.7032	31.6440	253.1520
9	45	.6729	30.2805	272.5245
10	45	.6439	28.9755	289.7550
11	45	.6162	27.7290	305.0190
12	45	.5897	26.5365	318.4380
13	45	.5643	25.3935	330.1155
14	45	.5400	24.3000	340.2000
15	45	.5167	23.2515	348.7725
16	45	.4945	22.1625	354.6000
17	45	.4732	21.2940	361.9980
18	45	.4528	20.3760	366.7680
19	45	.4333	19.4985	370.4715
20	1,045	.4146	433.2570	8,665.1400
			999.8707	13,591.0340
			or	or
			$1,000	$13,591

$$\text{Duration in half years} = \frac{13,591}{1,000}$$
$$= 13.591$$

$$\text{Duration in years} = \frac{13.591}{2}$$
$$= 6.79$$

Table 2–6 shows how the duration of a 9 percent coupon bond with 10 years to maturity and selling for $1,000 to yield 9 percent is computed assuming coupon interest is paid semiannually. The duration for this bond is 6.79 years.

The duration of a bond portfolio is equal to the weighted average of the duration of the individual bonds comprising the portfolio. For example, suppose a portfolio consists of three bonds with a market value of $2, $5 and $3 million and with a corresponding duration of 7, 5 and 9 years. The duration of this bond portfolio is 6.6 years (= (7)(2/10) + (5)(5/10) + (9)(3/10)).

Properties of duration. The following properties of a bond's duration should be noted. First, except for zero coupon bonds, the duration of a bond is less than its maturity. Second, with the exception of deep discount bonds, duration is larger the longer the maturity. For deep discount bonds there is a point at which duration will decrease as maturity increases. Third, the duration of a bond is shorter the greater the coupon rate. Finally, as market yields increase, the duration of a bond decreases. These properties are illustrated in Figure 2–6.

Figure 2–6
Duration versus Maturity

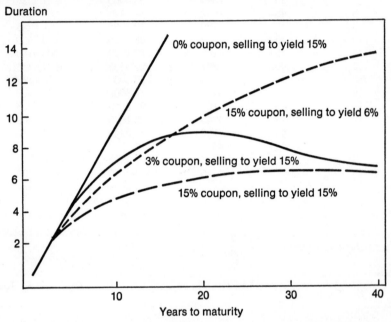

Source: William L. Nemerever, "Managing Bond Portfolios through Immunization Strategies," in *The Revolution in Techniques for Managing Bond Portfolios*, ed. Donald Tuttle (Charlottesville, Va.: The Institute for Chartered Financial Analysts, 1983).

Duration and bond price volatility. The specific link between a bond's duration and its price volatility for small changes in interest rates was demonstrated by Professors Michael Hopewell and George Kaufman.[12] They show that

---

[12] Michael H. Hopewell and George C. Kaufman, "Bond Price Volatility and Term to Maturity: A Generalized Respecification," *American Economic Review*, September 1973, pp. 749–53.

$$\text{Percentage change in bond's price} = -(\text{Modified duration}) \times \left(\frac{\begin{array}{c}\text{Change in market yield}\\ \text{in basis points}\end{array}}{100} \right)$$

where modified duration is duration divided by (1 + market yield/the number of coupon payments per year).

For example, the duration of the 9 percent coupon bond with ten years to maturity and selling to yield 9 percent is 6.79. Hence modified duration is 6.79/(1 + .09/2), or 6.50. The percentage decline in the bond's price if market yields rise by 50 basis points is 3.25 percent as shown below:

$$\text{Percentage change in bond's price} = -(6.50) \times \left(\frac{50}{100}\right)$$
$$= -3.25 \text{ percent}$$

Notice that the percentage change in a bond's price is a linear function of duration. As noted earlier in this section, a bond's price volatility was not proportional (linearly related) to coupon rate or maturity.

The linear relationship for bond price volatility as a function of duration derived by Hopewell and Kaufman employs the Macaulay definition of duration. However, the Macaulay definition of duration assumes (1) that the yield curve is flat and (2) that any changes in interest rates will correspond to a parallel shift in the yield curve. Consequently, alternative definitions of duration have been formulated based on different assumptions about how the yield curve will shift.

Offsetting interest-rate risk and reinvestment risk. The use of duration as a measure of the responsiveness of a bond's price to a change in market yields is only one application of how this concept can be used in bond portfolio management. Another important application deals with the trade-off that arises as interest rates change over the investor's investment horizon.

As interest rates increase, the price of the bond declines, but the portion of the total return from interest-on-interest increases. When interest rates decrease over the investor's investment horizon, the opposite is true. The portion of the total return resulting from interest-on-interest decreases, but the price of the bond increases. To immunize a bond or bond portfolio from this interest-rate risk so as to achieve a targeted return over an investment horizon, it can be demonstrated that the duration of the bond or bond portfolio should be set equal to the investment horizon. This application of duration is called immunization and is discussed in Chapter 6.

Portfolio Risk Characteristics

When securities are blended into a portfolio, the risk characteristics of the portfolio will differ from those of the individual securities comprising the portfolio. Risk can be decomposed into systematic risk and unsystematic risk. For fixed income securities systematic risk arises from the influence of overall changes in interest rates, affecting both capital changes as well as reinvestment return. Because a change in interest rates can affect returns on all bonds, systematic risk is a pervasive characteristic of bond investing. While stocks are also exposed to systematic risk, the effects of overall market conditions are less pervasive because they are far more heterogeneous than bonds. Thus stocks have much more risk specific to the individual security (unsystematic risk).

Specific or unsystematic risk. If interest rates do not change and the security is held to maturity, then the only source of risk in nominal terms is that of default. In this sense, then, the importance of unsystematic

Table 2–7
Composite Total Annual Returns (in percent). Based on Monthly Returns from January 1 to December 31 of Years Shown for a High-Grade Corporate Bond Index

From	1960	1961	1962	1963	1964	1965	1966	1967	1968	1969	1970
1960	9.1										
1961	6.9	4.8									
1962	7.3	6.4	7.9								
1963	6.0	5.0	5.0	2.2							
1964	5.7	4.9	4.9	3.5	4.8						
1965	4.7	3.8	3.6	2.1	2.1	−0.5					
1966	4.0	3.2	2.9	1.7	1.5	−0.1	0.2				
1967	2.9	2.0	1.5	0.3	−0.2	−1.9	−2.4	−5.0			
1968	2.8	2.1	1.7	0.7	0.4	−0.7	−0.8	−1.3	2.6		
1969	1.7	0.9	0.4	−0.6	−1.1	−2.2	−2.7	−3.6	−2.9	−8.1	
1970	3.1	2.5	2.3	1.6	1.5	0.9	1.2	1.5	3.7	4.3	18.4
1971	3.7	3.3	3.1	2.6	2.6	2.3	2.8	3.3	5.5	6.5	14.6
1972	4.0	3.6	3.5	3.0	3.1	2.9	3.4	4.0	5.8	6.7	12.1
1973	3.8	3.4	3.3	2.9	2.9	2.7	3.1	3.6	5.0	5.6	9.3
1974	3.3	2.9	2.8	2.4	2.4	2.1	2.4	2.7	3.9	4.1	6.7
1975	4.0	3.7	3.6	3.3	3.3	3.2	3.6	4.0	5.1	5.5	8.0
1976	4.8	4.5	4.5	4.3	4.4	4.4	4.9	5.4	6.6	7.1	9.4
1977	4.6	4.4	4.3	4.1	4.2	4.2	4.6	5.0	6.1	6.5	8.4
1978	4.4	4.1	4.1	3.8	4.0	3.9	4.2	4.6	5.5	5.8	7.5
1979	3.9	3.7	3.6	3.4	3.4	3.3	3.6	3.9	4.7	4.9	6.2
1980	3.6	3.3	3.3	3.0	3.1	3.0	3.2	3.4	4.1	4.2	5.4
1981	3.4	3.2	3.1	2.8	2.9	2.9	3.0	3.2	3.8	3.9	4.9

Source: Gifford Fong Associates.

risk vis-à-vis systematic risk is much less for fixed income securities than for stocks. Through diversification of issuers and classes of fixed income securities, unsystematic risk can be minimized.

Another manifestation of this risk source is in the yield spread relationship that may exist between securities. For example, a corporate bond that appears to be similar in all respects to another corporate bond but is selling at a higher yield reflects an issuing sector difference of some kind—typically in quality grade—that has gone undetected by the rating agencies. The variation in yield spread resulting from quality grade adjustments is an additional source of unsystematic risk.

By staying with high quality securities, the risk of default or unsystematic risk can be essentially eliminated under all but the most dire economic circumstances. For example, Treasury securities can be considered default-free. A portfolio of Treasury securities can therefore be thought of as having only systematic risk and subject only to price and return variation due to changes in interest rates.

1971	1972	1973	1974	1975	1976	1977	1978	1979	1980	1981
11.0										
9.1	7.3									
6.4	4.2	1.1								
3.9	1.7	−1.0	−3.1							
6.0	4.8	4.0	5.4	14.6						
8.0	7.4	7.5	9.7	16.6	18.6					
7.1	6.4	6.3	7.6	11.4	9.9	1.7				
6.2	5.5	5.2	6.0	8.4	6.4	0.8	−0.1			
5.0	4.2	3.8	4.3	5.8	3.7	−0.8	−2.1	−4.1		
4.2	3.5	3.0	3.3	4.3	2.4	−1.3	−2.3	−3.4	−2.7	
3.8	3.1	2.6	2.8	3.7	2.0	−1.1	−1.8	−2.3	−1.4	−0.2

Market or systematic risk. A central issue is how one controls market or systematic risk, which is the dominant influence on marginal return, positive or negative, that is implied by a bond's current yield to maturity. Traditionally, systematic risk has been controlled by varying the effective maturity (more accurately, duration or weighted average maturity) over time. In effect, diversifying maturities provides one way to control systematic risk. Maximum systematic risk exposure as measured in terms of standard deviation of return, given a specified interest rate change, is achieved with the longest maturity (duration) portfolio. Conversely, the minimum exposure to systematic risk is achieved by a short maturity (duration) portfolio. This holds assuming there is an equal basis point move across all maturities, i.e., a parallel shift in the yield curve. If there is a nonparallel change in rates, then a closer evaluation of return and risk impact is necessary. Return simulation analysis, described in Chapter 7, is a useful tool for this.

Alternatively, systematic risk may be controlled by investment strategies that seek to match maturity or duration of the securities (assets) with

Table 2–8
Annual Standard Deviations (in percent). Calculated from Composite Total Returns Based on Monthly Returns from January 1 to December 31 of Years Shown for a High-Grade Corporate Bond Index

From	1960	1961	1962	1963	1964	1965	1966	1967	1968	1969	1970
1960	3.5										
1961	3.4	3.3									
1962	3.1	2.8	2.0								
1963	2.8	2.4	1.8	1.2							
1964	2.6	2.2	1.7	1.3	1.3						
1965	2.5	2.2	1.9	1.6	1.8	1.9					
1966	3.0	2.8	2.7	2.7	3.0	3.5	4.6				
1967	3.9	3.9	3.9	4.1	4.6	5.1	6.2	7.3			
1968	4.3	4.4	4.5	4.7	5.1	5.7	6.4	7.2	6.9		
1969	4.8	4.8	5.0	5.2	5.6	6.1	6.7	7.2	7.2	7.1	
1970	5.5	5.6	5.8	6.1	6.5	7.0	7.6	8.2	8.4	9.0	9.2
1971	6.0	6.1	6.3	6.6	7.0	7.5	8.1	8.6	8.7	9.3	9.5
1972	5.8	5.9	6.1	6.4	6.7	7.1	7.5	7.9	7.9	8.2	8.0
1973	5.9	6.0	6.2	6.5	6.8	7.1	7.5	7.8	7.8	8.0	7.9
1974	6.4	6.6	6.7	7.0	7.3	7.6	8.0	8.3	8.4	8.6	8.7
1975	6.7	6.9	7.0	7.3	7.6	7.9	8.2	8.6	8.6	8.9	8.9
1976	6.6	6.8	7.0	7.2	7.4	7.7	8.0	8.3	8.3	8.5	8.5
1977	6.5	6.7	6.8	7.0	7.3	7.5	7.8	8.0	8.0	8.1	8.1
1978	6.4	6.6	6.7	6.9	7.1	7.4	7.6	7.8	7.8	7.9	7.8
1979	6.7	6.8	7.0	7.2	7.4	7.6	7.8	8.0	8.1	8.2	8.2
1980	7.9	8.0	8.2	8.4	8.6	8.9	9.2	9.4	9.5	9.7	9.8
1981	8.6	8.8	9.0	9.2	9.4	9.7	10.0	10.2	10.4	10.6	10.8

Source: Gifford Fong Associates.

the investment need (liabilities) of the portfolio. By virtue of the size and certainty of cash flows, it is possible to minimize the adverse effects of systematic risk via immunization strategies.

To summarize, since the investor who is very concerned with systematic risk can effectively immunize his bond portfolio, the only risk that remains is unsystematic risk, which can be essentially eliminated by diversifying the portfolio across a spectrum of high quality bond issues.

Measures of risk. As explained in Chapter 4, for asset allocation purposes, suitable risk measures are standard deviation and covariance of returns. In the context of fixed income securities these are directly related to the volatility of interest rates. As the magnitude of interest rate change increases, this will directly increase the standard deviation of fixed income returns. Since systematic risk is attributable to changes in interest rates, this implies a need to evaluate the standard deviation of interest rate changes.

Tables 2–7 and 2–8 reflect the total returns and standard deviations of a high-grade corporate bond index's monthly returns for holding peri-

1971	1972	1973	1974	1975	1976	1977	1978	1979	1980	1981
9.6										
7.1	2.9									
7.2	5.5	7.1								
8.5	7.9	9.4	11.2							
8.8	8.5	9.7	10.7	9.6						
8.3	8.0	8.8	9.2	7.5	4.3					
7.9	7.5	8.1	8.3	6.9	4.8	4.3				
7.5	7.2	7.7	7.7	6.5	4.8	4.3	4.3			
7.9	7.7	8.1	8.3	7.5	6.8	6.9	7.9	10.3		
9.8	9.8	10.4	10.8	10.7	10.8	11.6	13.2	15.9	19.9	
10.9	11.0	11.5	11.9	12.0	12.3	13.2	14.6	16.6	19.0	18.1

ods ranging from 1 year to 20 years over the two-decade-plus period 1960–81. Table 2–9 reflects the correlation of monthly total returns between bonds and stocks (represented by the S&P 500 Stock Composite Index) for similar combinations of holding periods.

Specifically, in Table 2–7, the numbers down the diagonal are the geometric mean (compound average) returns of the monthly total returns on the bond index from January to December of each year. As such, they represent the annual wealth increments of the index. The numbers in each column below the first number (the diagonal element defined in the previous sentence) are the geometric means of the corresponding numbers down the diagonal. For example, the 1963 value of 6.0 in the 1960 column is equal to $[(1.091 \times 1.048 \times 1.079 \times 1.022)^{1/4} - 1] \times 100$.

By contrast, in Table 2–8, the numbers down the diagonal are the standard deviations of the 12 monthly returns in each year, and the numbers in each column below the diagonal element are the standard deviations of the monthly returns from January of the column-heading year to December of the row-heading year. Hence, in the 1960 column the num-

Table 2–9
Correlations (in percent) of Monthly Total Returns on Standard & Poor's 500 Stock Composite Index with Returns on a High-Grade Corporate Bond Index

From	1960	1961	1962	1963	1964	1965	1966	1967	1968	1969	1970
1960	−7.0										
1961	6.0	41.3									
1962	3.5	10.2	2.5								
1963	−0.0	5.8	−9.9	−1.2							
1964	−0.0	5.8	−8.1	−1.4	9.0						
1965	1.6	7.8	−3.2	11.8	19.4	21.3					
1966	18.7	26.8	23.9	45.1	55.3	56.3	76.3				
1967	28.3	35.4	34.2	52.9	59.1	60.2	66.0	79.7			
1968	17.3	21.5	19.3	28.4	30.6	30.5	31.8	23.0	−27.9		
1969	20.9	24.5	22.7	30.6	32.1	31.6	32.4	27.3	5.5	28.3	
1970	33.2	36.5	36.2	43.2	45.2	45.3	46.8	44.2	40.5	61.1	79.0
1971	33.0	35.8	35.6	41.4	43.2	43.4	44.7	42.3	39.4	53.3	58.2
1972	34.0	36.8	36.7	42.4	44.3	44.5	45.7	43.4	40.5	53.8	57.6
1973	28.6	30.8	30.5	34.6	36.0	36.1	37.0	34.4	31.1	40.6	41.4
1974	34.1	35.8	35.7	38.7	39.7	39.8	40.5	38.9	37.6	43.9	45.7
1975	37.2	38.8	38.8	41.7	42.7	42.8	43.4	42.1	41.2	46.7	47.9
1976	37.8	39.3	39.4	42.1	43.1	43.2	43.9	42.5	41.7	47.0	47.9
1977	38.4	39.9	40.0	42.6	43.6	43.7	44.4	43.1	42.5	47.6	48.7
1978	38.5	40.0	40.0	42.5	43.4	43.5	44.1	42.9	42.2	46.9	47.9
1979	39.8	41.2	41.3	43.8	44.5	44.6	45.1	44.1	43.4	47.6	48.4
1980	32.2	33.3	33.2	35.1	35.6	35.7	36.0	35.0	33.8	36.6	36.3
1981	33.9	34.9	34.9	36.7	37.2	37.3	37.6	36.8	35.9	38.4	38.3

Source: Gifford Fong Associates.

ber 2.8 in the 1963 row is the standard deviation of the 48 monthly returns from January 1960 to December 1963.

Finally, in Table 2–9, the diagonal numbers are the coefficients of correlation (in percentage terms) of the 12 monthly returns on stocks and bonds from January to December of each year. The numbers in each column below the diagonal element are the correlation coefficients of the monthly paired stock and bond returns from January of the column-heading year to December of the row-heading year. For example, in the 1960 column, 1966 row, the number 18.7 indicates there was 0.187 correlation between the paired monthly returns on a stock and bond index over the period January 1960 to December 1966.

Looking down the diagonal of each of the tables, it can be seen that bond returns have varied on a yearly basis from −8.1 to 18.6 percent; the standard deviation from 1.2 to 19.9 percent; and the correlation from −.279 to .797. The compound or geometric average return for the entire period was 3.4 percent. Average and standard deviation numbers such as those generated in these tables usually provide the basis for forecasting

1971	1972	1973	1974	1975	1976	1977	1978	1979	1980	1981
34.8										
39.0	75.8									
17.2	−2.8	−26.5								
36.1	36.2	32.5	49.5							
41.6	43.4	42.4	54.1	55.8						
42.2	44.3	43.7	53.6	49.6	41.3					
43.4	45.4	44.8	54.5	55.5	56.2	59.7				
43.0	44.9	44.2	52.9	52.9	50.2	49.2	49.2			
44.4	45.9	45.3	52.7	54.3	51.8	53.2	55.6	71.6		
32.3	32.0	31.4	35.4	31.6	25.4	23.8	23.3	23.1	4.7	
35.1	35.1	34.6	38.1	37.1	33.7	33.3	33.3	35.1	27.8	69.6

expectations of future return and risk. But in the case of these distributions of returns, the range of the numbers shown is so wide that the average is not really representative or descriptive of the underlying distribution. It is important to keep in mind that it is the underlying economic process that is important for providing a credible basis for forecasting purposes. Identification of clear and unambiguous trends in the data—not present here—can be helpful in better understanding the process.

The recent increase in the standard deviation of bond returns reflects a sharp change in the riskiness of fixed income securities. If this represents secular rather than cyclical change in the risk characteristics of these securities, investors will have to reassess the role of bonds within the risk spectrum of all investable assets. The traditional role of bonds as a "safe" asset, with low price volatility and predictable cash flow, has been clouded by recent experience. Such abrupt changes in the characteristics of a class of securities like bonds are difficult to forecast with implicit or explicit models. But even though return and risk are not static phenomena, it is of some comfort to know that time has a way of smoothing out the peaks and valleys in bond market prices and returns. Risk, in particular, has a tendency to increase at a slower rate than return increases as the investor's time horizon is extended. Hence for investors with relatively long future time horizons, portfolio strategies allow and even encourage the inclusion of higher-return, higher-risk assets such as long maturity bonds.

Understanding the return and risk characteristics leads to the consideration of alternative strategies making use of these features. □

3

Portfolio Constraints

The return objectives and risk tolerance of investors is modified by investor constraints, some of which are characteristic of a class of investors while others may be unique to a particular institutional or individual investor. In this chapter we relate the characteristics of fixed income securities and fixed income markets to these investor constraints. Before doing so, however, we provide a brief overview of the federal and state regulations governing the activities of investment managers.

■ Regulation of Investment Managers

An investment manager's fiduciary responsibility to his clients is viewed by law as consisting of two duties. The first duty is that of reasonable care. The standard of reasonable care for a fiduciary is commonly referred to as "prudence." The second duty of a fiduciary is that of loyalty. This means that the fiduciary must provide advice that is not self-serving and that any decisions made by the fiduciary must be carried out for the sole benefit of the client. In the balance of this section, we will discuss the standard of prudence for investment managers and its implications. Our exclusion of loyalty, however, should not be construed as minimizing its importance in an investment manager's discharge of his or her responsibility.[1]

The duties of a fiduciary with respect to reasonable care are guided by the "prudent man" rule which has developed as part of the law of trusts, which is a matter of state law. The prudent man rule was first articulated in 1830 in the case of *Harvard College* v. *Amory*. In that decision, the Supreme Court of Massachusetts stated:

> All that can be required of a trustee to invest, is, that he shall conduct himself faithfully and exercise a sound discretion. He is to observe how men of prudence, discretion, and intelligence manage their own affairs, not in regard to speculation, but in regard to the permanent disposition of their funds, considering the probable income, as well as the probable safety of the capital to be invested.

This rule does not establish what is prudent or imprudent per se. Instead, it states that a factual determination must be made under the circumstances. One of the problems with the prudent man rule is that it has been interpreted as a rule that requires that each security holding in a portfolio must be prudent on its own rather than in terms of its role in a portfolio. As we shall see throughout this book, modern portfolio theory indicates that the risk of a security in the context of a portfolio should serve as the basis for judging whether a particular security holding is imprudent.

In 1975, the New York Court of Appeals in the case of *The Bank of New York* v. *Spitzer* reaffirmed the traditional "security-by-security" approach as a test of prudence but did recognize the role of a security within a portfolio when it stated:

> The record of any individual investment is not to be viewed exclusively, of course, as though it were in its one watertight compartment since to some extent individual investment decisions may properly be affected by considerations of the performance of the fund as an entity, as in the instance, for example, of individual security decisions based in part on considerations of diversification of the fund or capital transactions to achieve sound tax planning for the fund as a whole. The focus of inquiry, however, is nonetheless on the individual security as such and factors relating to the entire portfolio are to be weighted along with others in reviewing the prudence of the particular investment decision.

The view that prudence should be judged using a "whole portfolio approach" rather than a "security-by-security approach" was adopted in July 1979 by the Department of Labor (DOL) which has the responsibility

---

[1] For a further discussion of the responsibility of investment managers under fiduciary law, see James L. Walters, "An Overview of Fiduciary Law," Chapter 21 in *The Investment Manager's Handbook*, ed. Sumner Levine (Homewood, Ill.: Dow Jones-Irwin, 1980).

for administering the Employee Retirement Income Security Act of 1974 (ERISA). According to the Department of Labor regulations supplementing ERISA, a fiduciary will satisfy a prudence test if:

> Appropriate consideration to those facts and circumstances that, given the scope of such fiduciary's investment duties, the fiduciary knows or should know are relevant to the particular investment or investment course of action involved, including the role the investment or investment course of action plays in that portion of the plan's investment portfolio with respect to which the fiduciary has investment duties.

As for the meaning of "appropriate consideration," the DOL regulations supplementing ERISA defines that as:

> (A) A determination by the fiduciary that the particular investment or investment course of action is reasonably designed, as part of the portfolio (or, where applicable, that portion of the plan portfolio with respect to which the fiduciary has investment duties), to further the purposes of the plan, taking into consideration the risk of loss and the opportunity for gain (or other return) associated with the investment or investment course of action, and (B) consideration of the following factors as they relate to such portion of the portfolio:
>
> (i) The composition of the portfolio with regard to diversification;
>
> (ii) The liquidity and current return of the portfolio relative to the anticipated cash flow requirements of the plan; and
>
> (iii) The projected return of the portfolio relative to the funding objectives of the plan.

Although the whole portfolio approach test of prudence is applicable for plans regulated by ERISA, the security-by-security approach interpretation under the prudent man rule may be applicable in non-ERISA matters.

While prudence under the Department of Labor regulations supplementing ERISA provides general guidelines, the investment technology at the time will provide a specific benchmark for quantifying these guidelines. For example, the concepts of portfolio risk and diversification have been quantified based on the concepts of modern portfolio theory using various statistical measures.

More accurate techniques for measuring return and evaluating performance have been developed. As these techniques become accepted they will serve as benchmarks for tests of prudence, since under ERISA the prudent man rule provides that a fiduciary discharge his duties "with the care, skill, prudence, and diligence under the circumstances then prevailing that a prudent man acting in a like capacity and familiar with such matters would use in the conduct of an enterprise of a like character and with like aims." This is known as the "prudent expert" rule. Thus, investment managers of institutions will be judged by the standard existing for other investment managers of institutions. The investment tools we describe in this book represent the latest investment technology as well as new techniques that we hope will be accepted as the investment technology of the future.

■ Portfolio Constraints

Liquidity Needs

Fixed income securities are looked upon primarily as providing a secure cash flow stream and a fixed maturity. With respect to the allocation of funds among the general investment classes, they are well suited to meeting an investor's needs for continuous and periodic cash flow from income and/or maturing principal. Within the bond portfolio, the degree of liquidity required by investors varies.

For example, despite periods when a life insurance company may encounter liquidity problems due to an aggressive schedule of forward investment commitments, the liquidity needs of this segment of the insurance industry are considerably less than those of property and casualty companies. Even within a given industry, liquidity needs vary. For example, mature property and casualty insurance companies may be less concerned with liquidity than are newly created companies. In the pension area, the liquidity needs of a pension fund will depend on the current age distribution of future beneficiaries, with relatively young plans of growing firms having less need for liquidity than older plans where considerable benefits must be paid in the near future. Consequently, investors must modify their return objective and risk tolerance because of a basic need for an assured schedule of cash flow from their investment portfolio.

A liquidity reserve may be derived from the cash flow from coupons and maturing fixed income instruments or created and maintained by holding money market instruments, such as Treasury bills and commercial paper. Furthermore, liquidity may be derived from a spaced schedule of maturing obligations over a few months or a few years.

Liquidity can also be achieved by emphasizing or limiting portfolio investments to the most readily marketable and liquid types of bonds; that is, those issues that could be sold quickly with little or no price concession from currently quoted prices. Emphasis on marketability is important, not only for satisfying unanticipated cash flow requirements, but also for pursuing an overall portfolio strategy. For example, to maximize their aftertax return, property and casualty companies constantly shift between taxable and tax-exempts depending on underwriting profits which determine their marginal tax rate. The lack of marketability of portfolio holdings can jeopardize the success of this strategy. As another example, the immunization strategy that we will discuss in Chapter 6 requires the periodic disposition of bond issues. In an immunized portfolio, security holdings that must be disposed of at concession prices will reduce the likelihood that the strategy will satisfy its objective.

High credit quality and short maturity are the most dominant characteristics of readily marketable bonds. We should also note that round lot holdings—typically $500,000 par value of a corporate issue—are more marketable than odd lots—less than $500,000 par. The marketability of round lots is reflected in the narrower dealer spreads between bid and asked prices than occur for odd lots. Odd lot long bonds typically have wide spreads. On the other hand, Treasury bills and certain other money market instruments can be purchased in odd lots with little or no yield penalty. The yield penalty in the case of corporate bonds places restrictions on the allocation of funds among issues when designing a portfolio under a given strategy. For example, an optimal solution for some strategy may call for the purchase or sale of $200,000 par value of a particular corporate issue. Because of price concessions on odd lot transactions, constraints may have to be imposed to restrict a solution to only portfolio transactions of at least $500,000. We shall see examples of this when we discuss various strategies in this book. Actively managed bond portfolios develop periodic liquidity needs in the form of reserves held in anticipation of a change in yields and bond prices. Minimum market risk is sought with the least sacrifice in interest income.

Liquidity characteristics are determined by:

1. Amount outstanding (dollar amount of the issue of bonds outstanding)—the more the better.
2. Amount closely held (dollar amount of issue)—the less, the better.
3. Coupon level—the closer to the current coupon level the better because there is an investor preference for current coupon securities.
4. Age of issue—recently issued securities tend to be more actively traded.
5. Quality—the higher the better.
6. Terms (such as callability or sinking fund provisions)—tend to reduce liquidity but if a bond is redeemed by being called, the call feature provides a potential liquidity source.
7. Maturity (duration)—fixed income securities with a maturity or duration of less than one year tend to be more liquid than any longer maturity/duration securities for any given issue.

Tax Considerations

Unlike qualified pension funds, individual investors and financial institutions such as banks and insurance companies are subject to income taxes. Here we shall provide an overview of the federal income tax treatment of fixed income securities, highlighting the nuances of the tax code with respect to several financial institutions.

Terminology. The Internal Revenue Code (IRC) defines *gross income* as all income that is subject to income tax. For example, interest income and dividends are subject to taxation. However, there is a statutory exemption for interest income (not capital gains) earned from debt issued by any state or political subdivision thereof, the District of Columbia, any possession of the United States, and certain local and urban agencies operating under the auspices of the Department of Housing and Urban Development. *Taxable income* is the amount on which the tax liability is determined. An important deduction from gross income in determining taxable income is the long-term capital gains deduction which will be discussed later.

The IRC provides for a special tax treatment on the sale or exchange of a capital asset and for preferential tax treatment for certain gains on their disposal. Fixed income securities qualify as a capital asset in the hands of a qualified owner. In order to understand the tax treatment of a capital asset, the *tax basis* of an asset must be defined. In most instances the *original basis* of a capital asset is the price paid on the date it is acquired. The *adjusted basis* of a capital asset is its original basis increased by capital additions and decreased by capital recoveries.

To determine if a transaction produced a capital gain or loss, the proceeds received from the sale or exchange of a capital asset are compared to the adjusted basis. If the proceeds exceed the adjusted basis, the taxpayer realizes a capital gain. If the opposite occurs, the taxpayer realizes a capital loss. Just how any capital gains or losses are treated will be discussed below.

Tax treatment of interest income. Interest received by a taxpayer is included in gross income, unless there is a specific statutory exemption indicating otherwise. As we explained in Chapter 2, a portion of the total return from holding a bond may be in the form of capital appreciation. Prior to the Tax Reform Act of 1984, the capital appreciation portion of the total return was treated as a capital gain (with the exception of original-issue discount bonds). As explained later, the 1984 Act specifies that upon disposition of a bond, any capital appreciation must be separated into an interest income component and a capital gain component. The former is taxed as ordinary income. The capital gain component, on the other hand, may qualify for preferential tax treatment depending upon how long the bond was held. This treatment will be discussed later.

Consequently, the composition of the total return will have an impact on the aftertax return for a taxable entity. Since the maximum tax rate on ordinary income is 50 percent for individuals and 46 percent for corporations while the maximum tax rate on certain capital gains as explained later is 20 percent for individuals and 28 percent for corporations, the greater the portion of the total return that is classified as a capital gain, the greater the aftertax return that will be realized by a taxable entity.

Bond purchased at a premium. When a bond is purchased at a price greater than its redemption value at maturity, the bond is said to be purchased at a premium. For a taxable bond, the tax entity may elect to amortize the premium ratably over the remaining life of the security.[2] The amount amortized reduces the amount of the interest income that will be taxed. In turn, the basis is reduced by the amount of the amortization. For a tax-exempt bond, the premium *must* be amortized. Although the amount amortized is not a tax-deductible expense since the interest is exempt from taxation, the amortization reduces the original basis.

Bond purchased at a discount. A bond purchased at a price less than its redemption value at maturity is said to be bought at a *discount*. The tax treatment of the discount depends upon whether the discount represents *original-issue discount* or *market* discount (i.e., a bond that was *not* sold at an original-issue discount but is purchased in the secondary market at a discount).

The tax treatment of an original-issue discount depends on the issuance date. For obligations issued prior to July 2, 1982, the ratable monthly portion of the original-issue discount must be amortized and included in gross income. For obligations issued after July 2, 1982, the amount of the amortization is determined by the effective or so-called scientific interest method. This means that amortization is lower in the earlier years, gradually increasing over the life of the obligation on a compounding basis. Regardless of the issuance date, the amount amortized is added to the adjusted basis. The foregoing rules for original-issue discount bonds are not applicable to noninterest-bearing municipal and federal obligations maturing in one year or less from the date of the issuance. In such cases, the interest is recognized as earned only when the obligation is redeemed or sold.

An important point that the investor should bear in mind when considering original-issue discount bonds is that taxes must be paid *each year* on interest accrued as well as coupon interest received. For taxable entities holding zero coupon bonds, this will result in a negative cash flow. Consequently, original-issue deep discount bonds are unattractive for portfolios of individual investors and institutions subject to taxation.

The tax treatment of a market discount bond has been changed by the 1984 Act. *Upon the sale* of a market discount bond, any capital appreciation that is the result of accrued market discount is treated as interest income and therefore taxed as ordinary income. The excess of the capital appreciation over the accrued market discount is classified as a capital gain. Prior to the 1984 Act, the entire capital appreciation was classified as a capital gain. Consequently, before the passage of the 1984 Act bonds

---

[2] In the case of a convertible bond selling at a premium, however, the amount attributable to the conversion feature may not be amortized.

selling at a market discount were more attractive than bonds selling near par (current coupon bonds) to taxable entities because they offered the potential for a higher aftertax return.

Capital gain and loss treatment. Once a capital gain or capital loss is determined for a capital asset, there are special rules for determining the impact on adjusted gross income. The tax treatment for individuals and nondealer corporations is explained here.

To determine the impact of transactions involving capital assets on adjusted gross income, it is first necessary to ascertain whether the sale or exchange has resulted in a capital gain or loss that is long term or short term. The classification depends upon the length of time the capital asset is held by the taxpayer. For a capital asset acquired after June 22, 1984 and held for less than six months, the gain or loss is a short-term capital gain or loss.[3] A long-term capital gain or loss results when a capital asset is held for more than six months. The long-term holding period for a capital asset acquired before June 22, 1984 is one year.

Second, all short-term capital gains and losses are combined to produce either a *net short-term capital gain* or a *net short-term capital loss*. The same procedure is followed for long-term capital gains and losses. Either a *net long-term capital gain* or a *net long-term capital loss* will result.

Third, an overall *net capital gain* or *net capital loss* is determined by combining the amounts in the previous step. If the result is a net capital gain, the entire amount is added to gross income. However, net long-term capital gains are given preferential tax treatment. For individuals, a deduction is allowed from gross income in determining adjusted gross income. The permissible deduction is 60 percent of the excess of net long-term capital gains over net short-term capital losses.[4] Table 3–1 provides six illustrations of the treatment of a net capital gain.

The tax treatment of any net capital gain is different for a nondealer corporation. No net capital gain deduction is allowed. Instead the excess is subject to an alternative tax computation that limits the tax to 28 percent of the gain. The tax attributable to the excess of net long-term capital gains over net short-term capital losses is the lesser of (1) the tax liability on the taxable income when the excess is included in taxable income (i.e., regular tax computation) and (2) the tax liability on taxable income that is reduced by the excess, plus a 28 percent tax on the excess. The latter tax computation is the alternative tax computation.

---

[3] An exception to this rule applies to wash sales. A wash sale occurs when "substantially identical securities" are acquired within 30 days before or after a sale of the securities *at a loss*. In such cases, the loss is not recognized as a capital loss. Instead, the loss is added to the basis of the securities that caused the loss. The holding period for the new securities in connection with a wash sale then includes the period for which the original securities were held. The rule is not applicable to an individual who is a trader, nor to an individual or corporate dealer.

[4] A capital gain deduction taken by an individual could result in a minimum tax liability.

Table 3–1
Tax Treatment of a Net Capital Gain

	Illustration Number					
	(1)	*(2)*	*(3)*	*(4)*	*(5)*	*(6)*
1. Net long-term capital gain (loss)	$ 35,000	$ 35,000	$ 35,000	$ 0	$ (3,000)	$ (8,000)
2. Net short-term capital gain (loss)	(15,000)	15,000	0	15,000	15,000	15,000
3. Net capital gain: increase in gross income	20,000	50,000	35,000	15,000	12,000	7,000
4. Excess of net long-term capital gain over net short-term capital loss	20,000	35,000	35,000	0	0	0
5. Capital gains deduction (60 percent of line 4)	(12,000)	(21,000)	(21,000)	0	0	0
6. Increase in adjusted gross income (line 3 minus line 5)	8,000	29,000	14,000	15,000	12,000	7,000

For an individual, if there is a net capital loss, it is deductible from gross income. The amount that may be deducted, however, is limited to the lesser of (1) $3,000 (but $1,500 for married taxpayers filing separate returns), (2) taxable income without the personal exemption and without capital gains and losses minus the zero bracket amount, and (3) the total of net short-term capital loss plus half the net long-term capital loss. The third limitation is the so-called $1 for $2 rule and is the basic difference between the tax treatment of net short-term capital losses and net long-term capital losses. The former is deductible dollar for dollar, but the latter requires $2 of long-term capital loss to obtain a $1 deduction.

Because of the difference in the tax treatment of net long-term capital losses and net short-term capital losses, the order in which these losses are deductible in a tax year is specified by the Treasury. First, net short-term capital losses are used to satisfy the limitation. Any balance to satisfy the limitation is then applied from net long-term capital losses using the $1 for $2 rule. Any unused net short-term or net long-term capital losses are carried over on a dollar-for-dollar basis. When they are carried over, they do not lose their identity but remain either short-term or long-term. These losses can be carried over indefinitely until they are all utilized in subsequent tax years.

Table 3–2 provides 10 illustrations of the net capital loss deduction rule. In the illustrations it is assumed that taxable income as defined in (2) above is greater than $3,000, and the taxpayer, if married, is not filing a separate return.

For a nondealer corporation, on the other hand, no deduction is allowed for a net capital loss. However, net capital losses can be carried back to three preceding taxable years and carried forward five taxable years to offset any net capital gains in those years.[5] Although there are exceptions, the general rule is that any unused net capital loss after the fifth subsequent year can never be used by a corporate taxpayer. Net capital losses are not carried over in character. Instead, they are carried over as a short-term capital loss.

Special tax treatment for financial institutions. The IRC sets forth special tax treatment for certain financial institutions. Pension funds are afforded special tax treatment that results in a zero marginal tax rate for qualified plans. Another example is the taxation of life insurance companies which is governed by the complex rules of the Life Insurance Income Tax Act of 1959. According to this act, the investment income is not all taxable. Only that portion of investment income that is transferred

---

[5] There is a limitation on the amount that can be carried back. The amount cannot cause or increase a net operating loss in the taxable year it is carried back to. Net capital losses are applied to the earliest year as a carry-back or carry-over.

Table 3–2
Tax Treatment of a Net Capital Loss

					Illustration Number					
	(1)	(2)	(3)	(4)	(5)	(6)	(7)	(8)	(9)	(10)
1. Net long-term capital gain (loss)	$ 0	$(7,000)	$(7,000)	$(7,000)	$(3,000)	$(4,000)	$ 6,000	$(4,000)	$(12,000)	$ 4,000
2. Net short-term capital gain (loss)	(5,000)	0	(5,000)	(2,000)	(1,000)	0	(7,000)	1,000	2,000	(14,000)
3. Net capital loss	5,000	7,000	12,000	9,000	4,000	4,000	1,000	3,000	10,000	10,000
4. Capital loss deduction*	3,000	3,000	3,000	3,000	2,500	2,000	1,000	1,500	3,000	3,000
5. Long-term capital loss carryover	0	1,000	7,000	5,000	0	0	0	0	4,000	0
6. Short-term capital loss carryover	2,000	0	2,000	0	0	0	0	0	0	7,000

* Assumes that the taxpayer (1) is not married or if married is not filing a separate return and (2) has taxable income without the personal exemption and without capital gains and losses minus the zero bracket amount greater than $3,000.

to surplus, not the portion added to fund reserves, is taxable. Moreover, the complicated formula employed by the IRC to determine the taxable portion may result in instances where the marginal tax exceeds 46 percent.

Time Horizon

Each investor has a specified time horizon or period over which the return objectives are intended to be satisfied. The life cycle of the individual investor or the pension fund or the operating cycle of a financial institution or endowment fund largely determines the portfolio time horizon. Fixed income securities have a definite investment life or maturity that can be matched or related to the investor's time horizon. In fact, this certainty of term to maturity provides the portfolio manager with a base for fitting expected returns with investor return objectives. Preferred and common stocks, which have a perpetual life, provide no similar certainty or structure.

The essence of fixed income management is to take advantage of this structure. In its most basic form quality analysis ensures against experiencing default, while more active forms of management seek to exploit cyclical or temporary return opportunities. Time horizon trade-offs, where the relatively certain returns of holding a security to maturity are balanced against a more active trading strategy, must be a continual consideration. For example, if you begin to actively manage a portfolio that has employed a buy-and-hold approach, you may jeopardize the high cash flows that had been expected from buying and holding. Similarly, if you decide to actively manage a previously immunized portfolio where coupon reinvestment risk has been balanced against discount accretion, you may jeopardize the original objective sought via immunization. It can be seen from these examples that both the decision to change strategy—and to begin to actively manage—*and* the timing of that decision can be critical to the attainment of fixed income portfolio objectives.

Active strategies are concerned with planning horizons within the portfolio time horizon; hence, the manager is faced with a sequence of decision horizons. Logically, each of these would be concurrently, rather than sequentially, optimized, so that the decision-making process would span multiple horizons instead of one period at a time. However, because of the uncertainty of expectations, considerations beyond the next planning period become very complicated. For example, a three-scenario forecast leads to a nine-scenario projection if two periods are considered at once, since each period-one scenario can lead to three possible period-two scenarios. This would continue to increase by a factor of three with each additional time period. Providing the inputs to and understanding the outputs from such a process would be beyond the capacity of most managers. The solution has been to retain the one-period framework, to continuously monitor the analysis, and to be open to adjustments with the passage of time—especially whenever a change in expectations takes place. A moving window of a desired planning horizon emerges within the overall portfolio time horizon.

Regulatory or Legal Considerations

The environment in which fixed income management must operate includes a number of exogenous constraints.

Regulation of asset allocation. Certain financial institutions are regulated as to the eligible class of assets, the minimum and/or maximum amount that may be placed in a particular asset class, and the maximum amount that may be invested in a given asset. Within an asset class, there may be restrictions on the particular assets eligible for investment.

The life insurance industry is an excellent example. The portfolios of firms in this industry are heavily influenced by state insurance regulations. The New York State Insurance Law, for example, does not allow a life insurance company to invest more than 5 percent of its admitted assets in the bonds of any one institution and no more 2 percent of its admitted assets in the preferred stock of any one corporation. There are quantitative standards that must be satisfied by an issue in order to be eligible. For bonds, these tests deal with minimum coverage ratios or earnings tests. Yet, there is some flexibility built in for bonds that would not qualify according to quantitative standards. New York, as well as other states, has a "basket" or "leeway" provision. This provision permits a certain amount to be invested in otherwise ineligible investments such as lower rated quality bonds.

Regulatory restrictions on the inclusion of certain types of investment vehicles will reduce a portfolio manager's ability to provide a better risk-return trade-off for his client. For example, strategies involving futures and options, as we explain in Chapter 8, allow a portfolio manager to provide a better risk-return trade-off for his clients. Yet, because futures and options are viewed as speculative by some regulators, rather than as tools for controlling portfolio risk, there has often been considerable lag time between the introduction of a new contract and its acceptance by regulators as an eligible investment vehicle. Fortunately, in recent years, as some regulators have become more familiar with the economic role of these instruments, they have broadened their position regarding the use of these relatively new vehicles by the institutions they regulate. For example, it took years before many state insurance regulators permitted the use of certain strategies involving exchange-traded equity options. As another example, consider the position of the Comptroller of the Currency on the use of exchange-traded equity options by national banks. In late 1973, just after exchange-traded equity options began trading, the Comptroller's position was that all option transactions may be speculative as a matter of law and, as a result, subject to criticism as investments for a trust account. Nine months later the Comptroller expanded his position by permitting trust accounts to employ a certain option strategy known as a covered call, but left other forms of option positions subject to criticism. It took until the end of 1979 for the Comptroller to accept that options, as an investment tool, were neither inherently prudent nor imprudent.[6]

As new instruments, such as futures and options, are introduced, there may not be a clear-cut position taken by a regulatory body. In such circumstances, interpretation of the existing laws governing prudence are required by counsel. ERISA, for example, does not specifically mention the use of futures and options by private pension plans. However, because of the prudent expert rule under ERISA certain strategies involving options and futures are generally believed to be permissible for private pension plans.

Taking losses. Because bonds eventually mature at par value, investors, even those who are not legally constrained, are often reluctant to sell a bond at a price below the cost of the bond and realize a capital loss.[7] This preoccupation with book loss (the difference between cost and market) or even par value loss (the difference between par and market) may appear prudent on the surface. However, for an income-oriented investor in particular, such concerns ignore the opportunity costs involved.

These opportunity costs represent the loss of increase in investment income that could be realized from the sale of a bond and reinvestment of the proceeds in another suitable and higher yielding bond. Such higher yielding opportunities often arise if the investor is willing to lengthen matur-

---

[6] For a discussion of the use of options by institutions, see Beverly S. Gordon, "Market Participants: Institutions," Chapter 30 in *The Handbook of Financial Markets: Securities, Options and Futures,* ed. Frank J. Fabozzi and Frank G. Zarb (Homewood, Ill.: Dow Jones-Irwin, 1981). For a discussion of the use of futures by institutions, see Stephen F. Selig, "Regulation of Users of Stock Index Futures," Chapter 20 in *Stock Index Futures,* ed. Frank J. Fabozzi and Gregory M. Kipnis (Homewood, Ill.: Dow Jones-Irwin, 1984).

[7] Many pension funds have bookkeeping practices that inhibit portfolio managers from taking capital losses. This policy is one of the reasons why original-issue deep discount bonds are popular with pension funds despite the yield sacrifice. If an original deep discount bond is selling at a favorable spread over prevailing nonoriginal deep discount bonds held in their portfolio, a swap can be undertaken without having an adverse impact on the fund's financial statements. Bond swaps that enhance a portfolio's return without incurring any additional risk or improve the quality with no sacrifice of return may be shunned by a portfolio manager if it means that a capital loss may result. Yet a capital loss may not occur or may be negligible if the newly acquired bond is an original-issue deep discount bond.

ity (assuming a positively sloped yield curve) or reduce quality. Less frequently, market inefficiencies provide the observant investor with the opportunity to reinvest at a higher yield without extending or downgrading. For example, sinking-fund bids for industrial bonds frequently provide the opportunity to sell older issues at a premium over current market prices on similar bonds except for sinking-fund purchasing activity.

Most importantly, the opportunity cost must be sufficiently great or, in other words, the yield advantage must be sufficiently large to allow the investor to recover the loss (book or par) out of the additional interest income at or prior to the maturity of the bond sold. Because tax regulation allows the offset of capital gains and losses, as explained earlier in this chapter, some taxable investors might adjust the realized loss by the amount of the capital gains tax that could be saved. Table 3–3 provides an

Table 3–3
Example of Loss Makeup on a Corporate Bond Sold

Sold: American Telephone and Telegraph Company
2⅝% Debentures due 7-1-86
Price: 73½   Yield-to-maturity: 10.66%

Purchased: U.S. Treasury
12¾% Notes due 2-15-87
Price: 96.469   Yield-to-maturity: 13.76%

Investment Results

	Including Capital Gains Tax Savings	Excluding Capital Gains Tax Savings
I. CAPITAL LOSS		
Tax basis of bonds sold	$208,000	$208,000
Less: Proceeds	152,880	152,880
Gross loss	$ 55,120	$ 55,120
II. INCOME RESULTS		
Proceeds	$152,880	$152,880
Add: Prospective capital gains tax savings at 28% corporate rate	15,434	—
Total reinvested	168,314	152,880
New annual income at 13.76%	23,160	21,036
Less: Previous income	5,460	5,460
Annual increase	$ 17,700	$ 15,576
Percent increase	324%	260%
III. LOSS MAKEUP TIME		
Time required to recover gross loss	3.1 years	3.3 years
Time to maturity of sold bonds	4.2	4.2
Maturity of Treasury bond purchased	4.8	4.8

example that illustrates that taking losses can be both prudent and profitable when market inefficiencies provide such opportunities.

GIC valuation. Another example of this type of constraint is the special treatment afforded guaranteed investment contracts (GICs) by actuaries who will accept valuation of GICs at book. Immunized portfolios on the other hand are usually valued at market. This makes GICs appear more attractive because of their resulting lack of principal volatility. There does appear to be some movement toward having immunized portfolios treated similarly.

The point to be made in this discussion is that fixed income strategies cannot be considered in the abstract. Realistically, depending on the type of investor and the jurisdiction(s) that may be controlling, theoretical optimality may be modified via regulator constraints.

Unique Considerations of the Investor

Portfolio construction would be sterile without provision for the special requirements of each investor. Some of these have already been covered in the other sections on fixed income portfolio constraints. Beyond these, institutional investors may be concerned with such things as social responsibility issues that may preclude investing in firms that make objectionable products or do business in certain countries;[8] predefined portfolio structures where the quality and/or maturity range of the portfolio holdings may be restricted; and special strategy arrangements, as described by Black and Dewhurst, that suggest an all-bond portfolio for pension funds because of tax arbitrage reasons.[9] For the individual investor, the status of his or her estate, retirement objectives, and cash flow needs should be taken into account.

------

[8] Advocates of social investing have argued that public pension funds should use their economic clout as a mechanism for increasing the supply of affordable mortgage money for state residents. As of mid-1983, at least 25 states have programs requiring state administered pension funds to invest a portion of their portfolio in publicly or privately insured mortgage-backed securities in order to increase the supply of mortgage funds for homeownership. Although advocates believe that social investing programs can achieve desirable objectives without foregoing return or increasing risk, an analysis of state-administered pension funds' experience with privately insured mortgage-backed securities does not support this position. (See Alicia H. Munnell (with the assistance of Lynn E. Blais and Kristine M. Keefe), "The Pitfalls of Social Investing: Public Pensions and Housing," *New England Economic Review* (September–October 1983), pp. 20–41.

[9] Fischer Black and Morey Dewhurst, "A New Investment Strategy for Pension Funds," *The Journal of Portfolio Management*, Summer 1981, pp. 26–34. See also Fischer Black, "The Consequences of Long-Run Pension Policy," *Financial Analysts Journal* (July–August 1980), pp. 21–29.

■ *Summary*

The important point that an investment manager must recognize is that portfolio construction process does not proceed in a vacuum. Optimal return-risk trade-offs may have to be compromised to adhere to the investor's preferences. In the final analysis, however, it is the client's portfolio and if an effective relationship is to be maintained, the portfolio manager and the client will have to come to a meeting of the minds on these issues. □

4

Asset Allocation Decision

Portfolio management can be viewed as a two-level process: the macro decision on the proportion of the portfolio to be held in various asset classes (stocks, bonds, treasury bills, etc.), and the micro decision on which individual securities will make up the respective components. While both steps have similar concerns relating to return and risks, the first step, or macro decision, deserves special attention because it is probably the most important portfolio decision in terms of maximizing return and minimizing risk. We refer to this process as *asset allocation*.[1]

If an investor is risk-averse, the problem of how to achieve alternative return levels at minimum risk is important. If minimizing risk is the only objective, then investment in Treasury bills will achieve a return which is accepted as being relatively risk-free. If maximizing return is the only objective, then investment in the highest expected return asset is the answer. Given the usual range of alternatives, this is common stock. The real problem occurs when a trade-off is desired between return and risk. This can be expressed as maximizing expected return at a given level of risk or minimizing risk at a given level of expected return. Any departure from simple consideration of the lowest or highest return confronts the problem

---

[1] See H. Gifford Fong, "An Asset Allocation Framework," *The Journal of Portfolio Management,* Winter 1980, pp. 58–66.

of the best trade-off and, consequently, the best mix of portfolio selections.[2]

The two principal uses of asset allocation models are for assistance in setting investment policy and evaluation of the implications of strategic decisions by the asset manager. The basic difference between the two is the time horizon of interest. Pension funds, for example, are generally oriented toward the long term, with a three- to five-year minimum. In some cases, the analysis may be for 20 or even 30 years. Asset managers are usually concerned with periods of less than a year for purposes of altering the portfolio mix in anticipation of changes in return expectations.

The purpose of this chapter is to explain several asset allocation models that can be employed to guide those who are responsible for making the asset allocation decision. We will then explain how to apply the asset allocation model in setting investment policy and evaluating the implications of strategic decisions by the asset manager.

■ Measuring Risk and Return for Individual Securities and Portfolios

We have used the terms *return* and *risk* in a very casual manner thus far. But in order to make asset allocation decisions, as well as other bond portfolio management decisions that will be discussed in this book, we must provide more precise mathematical definitions for return and risk.

We will begin with an explanation of how to measure the expected return and risk of an individual security. We then can explain how the return and risk are determined for a portfolio consisting of two securities. Building on the two-security case, we explain how the return and risk of a portfolio comprising any number of securities are computed. The fundamental principle that you should learn from this exercise is that, although the expected return for a portfolio is merely the weighted average of the expected returns of the securities comprising the portfolio, the risk for the portfolio depends not only on the risk associated with the individual securities comprising the portfolio but also on the correlation of returns of the

---

[2] The foundation for the selection of a portfolio that would have a maximum expected return for a given level of risk for risk-averse investors was developed by Harry M. Markowitz in 1952. (See Harry M. Markowitz, "Portfolio Selection," *The Journal of Finance*, March 1952, pp. 77–91 and *Portfolio Selection: Efficient Diversification of Investment* (New York: John Wiley & Sons, 1959). In the mid-1960s, Professor Markowitz's work was extended by several individuals who demonstrated that a "market portfolio" offered the highest level of return per unit of risk in an *efficient* market. See William F. Sharpe, "Capital Asset Prices: A Theory of Market Equilibrium under Conditions of Risk," *The Journal of Finance*, September 1964, pp. 425–42; John Lintner, "Security Prices, Risk and Maximal Gains from Diversification," *The Journal of Finance*, December 1965, pp. 587–616; and Jan Mossin, "Equilibrium in a Capital Asset Market," *Econometrica*, October 1966, pp. 768–83.

individual securities with each other. As long as the correlation between securities in a portfolio is less than one, the risk of the portfolio will be less than the weighted average of the risk of the individual securities comprising the portfolio.

Risk and Return for an Individual Security

Investors are exposed to risk because the return from holding a security is not known with certainty. That is, at the time the investment is made, the investor believes that it is possible that one of several possible returns may be realized at the end of the investment horizon. If an investor can estimate the probability of each return occurring, an *expected return* can be computed by weighting each possible return (outcome) by the probability associated with the return. Mathematically, the expected return can be expressed as follows:

$$E(R) = \sum_{k=1}^{K} R_k P_k \qquad (4-1)$$

where

$E(R)$ = expected return
R_k = the kth possible return
P_k = probability of the kth possible return
K = number of possible returns

For example, suppose that there are five possible returns for a hypothetical security. The possible returns and the probability associated with each return are shown in Table 4–1. The expected return for the hypothetical security in Table 4–1 is 10 percent, as shown below.

$$E(R) = -.10(.10) + .0(.20) + .10(.40) + .20(.20) + .30(.10)$$
$$= .10$$

The risk faced by an investor is the extent to which the return realized will deviate from the expected return. Therefore, the dispersion of the

Table 4–1
Possible Returns for a Hypothetical Security

Possible Return	Probability of Return
−.10	.10
0	.20
.10	.40
.20	.20
.30	.10

possible returns around the expected return can be used as a measure of risk. The greater the dispersion of the possible returns from the expected return, the greater the risk.

There are three commonly accepted ways to measure the dispersion of the possible returns around the expected return—variance, semivariance, and mean absolute deviation. The variance (or its square root, the standard deviation) is the usual measure of risk employed in investment management. The variance is simply the weighted average of the square of the deviation of each possible return from the expected return, where the weights are the probabilities associated with each possible return. The rationale for squaring the deviations is to keep deviations above and below the expected return from canceling each other out. Mathematically, this can be expressed as follows:[3]

$$\text{Var}(R) = \sum_{k=1}^{K} [R_k - E(R)]^2 P_k \qquad (4\text{-}2)$$

For the hypothetical security shown in Table 4–1 whose expected return is 10 percent, the variance is 1.2 percent, as shown below.

$$
\begin{aligned}
\text{Var}(R) &= [-.10 - (.10)]^2 (.10) + [.0 - (.10)]^2 (.20) \\
&\quad + [.10 - (.10)]^2 (.40) + [.20 - (.10)]^2 (.20) \\
&\quad + [.30 - (.10)]^2 (.10) \\
&= .004 + .002 + 0 + .002 + .004 \\
&= .012
\end{aligned}
$$

The variance is a difficult number to interpret because it is in terms of squared units. To convert this measure into a more intuitively appealing

---

[3] An alternative formula for the expected return and variance that can be more conveniently applied when historical returns are used is given below.

$$F(R) = \frac{1}{T} \sum_{t=1}^{T} R_t$$

and

$$\text{Var}(R) = \frac{1}{T} \sum_{t=1}^{T} [R_t - E(R)]^2$$

where

R_t = observed return for period t
T = number of observations

Notice that if there are T historical returns, each one will have a probability of $1/T$. Substituting $1/T$ for P_k in Equations (4–1) and (4–2) gives the above two equations for the expected return and variance.

number, the square root of the variance can be computed. The resulting number is called the *standard deviation*. The standard deviation for the hypothetical security in Table 4–1 is 10.95 percent (square root of .012).

There are two problems with using the variance or standard deviation as a measure of risk. First, because the deviations are squared, the variance is sensitive to possible returns that are distant from the expected return. A measure of risk that overcomes this shortcoming is the mean absolute deviation. Rather than squaring the deviations and weighting by the associated probability, the absolute mean deviation is computed by taking the weighted average of the absolute value of the deviations. Using the absolute value avoids the problem of deviations above and below the expected return offsetting each other. Despite the advantage of the mean absolute deviation over the variance, the latter is used in portfolio management.

The second problem with employing the variance as a measure of risk is that it considers deviations above the expected return. However, possible returns greater than the expected return are outcomes that investors would like to realize.

The semivariance, the third candidate as a measure of risk, considers only those deviations below the expected return.[4] The logic of this measure of risk is that investors are only concerned with the possibility of realizing a return that is less than the expected return. That is, the semivariance measures downside risk. However, if the underlying probability distribution of returns for a security is normal (i.e., a bell-shaped curve), then the semivariance and variance would be equivalent.

Risk and Return for a Two-Security Portfolio

When two securities are combined to form a portfolio, the expected return for the portfolio is simply the weighted average of the expected return for the two securities. The weight for each security is equal to the dollar value of the security relative to the total dollar value of the portfolio. The sum of the weights, of course, must equal one.

Mathematically, the expected return for a two-security portfolio can be expressed as follows:

$$E(R_p) = W_1 E(R_1) + W_2 E(R_2) \tag{4–3}$$

where

$E(R_p)$ = expected return for the portfolio

$E(R_1)$ = expected return for security 1

---

[4] The semivariance suffers from the problem pointed out for the variance—it is sensitive to possible returns distant from the expected return.

$E(R_2)$ = expected return for security 2
W_1 = percentage of the portfolio invested in security 1
W_2 = percentage of the portfolio invested in security 2

and

$$W_1 + W_2 = 1$$

Unlike the portfolio's expected return, the portfolio's variance (standard deviation) is not simply a weighted average of the variance (standard deviation) of the two securities. Instead, the portfolio variance is equal to

$$\text{Var}(R_p) = W_1^2 \, \text{Var}(R_1) + W_2^2 \, \text{Var}(R_2) + 2W_1W_2 \, \text{Covar}(R_1, R_2) \quad (4\text{--}4)$$

where

$\text{Covar}(R_1, R_2)$ = the covariance between securities 1 and 2

The covariance measures the extent to which the returns on two securities move together. A positive covariance means that the returns for the two securities tend to move together; a negative covariance means that the returns for the two securities tend to move in opposite directions. As should be clear from Equation (4–4), the portfolio variance is higher the greater the covariance between the two securities.

Since it may be difficult to grasp the notion of a covariance, it is helpful to recast the mathematical expression for the portfolio variance in terms of a concept that may be more familiar. Correlation is a measure of the association between two random variables. The correlation can take on any value between -1 and $+1$. The correlation is equal to the covariance divided by the product of the standard deviation of the two random variables. When the random variables are the returns of two securities, the correlation can be expressed as follows:

$$\text{Corr}(R_1, R_2) = \frac{\text{Covar}(R_1, R_2)}{\text{Std}(R_1)\text{Std}(R_2)} \quad (4\text{--}5)$$

where

$\text{Corr}(R_1, R_2)$ = correlation between security 1 and security 2
$\text{Std}(R_1)$ = standard deviation for security 1
$\text{Std}(R_2)$ = standard deviation for security 2

From (4–5) it can be seen that the covariance is equal to the correlation times the standard deviation of the two securities. Therefore, the portfolio variance can be expressed in terms of the correlation as shown below:

$$\text{Var}(R_p) = W_1^2 \, \text{Var}(R_1) + W_2^2 \, \text{Var}(R_2)$$
$$+ 2W_1W_2 \, \text{Std}(R_1) \, \text{Std}(R_2) \, \text{Corr}(R_1, R_2) \quad (4\text{--}6)$$

To illustrate the computation of the expected return and variance of a two-security portfolio, consider the two hypothetical securities shown in Table 4–2.

Table 4–2
Expectational Inputs for Two Hypothetical Securities

Security	Expected Return	Variance	Standard Deviation
1	.13	.0342	.185
2	.08	.0036	.060

Correlation between security 1 and security 2 = .20

If all funds are placed in security 1 (i.e., $W_1 = 1$ and $W_2 = 0$), the portfolio's expected return is simply 13 percent, the expected return for security 1. The portfolio's variance and standard deviation are equal to that of security 1, .0342 and .185, respectively. At the other extreme, if all the portfolio's funds are invested in security 2, the portfolio's expected return, variance, and standard deviation would be .08, .0036 and .06, respectively.

Suppose that the portfolio's funds are evenly divided between the two securities (i.e., W_1 and $W_2 = .50$). From Equation (4–3), the portfolio expected return is:

$$E(R_p) = .5(.13) + .5(.08)$$
$$= .105 \text{ or } 10.5 \text{ percent}$$

From Equation (4–6), the portfolio variance is:

$$Var(R_p) = (.5)^2(.0342) + (.5)^2(.0036)$$
$$+ 2(.5)(.5)(.185)(.06)(.20)$$
$$= .01056$$

The portfolio standard deviation is equal to .1028. Notice that the portfolio standard deviation of .1028 is less than the weighted average of the standard deviation of the two securities which is .1225 [= .5(.185) + .5(.06)]. However, if the correlation between security 1 and security 2 is equal to +1, then from Equation (4–6) the variance is .0150 and therefore the portfolio standard deviation is .1225. But this is precisely the portfolio standard deviation found by the weighted average of the standard deviation of the two securities. In fact, *when the correlation is equal to one, the portfolio's standard deviation will always be a weighted average of the* standard deviations of the two securities.[5] Consequently, by combining securities that have a correlation of less than one into a portfolio, the portfolio standard deviation will always be less than the weighted average of the standard deviation of the individual securities.

Table 4–3 summarizes the portfolio expected return, variance, and standard deviation for different allocations of funds between the two securities.

Table 4–3
Portfolio Expected Return, Variance, and Standard Deviation for Different Allocations of Funds between the Two Hypothetical Securities*

Allocation		Expected Return	Variance	Standard Deviation
W_1	W_2	$E(R_p)$	$Var(R_p)$	$Std(R_p)$
.0	1.0	.080	.0036000	.0600000
.1	.9	.085	.0036570	.0604769
.2	.8	.090	.0043820	.0661978
.3	.7	.095	.0057740	.0759872
.4	.6	.100	.0078330	.0885054
.5	.5	.105	.0105596	.1027600
.6	.4	.110	.0139532	.1181240
.7	.3	.115	.0180141	.1342160
.8	.2	.120	.0227421	.1508050
.9	.1	.125	.0281375	.1677420
1.0	.0	.130	.0342000	.1849320

* See Table 4–2 for the expectational inputs for the two hypothetical securities.

[5] This can be demonstrated as follows. Substitute the following into Equation (4–6):

$$W_2 = (1 - W_1)$$
$$Corr(R_1, R_2) = 1$$
$$Var(R_1) = [Std(R_1)]^2$$
$$Var(R_2) = [Std(R_2)]^2$$

Equation (4–6) then becomes

$$Var(R_p) = W_1^2[Std(R_1)]^2 + (1 - W_1)^2[Std(R_2)]^2 + 2W_1(1 - W_1) Std(R_1) Std(R_2)$$

$Var(R_p)$ can then be factored as follows:

$$Var(R_p) = [W_1 Std(R_1) + (1 - W_1) Std(R_2)]^2$$

Therefore, the portfolio standard deviation is

$$Std(R_p) = W_1 Std(R_1) + (1 - W_1) Std(R_2)$$

which is simply a weighted average of the standard deviation of the two securities.

Risk and Return for an N-Security Portfolio

The expected return of a portfolio comprised of N-securities, as in the two-security portfolio case, is simply the weighted average of the expected return of the N-securities in the portfolio. The formula is as follows:

$$E(R_p) = \sum_{i=1}^{N} E(R_i) W_i \qquad (4-7)$$

where

$E(R_i)$ = expected return for security i
W_i = percent of the portfolio invested in security i

and

$$\sum_{i=1}^{N} W_i = 1$$

That was simple, right? The formula for the portfolio variance, however, is more difficult:

$$\text{Var}(R_p) = \sum_{i=1}^{N} W_i^2 \, \text{Var}(R_i) + \sum_{i=1}^{N} \sum_{j=1}^{N} W_i W_j \, \text{Covar}(R_i, R_j) \qquad (4-8)$$
$$\text{for } i \neq j$$

Once again we see that the portfolio variance is a function of the covariance between each pair of the N securities. Recasting our formula for the portfolio variance in terms of the correlation between securities, we have:

$$\text{Var}(R_p) = \sum_{i=1}^{N} W_i^2 \, \text{Var}(R_i)$$
$$+ \sum_{i=1}^{N} \sum_{j=1}^{N} W_i W_j \, \text{Std}(R_i) \, \text{Std}(R_j) \, \text{Corr}(R_i, R_j) \qquad (4-9)$$
$$\text{for } i \neq j$$

To illustrate the computation of the portfolio expected return using Equation (4–7) and the portfolio variance using Equation (4–9), consider the three hypothetical securities shown in Table 4–4. Assuming that 40 percent of the funds are invested in security 1 ($W_1 = .40$), 35 percent are invested in security 2 ($W_2 = .35$), and 25 percent are invested in security 3 ($W_3 = .25$), then

$$\begin{aligned} E(R_p) &= E(R_1)W_1 + E(R_2)W_2 + E(R_2)W_2 \\ &= .13(.40) + .08(.35) + .06(.25) \\ &= .095 = 9.5 \text{ percent} \end{aligned}$$

$$Var(R_p) = W_1^2\, Var(R_1) + W_2^2\, Var(R_2) + W_3^2\, Var(R_3)$$
$$+ W_1W_2\, Std(R_1)\, Std(R_2)\, Corr(R_1, R_2)$$
$$+ W_1W_3\, Std(R_1)\, Std(R_3)\, Corr(R_1, R_3)$$
$$+ W_2W_1\, Std(R_2)\, Std(R_1)\, Corr(R_2, R_1)$$
$$+ W_2W_3\, Std(R_2)\, Std(R_3)\, Corr(R_2, R_3)$$
$$+ W_3W_1\, Std(R_3)\, Std(R_1)\, Corr(R_3, R_1)$$
$$+ W_3W_2\, Std(R_3)\, Std(R_2)\, Corr(R_3, R_2)$$

$$= (.40)^2(.0342) + (.35)^2(.0036) + (.25)^2(.000016)$$
$$+ (.40)(.35)(.185)(.060)(.20)$$
$$+ (.40)(.25)(.185)(.004)(-.15)$$
$$+ (.35)(.40)(.060)(.185)(.20)$$
$$+ (.35)(.25)(.060)(.004)(-.12)$$
$$+ (.25)(.40)(.004)(.185)(-.15)$$
$$+ (.25)(.35)(.004)(.060)(-.12)$$
$$= .0065072$$

The portfolio standard deviation is .0807. The weighted average of the standard deviation of the three securities is .096 [= .40(.185) + .35(.060) + .25(.004)] which is greater than the portfolio standard deviation. As explained in the two-security portfolio case, as long as the pairwise correlation between the securities in the portfolio is less than one, the portfolio standard deviation will be less than the weighted average of the individual securities.

Table 4–4
Expectational Inputs for Three Hypothetical Securities

Security	Expected Return	Variance	Standard Deviation
1	.13	.034200	.185
2	.08	.003600	.060
3	.06	.000016	.004

Correlations $[Corr(R_i, R_j)]$

Security i	Security j 1	2	3
1	1.00	.20	−.15
2	.20	1.00	−.12
3	−.15	−.12	1.00

■ The Role of Bonds in the Macro Analysis

The foregoing discussion focused on the allocation of funds to individual securities. However, the principles discussed are just as appropriate for determining how to allocate funds among broad asset classes (stocks, bonds, Treasury bills, etc.).

We now understand that there are two sources of overall portfolio risk. The first source is the individual risk characteristics of each asset class, and the second source is the relative interaction between asset classes. The standard deviation of asset alternatives will not merely be a function of their individually measured standard deviations, but also the result of the risk due to common factors affecting returns, as measured by the correlation or covariance of returns. This additional source of risk (for example, the effect of interest rate change on bond and stock returns) holds the potential for risk minimization beyond the risk from individual asset standard deviations. By combining asset categories whose correlation is less than one, the portfolio risk, as measured by the standard deviation, will be less than the weighted average standard deviation of the individual asset classes. The lower the correlation between asset classes included in a portfolio, the lower will be the portfolio risk compared to the weighted average of the risk of the individual asset classes.

We discussed the role of bonds in an overall portfolio strategy in the two previous chapters. As demonstrated, the characteristics of bonds in a portfolio reveal a number of reasons for the continued interest in this asset class. In particular, as higher returns are achieved, the amount of risk per unit of return (coefficient of variation) increases. The implication is that, although the expectations over sufficiently long periods of time are for stocks to outperform bonds and bonds to outperform Treasury bills, the associated risk over a one-year time frame rises rapidly as higher return asset classes are held. For every rule there is an exception. Whether the risk preference of the investor can tolerate the associated short-term risk of ownership of equity is a significant issue. For example, pension funds, because of the nature of their cash flows, typically have a long-term perspective; yet, many sponsors are sensitive only to short-term asset fluctuations. By contrasting the long-term benefits of higher return/higher risk portfolio allocations, a basis for understanding the trade-off between return and risk and time horizon can be evaluated. Asset allocation models can thus aid in correcting myopic responses to a condition requiring foresight. This issue has helped stimulate the concern in the asset allocation process and the role bonds can play.[6]

There has been a historical positive covariance relationship between

---

[6] Whether the analysis is for setting a policy for a corporate pension fund or for assisting in setting strategy for an investment manager, the time dimension is important. Assuming serial independence of return distributions, risk varies with the square root of time, while return increases proportionately with time. (See M. F. M. Osborne, "Brownian Motion in the Stock Market," *Operations Research*, March–April 1959, pp. 145–73.) Hence, as one extends the analysis horizon, risk increases at a slower rate than return. This relationship provides the basis for higher risk, higher return portfolio allocations where one has a longer-term orientation.

stocks and bonds as shown in Table 2–9. However, the correlation has been significantly less than unity. Since Treasury bills have only nominal price risk, there has not been a strong relationship between Treasury bills and changes in returns on stocks or on bonds.

Over time, the magnitude of the covariance between stocks, bonds, and Treasury bills may change. However, there may be an economic basis for this characteristic. For example, as interest rates rise, the return from Treasury bills will increase and there may be a tendency for the stock market return to decrease. Interest rate changes can become a fundamental cause of both the magnitude and sign of the covariance. For stocks, increased interest rates increase the discount factor on the stream of future cash flows resulting in a lower intrinsic value unless offset by increased expected earnings or other changes resulting from inflation; for Treasury bills, increased interest rates will increase the return, assuming the instrument is held to maturity and rolled over. These tendencies over subperiods within the time horizon contribute to the relative fluctuation in return. For the entire time horizon, both asset classes will presumably have a positive return, and by taking into account short-run tendencies, the interim portfolio fluctuations can be minimized.

Of course, if the portfolio were always held to the end of the horizon, and all the return expectations were met, the problem would become academic. In the face of uncertainty, however, and the expectation that the portfolio will not be held for the entire period, minimizing portfolio return fluctuation is desirable.

The correlation coefficients between bonds and Treasury bills for various subperiods demonstrates that the covariance between these two asset classes is weak and may be negative. As explained in the previous section, one of the fundamental principles of efficient diversification is the combination of assets to take advantage of the existence of low or negative correlated assets to minimize overall portfolio risk. Bonds and Treasury bills with their low or negatively correlated returns are therefore attractive portfolio candidates.

■ Asset Allocation Models

In this section we shall describe several asset allocation models. We begin with the two-asset class problem and introduce the notion of an efficient portfolio and an efficient set (frontier). The asset allocation model with more than two asset classes is then explained and extended to (1) provide supplementary measures of risk, which we refer to as the *risk-of-loss,* (2) multiple scenarios, and (3) short-term/long-term asset allocations.

The basic inputs for the asset allocation models discussed are the expected returns, expected yields, risk estimates, and correlations (or covariances) for each asset class included in the analysis. The appropriate source for these inputs is the asset manager, since he is most directly concerned with these factors on a day-to-day basis. Additional insights can be achieved by using historical estimates, either from a lengthy past period or from more recent experience. The objective is to use the proxy that will best represent the future horizon of interest.

Typically, the asset manager will use his own return expectation in conjunction with historical risk measures based on the variance and co-variance from a historical series. Of course, other inputs may include constraints such as target minimum or maximum concentration constraints of individual or group-of-asset types and corresponding yield constraints on part or all of the portfolio.

Two Asset Class Allocation Model

In order to introduce the concept of an efficient set (frontier) let us consider the asset allocation model when funds are to be allocated between only two assets classes, stocks and bonds. The proxy for stocks will be the Standard & Poor's 500 and for bonds the Kuhn Loeb Bond Index. Table 4–5 summarizes the expectational input (expected return, variance, stan-

Table 4–5
Expectational Inputs for Two Asset Classes

Asset Class	Expected Return	Variance	Standard Deviation
Stock (S&P 500)	.13	.0342	.185
Bonds (Kuhn Loeb Bond Index)	.08	.0036	.060

Correlation between stocks and bonds = .20

dard deviation and correlation of returns). Notice that the expectational inputs in Table 4–5 for stocks and bonds are identical to those in Table 4–2 for security 1 and security 2, respectively. For purposes of this illustration, we shall assume that there are no constraints. Since the expectational inputs in Table 4–5 are identical to those in Table 4–2, the portfolio expected return and standard deviation for various combinations of concentration of funds (weights) will be the same as those shown in Table 4–3. Figure 4–2 graphically portrays the portfolio expected return and standard deviation presented in Table 4–3. With respect to Figure 4–2, the following should be noted.

1. Every point on XYZ denotes a portfolio consisting of a specific allocation of funds between stocks and bonds. Not all of the portfolios are shown in Table 4–3. We filled in the gaps when we plotted the results.

2. XYZ represents all possible portfolios consisting of these two security classes. XYZ is therefore called the *investment opportunity set* or the *feasible set.*[7]

3. It would never be beneficial for an investor to allocate his funds between stocks and bonds to produce a portfolio on that portion of XYZ between Y and Z (excluding portfolio Z).[8] The reason is that for every portfolio on segment YZ there is a portfolio that dominates it on the XY segment of the investment opportunity set. By *dominates,* we mean that for a given portfolio standard deviation (risk level), an investor can realize a higher portfolio expected return. This can be seen on Figure 4–1 by examining portfolios A and A'. Portfolios A and A' have the same portfolio standard deviation; however, the expected return for portfolio A is greater than that for portfolio A'. Consequently, all portfolios on XY of the investment opportunity set dominate the portfolios on YZ of the investment opportunity set. XY, therefore, is called the *efficient set* or *efficient frontier.* We use these two terms interchangeably. A portfolio in the efficient set is said to be an *efficient portfolio* or an *optimal portfolio.*

The efficient set indicates the expected trade-off between return and risk (standard deviation) faced by the investor. Just which portfolio in the efficient set the investor selects depends on the investor's preferences.

To see the impact of the correlation on the efficient set, Table 4–6 shows the expected return, variance, and standard deviation for portfolios consisting of stocks and bonds for various assumed correlation of returns. The efficient set for each assumed correlation is plotted on Figure 4–2. As can be seen, the lower the correlation of returns, the better off the investor is.[9] That is, for a given set of expected returns and standard deviations for the two asset classes, the investor will be exposed to a lower level of risk (standard deviation) for a given portfolio if the correlation of returns is

---

[7] The portfolios on XYZ include portfolios in which there is short selling of either asset class.

[8] The portfolio represented by point Y is the minimum variance that can be obtained by holding these two asset classes in any combination. It can be found in the two asset class case by using the following formula:

$$W_1 = \frac{\mathrm{Var}(R_1) - \mathrm{Corr}(R_1, R_2)\,\mathrm{Std}(R_1)\,\mathrm{Std}(R_2)}{\mathrm{Var}(R_1)\,\mathrm{Var}(R_2) - 2\,\mathrm{Corr}(R_1, R_2)\,\mathrm{Std}(R_1)\,\mathrm{Std}(R_2)}$$

$$W_2 = 1 - W_1$$

For our two asset classes, the minimum variance is .0035429 (minimum standard deviation is .05952) when W_1 is .0414 and W_2 is .9586.

[9] The minimum variance that can be achieved by any combination of the two asset classes is also reduced. For example, if the correlation is −.2, the minimum variance using the formula to obtain W_1 in the previous footnote is .0027983 and the minimum standard deviation is .0529. This occurs when W_1 is .138. By combining the riskier asset class (stocks) with the relatively safer asset class (bonds) it is possible to obtain a portfolio with less risk than one with bonds alone. Moreover, the expected return for this minimum variance portfolio is 8.69 percent which is greater than the expected return for a portfolio holding just bonds.

Figure 4–1
Investment Opportunity Set and Efficient Set for Two Asset Classes

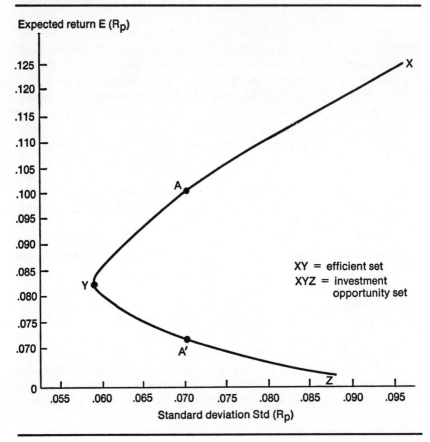

Expected return E (R_p)

XY = efficient set
XYZ = investment
       opportunity set

Standard deviation Std (R_p)

lower. Notice that, if the correlation is 1, the efficient set is a straight line and the portfolio standard deviation is therefore a weighted average of the standard deviations of the two asset classes.

N-Asset Class Allocation Model

The principles we have discussed for the efficient set for the two-asset class allocation model can easily be extended to the general case of N-asset classes.

Graphically, the efficient set of portfolios in the N-asset class case can be portrayed in the same manner as in the two-asset class case. Figure 4–3 shows all possible portfolios for the N-asset class case. This figure is analo-

Table 4–6
Portfolio Expected Return and Standard Deviation for Different Correlations between the Two Asset Classes

Weight for Each Asset Class		Expected Return	Portfolio Standard Deviation If the Correlation Is:				
W_1	W_2	$E(R_p)$	0.2	0.0	0.2	0.5	1.0
0.0	1.0	.080	.0600000	.0600000	.0600000	.0600000	.0600000
.1	.9	.085	.0534654	.0570789	.0604769	.0667560	.0724932
.2	.8	.090	.0544230	.0605970	.0661978	.0761736	.0849865
.3	.7	.095	.0625295	.0695845	.0759872	.0873967	.0974797
.4	.6	.100	.0755168	.0822679	.0885054	.0998180	.1099730
.5	.5	.105	.0913258	.0972111	.1027600	.1130430	.1224660
.6	.4	.110	.1087330	.1135250	.1181240	.1268210	.1349590
.7	.3	.115	.1270820	.1306980	.1342160	.1409900	.1474530
.8	.2	.120	.1460200	.1484320	.1508050	.1554430	.1599460
.9	.1	.125	.1653440	.1665470	.1677420	.1701070	.1724390
1.0	0.0	.130	.1849320	.1849320	.1849320	.1849320	.1849320

Figure 4–2
Comparison of Efficient Set for Different Correlations between Two Asset Classes

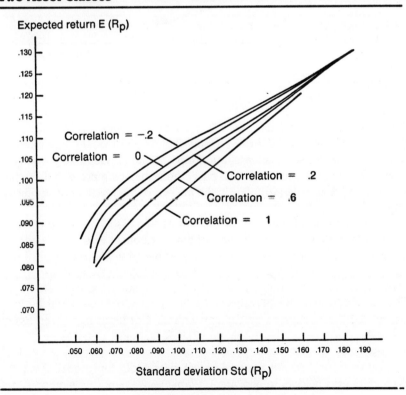

Figure 4–3
Investment Opportunity Set and Efficient Set in N-Asset Class Portfolio Case

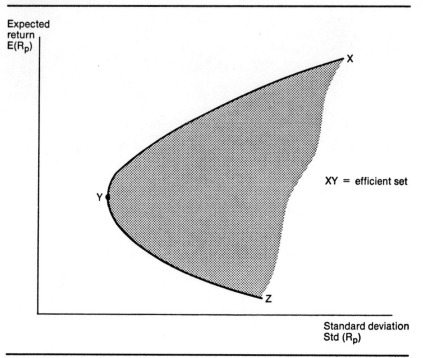

gous to Figure 4–1. The difference is that the investment opportunity set in the two-asset class case does not include points (portfolios) in the interior of XYZ. In the N-asset class case, interior points are also feasible portfolios. However, as in the two-asset class case, the portfolios represented by the segment XY dominate portfolios in the interior of the investment opportunity set.

Although the efficient set for the simple two-asset class case can be easily determined, the computation of the efficient set when funds are to be allocated to more than two asset classes becomes more difficult. Fortunately, the efficient set for the N-asset class problem can be solved using a mathematical programming technique called quadratic programming. This algorithm can also accomodate other constraints that might be imposed, such as limitations on the concentration of funds in a given asset class. Appendix A to this book provides a technical description of the process.

Let us now illustrate the three-asset class allocation model. Assume that an investor wishes to allocate available investment funds among the following three asset classes: stocks, bonds, and Treasury bills. As in the two asset class problem, a proxy for stocks, the Standard & Poor's 500 (S&P 500) is used. The Kuhn Loeb Bond Index is used as the proxy for bonds. The expectational inputs for stocks and bonds are the same as in the two-asset class problem illustrated above. For Treasury bills, we shall use the same expectational inputs as for security 3 in Table 4-4.

Table 4-7 presents the annual expected return, expected yield, standard deviation, and correlations for the three asset classes for two scenar-

Table 4-7
Expectational Inputs for Three Asset Classes for Two Scenarios

Asset Class	Expected Return	Expected Yield	Variance	Standard Deviation
Scenario 1:				
Stock (S&P 500)	.13	.05	.034200	.185
Bonds	.08	.08	.003600	.060
(Kuhn Loeb Bond Index)				
Treasury bills	.06	.06	.000016	.004
Scenario 2:				
Stock (S&P 500)	.15	.05	.034200	.185
Bonds	.08	.08	.003600	.060
(Kuhn Loeb Bond Index)				
Treasury bills	.05	.05	.000016	.004

	Correlations for Both Scenarios		
	Stocks	Bonds	Treasury Bills
Stocks	1.00	.20	−.15
Bonds	.20	1.00	−.12
Treasury bills	−.15	−.12	1.00

ios. (We will discuss the two scenarios later.) The expected yield component of the expected return is the amount of the return attributable to dividends in the case of stocks, and interest payments in the case of bonds. The difference between the expected return and expected yield is therefore the return attributable to capital appreciation.

Using quadratic programming, the efficient set can be determined. The results for scenario 1, assuming a one-year horizon and no contraints, are shown in Table 4-8 while the results for scenario 2 are shown in Table 4-9. For each identified level of portfolio expected return, the corresponding standard deviation, yield component of total return, and minimum risk concentrations (weights) of each asset class are shown on both tables. The

Table 4–8
Optimal Asset Allocation for Scenario 1: Sample Portfolios in the Efficient Set (12-month horizon)

Annual Expected Return	Annual Standard Deviation	Annual Expected Yield	Probability of Annual Return of Less than				Minimum Risk Asset Mix:		
			0.0 Percent	5.0 Percent	7.0 Percent	10.0 Percent	S&P500	KLLC	USTB
6.00%	0.400%	6.00%	0.0%	0.9%	99.1%	100.0%	0.0%	0.0%	100.0%
6.04	0.389	6.02	0.0	0.5	99.0	100.0	0.3	1.0	98.7
6.50	1.097	6.18	0.0	9.7	66.7	99.8	4.1	10.9	84.9
7.00	2.174	6.35	0.1	19.2	50.0	90.0	8.3	21.7	70.0
7.50	3.271	6.52	1.3	23.5	44.3	76.0	12.5	32.4	55.1
8.00	4.368	6.70	3.8	25.8	41.5	66.4	16.6	43.1	40.3
8.50	5.462	6.87	6.6	27.3	39.9	60.0	20.7	53.7	25.6
9.00	6.552	7.04	9.3	28.3	38.8	55.6	24.8	64.2	10.9
9.50	7.649	7.09	11.6	29.0	38.1	52.4	30.4	69.6	0.0
10.00	8.918	6.79	14.1	30.0	37.7	50.0	40.5	59.5	0.0
10.50	10.356	6.48	16.5	31.0	37.7	48.2	50.5	49.5	0.0
11.00	11.895	6.19	18.8	31.9	37.8	46.9	60.5	39.5	0.0
11.50	13.497	5.89	20.8	32.7	37.9	46.0	70.4	29.6	0.0
12.00	15.142	5.59	22.5	33.3	38.0	45.2	80.3	19.7	0.0
12.50	16.813	5.29	24.0	33.9	38.2	44.6	90.2	9.8	0.0
13.00	18.500	5.00	25.2	34.4	38.3	44.2	100.0	0.0	0.0

Table 4-9
Optimal Asset Allocation for Scenario 2: Sample Portfolios in the Efficient Set (12-month horizon)

Annual Expected Return	Annual Standard Deviation	Annual Expected Yield	Probability of Annual Return of Less than				Minimum Risk Asset Mix:		
			0.0 Percent	5.0 Percent	7.0 Percent	10.0 Percent	S&P500	KLLC	USTB
5.00%	0.400%	5.00%	0.0%	50.1%	100.0%	100.0%	0.0%	0.0%	100.0%
5.06	0.389	5.03	0.0	44.3	100.0	100.0	0.3	1.0	98.7
5.50	0.784	5.24	0.0	27.2	96.5	100.0	2.8	7.9	89.3
6.00	1.501	5.47	0.0	26.3	73.5	99.3	5.5	15.7	78.7
6.50	2.248	5.70	0.2	26.3	58.3	92.6	8.3	23.5	68.2
7.00	3.003	5.94	1.2	26.4	50.0	82.3	11.0	31.2	57.7
7.50	3.757	6.17	2.6	26.4	45.0	73.1	13.8	38.9	47.3
8.00	4.509	6.40	4.3	26.5	41.8	65.9	16.5	46.6	36.9
8.50	5.258	6.63	5.9	26.5	39.5	60.4	19.2	54.2	26.6
9.00	6.005	6.85	7.4	26.5	37.8	56.1	21.9	61.8	16.3
9.50	6.750	7.08	8.8	26.6	36.5	52.7	24.6	69.4	6.0
10.00	7.505	7.13	10.0	26.6	35.5	50.0	29.1	70.9	0.0
10.50	8.374	6.91	11.5	26.9	34.9	47.8	36.4	63.6	0.0
11.00	9.345	6.69	13.0	27.4	34.6	46.1	43.6	56.4	0.0
11.50	10.386	6.48	14.5	28.0	34.4	44.8	50.7	49.3	0.0
12.00	11.478	6.26	15.9	28.5	34.4	43.7	57.8	42.2	0.0
12.50	12.605	6.05	17.3	29.0	34.4	42.9	64.9	35.1	0.0
13.00	13.756	5.84	18.5	29.5	34.4	42.2	72.0	28.0	0.0
13.50	14.927	5.63	19.6	29.9	34.5	41.6	79.1	20.9	0.0
14.00	16.109	5.42	20.5	30.3	34.5	41.1	86.1	13.9	0.0
14.50	17.302	5.21	21.4	30.6	34.6	40.7	93.0	7.0	0.0
15.00	18.500	5.00	22.2	30.9	34.7	40.4	100.0	0.0	0.0

columns under the heading *Probability of Annual Return of Less than* will be explained shortly.

To make sure you understand the two tables, let's interpret one of the results. For scenario 1, the minimum risk (standard deviation) that the investor will be exposed to if he seeks a 9 percent return for the 12-month period is 6.552 percent. There is no other allocation producing a 9 percent return with a standard deviation less than 6.552 percent. The asset mix associated with this efficient or optimal portfolio is 24.8 percent in stocks, 64.2 percent in bonds, and 10.9 percent in Treasury bills. (The total does not equal one because of rounding.) The annual expected return of 9 percent will have an expected yield of 7.04 percent. Therefore, 1.96 percent of the total annual expected return will be attributable to capital appreciation.

Extension of the Asset Allocation Model to Risk-of-Loss

In the portfolio risk-minimization process, the variance (standard deviation) of returns was the proxy measure for portfolio risk. As a supplement, the probability of not achieving a portfolio expected return can be established. This type of analysis would be useful in determining the most appropriate mix from the set of optimal portfolio allocations.

We refer to this analysis as the *risk-of-loss*. A technical description of the analysis is described in Appendix B of this book. The columns under the heading *Probability of Annual Return of Less than* in Tables 4–8 and 4–9 show the results of the risk-of-loss analysis for four annual return levels. The interpretation of the results for the 9 percent expected return for scenario 1 (Table 4–8) is as follows. There is a 9.3 percent probability that the annual return will be negative, a 28.3 percent probability that the annual return will be less than 5 percent, a 38.8 percent probability that the annual return will be less than 7 percent, and a 55.6 percent probability that the annual return will be less than 10 percent.

Extension of the Asset Allocation Model to Multiple Scenarios

In Table 4–7 the expected return and expected yield are shown for two assumed scenarios. Each assumed scenario is believed to be an assessment of the asset performance in the long run, over the investment horizon. If a probability can be assigned to each scenario, an efficient set can be constructed for the composite scenario. The procedure for computing the optimal asset allocation when there are multiple scenarios which are discrete or mutually exclusive and each scenario can be assigned a probability of occurence is explained in Appendix C.

   Assuming a probability of 50 percent for each of the two scenarios in Table 4–7, Table 4–10 displays the optimal asset allocation for the composite scenario for a 12-month investment horizon. Table 4–11 provides the minimum risk portfolio for specified return levels for the composite scenario results for a 60-month horizon. In both tables, the risk-of-loss analysis results are also shown.
   Let's take a closer look at these results to see how useful they can be in the asset allocation decision. Figure 4–4 is an illustration of the optimal mixes for the 12-month horizon for the composite scenario. The vertical height of each of the three lines represents the amount that would be allocated to an asset for a given expected return level shown on the horizontal axis. For example, Figure 4–4 has the optimal concentrations for an expected return of 8 percent of about 12 percent stocks, 45 percent bonds, and 38 percent Treasury bills, corresponding to the results shown in Table 10 of 16.6 percent stocks, 45.2 percent bonds and 38.3 percent Treasury bills.[10]

Figure 4–4
Risk-of-Loss Analysis: Minimum-Risk Concentrations

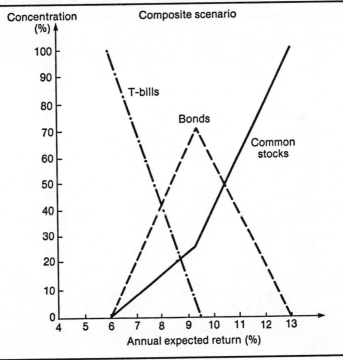

_____

[10] As noted earlier, the optimal mix may not equal one because of rounding.

Table 4-10
Optimal Asset Allocation for Composite Scenario: Sample Portfolios in the Efficient Set (12-month horizon)

Annual Expected Return	Annual Standard Deviation	Annual Expected Yield	Probability of Annual Return of Less than				Minimum Risk Asset Mix		
			0.0 Percent	5.0 Percent	7.0 Percent	10.0 Percent	S&P500	KLLC	USTB
5.50%	0.422%	5.50%	0.0%	24.8%	99.5%	100.0%	0.0%	0.0%	100.0%
5.55	0.412	5.53	0.0	21.8	99.4	100.0	0.3	1.1	98.6
6.00	0.918	5.71	0.0	16.7	82.4	100.0	3.3	9.2	87.5
6.50	1.777	5.92	0.0	21.3	59.9	96.3	6.6	18.3	75.1
7.00	2.666	6.13	0.6	23.8	49.7	84.8	10.0	27.3	62.8
7.50	3.560	6.34	2.1	25.2	44.5	73.9	13.3	36.2	50.5
8.00	4.452	6.55	4.1	26.2	41.5	65.8	16.6	45.2	38.3
8.50	5.342	6.75	6.3	26.8	39.5	59.9	19.8	54.0	26.1
9.00	6.228	6.96	8.3	27.3	38.1	55.6	23.1	62.9	14.0
9.50	7.113	7.16	10.0	27.6	37.1	52.4	26.3	71.7	2.0
10.00	8.063	6.98	11.8	28.1	36.4	49.8	33.9	66.1	0.0
10.50	9.168	6.73	13.7	28.7	36.1	47.8	42.3	57.7	0.0
11.00	10.377	6.48	15.6	29.5	36.0	46.4	50.7	49.3	0.0
11.50	11.655	6.23	17.4	30.2	36.0	45.2	59.0	41.0	0.0
12.00	12.981	5.98	19.0	30.8	36.1	44.3	67.3	32.7	0.0
12.50	14.338	5.73	20.5	31.4	36.2	43.6	75.5	24.5	0.0
13.00	15.715	5.49	21.7	31.9	36.3	43.1	83.7	16.3	0.0
13.50	17.110	5.24	22.9	32.3	36.4	42.6	91.9	8.1	0.0

Table 4–11
Optimal Asset Allocation for Composite Scenario: Sample Portfolios in the Efficient Set (60-month horizon)

Annual Expected Return	Annual Standard Deviation	Annual Expected Yield	Probability of Annual Return of Less than				Minimum Risk Asset Mix		
			0.0 Percent	5.0 Percent	7.0 Percent	10.0 Percent	S&P500	KLLC	USTB
5.50%	0.422%	5.50%	0.0%	23.7%	100.0%	100.0%	0.0%	0.0%	100.0%
5.55	0.412	5.53	0.0	17.3	100.0	100.0	0.3	1.1	98.6
6.00	0.918	5.71	0.0	4.0	95.3	100.0	3.3	9.2	87.5
6.50	1.777	5.92	0.0	4.5	70.2	100.0	6.6	18.3	75.1
7.00	2.666	6.13	0.0	5.8	49.4	98.8	10.0	27.3	62.8
7.50	3.560	6.34	0.0	6.8	38.0	92.3	13.3	36.2	50.5
8.00	4.452	6.55	0.0	7.7	31.6	81.8	16.6	45.2	38.3
8.50	5.342	6.75	0.0	8.3	27.6	71.3	19.8	54.0	26.1
9.00	6.228	6.96	0.1	8.8	25.0	62.4	23.1	62.9	14.0
9.50	7.113	7.16	0.2	9.2	23.1	55.3	26.3	71.7	2.0
10.00	8.063	6.98	0.4	9.7	21.9	49.6	33.9	66.1	0.0
10.50	9.168	6.73	0.7	10.6	21.4	45.2	42.3	57.7	0.0
11.00	10.377	6.48	1.2	11.5	21.3	41.9	50.7	49.3	0.0
11.50	11.655	6.23	1.8	12.4	21.3	39.4	59.0	41.0	0.0
12.00	12.981	5.98	2.6	13.2	21.4	37.5	67.3	32.7	0.0
12.50	14.338	5.73	3.3	14.0	21.6	36.0	75.5	24.5	0.0
13.00	15.715	5.49	4.1	14.7	21.7	34.8	83.7	16.3	0.0
13.50	17.110	5.24	4.9	15.4	21.9	33.9	91.9	8.1	0.0

The yield component of the optimal mixes is shown for each scenario and the composite scenario in Figure 4–5. As explained earlier, the yield is the amount of return attributable to dividends and interest payments for the range of optimal portfolios. For the 8 percent expected return level, Figure 4–5 indicates that the yield component is 6.55 percent, which leaves 1.45 percent as the return attributable to capital appreciation.

Figure 4–5
Risk-of-Loss Analysis: Yield of Minimum-Risk Portfolios

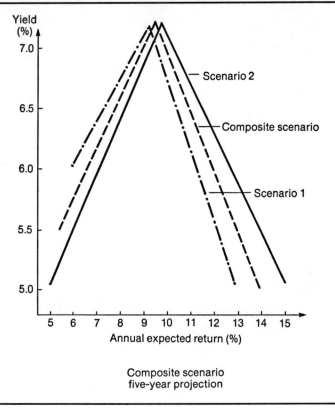

Composite scenario
five-year projection

Figure 4–6 depicts the risk of loss or probability of not achieving the specified return benchmarks of 0, 5, 7, and 10 percent over a one-year horizon for the composite case. From the expected return range on the horizontal axis, the probability of not achieving a given benchmark can be determined by proceeding vertically to the return benchmark curves. For example, if the 8 percent expected return optimal portfolio were assumed, there would be a 4 percent probability of not achieving a positive percent return over the next year (probabilities on the vertical axis). From Table

Figure 4–6
Risk-of-Loss Analysis: Probability of Loss for
Minimum-Risk Portfolios

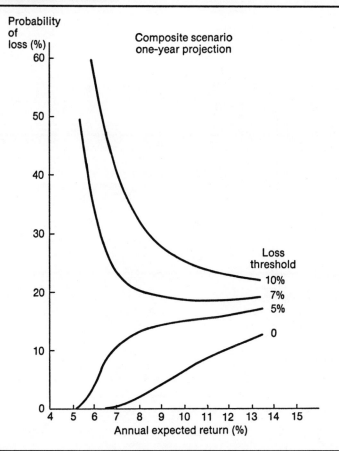

4–10 the tabular results reveal the more precise value of 3.8 percent. Figure 4–7 graphically characterizes the risk-of-loss for the composite scenario for the five-year horizon results shown in Table 4–11.

The comparison between Figure 4–6 and Figure 4–7 is particularly interesting. The influence of the passage of time is illustrated by comparing the 12-month horizon of Figure 4–6 and the 60-month horizon of Figure 4–7. The most striking difference is the significant downward shift of all risk-of-loss curves for the longer time horizon. This is consistent with the return increasing at a greater rate than risk over time.[11] The greater the

---

[11] See footnote 6.

Figure 4–7
Risk-of-Loss Analysis: Probability of Loss for
Minimum-Risk Portfolios

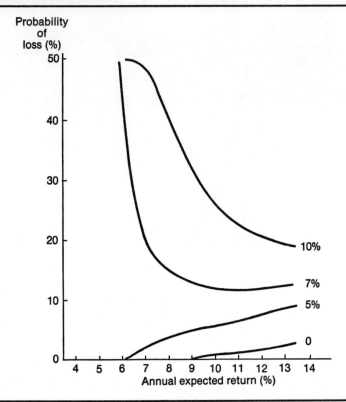

time horizon, the greater the incentive to seek higher expected return/
higher expected risk portfolios. The effect of the high risk associated with
high return portfolios is most significant during short time horizons. If the
risk exposure over short horizons is important, it is apparent that lower
return portfolios are appropriate. In other words, if the investor is concerned with near-term portfolio fluctuation, a portfolio consisting entirely
of common stock (highest expected return and risk class in our example) is
clearly not fitting. As the relevant horizon increases, however, a higher
proportion of stocks is possible and even desirable to achieve higher
return.

In practice, there probably will be a trade-off between short-term risk
tolerance and long-term return desirability. How much short-term risk is
tolerable may therefore control the proportion of higher return assets and

hence the expected return attainable. Using formats such as Figure 4–6 and Figure 4–7 and their supporting tables, Table 4–10 and Table 4–11, can assist the investor in choosing the most desirable return/risk trade-off.

As an alternative to visual inspection of the return/risk trade-off, the mathematically best trade-off in terms of the most return per unit of risk can be calculated. This procedure involves the evaluation of a chosen risk-of-loss curve for the point along the curve where the second derivative of the curve is zero (i.e., where its slope is steepest). This provides the greatest decrease in risk-of-loss for an increment of expected return.

Extension of the Asset Allocation Model to Short-Term/Long-Term Asset Allocation

In the multiple scenario case just described, it was assumed that the investor has certain expectations about the performance of the asset classes in terms of expected returns, expected yields, standard deviations, and correlations of return for each scenario. These values are used to assess, under various scenarios, the asset class performance in the long run, over the investment horizon.

It is often the case, however, that the investor expects a very different set of values to be applicable in the short run, say the next 12 months. For example, the investor may estimate the long-term expected annual return on stocks at 12 percent, but over the next year his expected return on stocks is only 5 percent. The investment objectives are still stated in terms of the portfolio performance over the entire investment horizon. The return characteristics of each asset class, however, are described by one set of values over a short period and another set of values over the remainder of the horizon.

In such a case, the investment strategy may involve investing in one portfolio over the short period and another portfolio over the remaining horizon. Naturally, the investor is mostly interested in the short-term portfolio since this addresses the current task of asset allocation. It is necessary to take into consideration the subsequent allocation as well, since both relate to the total horizon investment objectives.

To explain this point further, suppose that the investor wants to achieve a certain level of return, say 10 percent, with minimum risk over a five-year horizon. The 10 percent expected overall return may be accomplished by being very conservative in the first year and more aggressive over the remaining four years, or aggressive in the first year and more conservative thereafter. For the asset allocations in the two periods, there is a spectrum of choices that would produce the same 10 percent overall expected return. Not all of these choices, however, would have the same overall risk, as measured by the standard deviation of total returns. As a matter of fact, there would be one combination of the asset allocations over the first and the second periods that would have the minimum risk and overall expected return of 10 percent. Such a strategy represents a point on the overall efficient set. By varying the required total expected return, one can generate the whole efficient set for the investment horizon.

A procedure to identify the overall efficient frontier and characterize the investment strategies which comprise it has been developed by Gifford Fong Associates. Notice that in this context we refer to optimal strategies, rather than optimal asset allocations, because each strategy consists of two asset allocations over the two separate periods of the horizon.

This extension of basic asset allocation has considerable flexibility. It allows an investor to specify different values for the short period and for the remainder of the horizon for any of the basic data required for the asset allocation model. The investor can also specify different portfolio constraints in the two periods. In fact, it is even possible to consider different asset classes in the two periods comprising the horizon.

The techniques involved in the generation of the efficient strategies and their characterization in terms of return and risk, as well as probabilities of meeting threshold returns (risk-of-loss analysis), for the horizon and the two subperiods are fairly complex. Since the model simultaneously optimizes over two periods, quadratic programming alone is no longer sufficient. The computational procedure is beyond the scope of this book.[12]

To illustrate this extension of the asset allocation model, the following are assumed:

1. There are six asset classes over which funds are to be allocated. They are: (1) government agencies, (2) intermediate-term industrials, (3) long-term corporates, (4) S&P 500 stocks, (5) AMEX stocks, and (6) Treasury bills. The proxies for the first three asset classes are the Kuhn Loeb Government/Agency Index, Kuhn Loeb Intermediate Industrial Index, and Kuhn Loeb Long Corporate Index.

---

[12] Briefly, the approach used is as follows. For a given level of the total expected return, the overall standard deviation is expressed as a function of the first period expected return. This is possible since a value of the first period expected return determines the second period expected return necessary to generate the given overall return expectation required. Two separate quadratic algorithms give the two one-period minimum standard deviations corresponding to the one-period returns. These standard deviations are then combined by an appropriate formula to provide the overall standard deviation. Once the total standard deviation is expressed as a function of the first period return expectation, this function is minimized to obtain a point on the overall efficient set. (The method used for the minimization of this function is the three-point Newton iteration method.) The above process is repeated for different values of the total expected return in the feasible range to generate the whole efficient set. The optimal asset allocation strategies are obtained in the process. No assumptions beyond serial independence of returns are necessary for the calculation of the mean/variance efficient strategies. Lognormality of the return distributions is assumed for calculation of the probabilities of exceeding threshold returns.

Table 4–12
Long-Term/Short-Term Asset Allocation: Long-Term Specifications (60-month period)

Name	Annual Expected Return	Annual Expected Yield	Annual Standard Deviation	Correlation with					
				KLGA	KLII	KLLC	S&P500	AMEX	USTB
KLGA	8.00%	8.00%	4.00%	1.000					
KLII	9.00	9.00	6.00	0.974	1.000				
KLLC	10.00	10.00	12.00	0.965	0.965	1.000			
S&P500	15.00	5.00	16.00	0.353	0.401	0.387	1.000		
AMEX	20.00	5.00	25.00	0.281	0.356	0.327	0.845	1.000	
USTB	6.00	6.00	1.00	0.611	0.560	0.508	-0.032	-0.097	1.000

Constraints:

	KLGA	KLII	KLLC	S&P500	AMEX	USTB
Minimum concentration (percent)	20.00	0.0	0.0	0.0	0.0	0.0
Maximum concentration (percent)	100.00	100.00	100.00	80.00	80.00	60.00
Minimum yield (percent)	6.00					

Key: KLGA = Kuhn Loeb Government/Agency Index
KLII = Kuhn Loeb Intermediate Industrials Index
KLLC = Kuhn Loeb Long-Term Corporates
S&P500 = Standard & Poor's 500
AMEX = American Stock Exchange Index
USTB = U.S. Treasury bills

Table 4–13
Long-Term/Short-Term Asset Allocation: Short-Term Specifications (12-month period)

Name	Annual Expected Return	Annual Expected Yield	Annual Standard Deviation	Correlation with					
				KLGA	KLII	KLLC	S&P500	AMEX	USTB
KLGA	15.00%	8.00%	4.00%	1.000					
KLII	13.00	9.00	4.00	0.965	1.000				
KLLC	25.00	10.00	6.00	0.972	0.970	1.000			
S&P500	10.50	5.00	10.00	−0.200	−0.200	−0.300	1.000		
AMEX	5.00	5.00	12.00	−0.100	−0.200	−0.200	0.848	1.000	
USTB	7.00	7.00	0.0	0.0	0.0	0.0	0.0	0.0	1.000

Constraints:

	KLGA	KLII	KLLC	S&P500	AMEX	USTB
Minimum concentration (percent)	20.00	0.0	0.0	0.0	0.0	0.0
Maximum concentration (percent)	100.00	100.00	100.00	80.00	80.00	100.00
Minimum yield (percent)	6.00					

Key: KLGA = Kuhn Loeb Government/Agency Index
       KLII = Kuhn Loeb Intermediate Industrials Index
       KLLC = Kuhn Loeb Long-Term Corporates
     S&P500 = Standard & Poor's 500
       AMEX = American Stock Exchange Index
       USTB = U.S. Treasury bills

Table 4–14
Long-Term/Short-Term Asset Allocation: Optimal Initial Strategy (12-month period)

Strategy	Annual Expected Return	Annual Standard Deviation	Annual Expected Yield	Probability of Annual Return Less than					Minimum Risk Asset Mix					
				0.0 Percent	8.0 Percent	10.0 Percent	12.0 Percent	20.0 Percent	KLGA	KLII	KLLC	S&P500	AMEX	USTB
1	8.66%	0.784%	7.17%	0.0%	20.0%	95.7%	100.0%	100.0%	20.0%	0.0%	0.0%	1.6%	0.0%	78.4%
2	10.10	1.214	7.34	0.0	4.0	46.9	94.1	100.0	20.0	0.0	7.5	4.2	0.0	68.2
3	12.49	1.938	7.66	0.0	0.9	9.9	40.4	100.0	20.0	0.0	20.2	7.3	0.0	52.5
4	14.92	2.680	7.98	0.0	0.4	3.1	13.7	96.9	20.0	0.0	33.1	10.4	0.0	36.5
5	17.41	3.440	8.32	0.0	0.2	1.3	5.5	77.6	20.0	0.0	46.3	13.6	0.0	20.1
6	19.96	4.216	8.66	0.0	0.1	0.7	2.6	51.1	20.0	0.0	59.8	16.9	0.0	3.3
7	21.69	4.861	9.15	0.0	0.1	0.6	2.0	37.0	20.0	0.0	71.0	8.0	0.0	0.0
8	23.00	5.581	9.60	0.0	0.2	0.7	2.1	30.1	20.0	0.0	80.0	0.0	0.0	0.0
9	23.00	5.581	9.60	0.0	0.2	0.7	2.1	30.1	20.0	0.0	80.0	0.0	0.0	0.0
10	23.00	5.581	9.60	0.0	0.2	0.7	2.1	30.1	20.0	0.0	80.0	0.0	0.0	0.0
11	23.00	5.581	9.60	0.0	0.2	0.7	2.1	30.1	20.0	0.0	80.0	0.0	0.0	0.0
12	23.00	5.581	9.60	0.0	0.2	0.7	2.1	30.1	20.0	0.0	80.0	0.0	0.0	0.0
13	23.00	5.581	9.60	0.0	0.2	0.7	2.1	30.1	20.0	0.0	80.0	0.0	0.0	0.0
14	23.00	5.581	9.60	0.0	0.2	0.7	2.1	30.1	20.0	0.0	80.0	0.0	0.0	0.0
15	23.00	5.581	9.60	0.0	0.2	0.7	2.1	30.1	20.0	0.0	80.0	0.0	0.0	0.0
16	23.00	5.581	9.60	0.0	0.2	0.7	2.1	30.1	20.0	0.0	80.0	0.0	0.0	0.0
17	23.00	5.581	9.60	0.0	0.2	0.7	2.1	30.1	20.0	0.0	80.0	0.0	0.0	0.0
18	23.00	5.581	9.60	0.0	0.2	0.7	2.1	30.1	20.0	0.0	80.0	0.0	0.0	0.0
19	23.00	5.581	9.60	0.0	0.2	0.7	2.1	30.1	20.0	0.0	80.0	0.0	0.0	0.0
20	23.00	5.581	9.60	0.0	0.2	0.7	2.1	30.1	20.0	0.0	80.0	0.0	0.0	0.0
21	23.00	5.581	9.60	0.0	0.2	0.7	2.1	30.1	20.0	0.0	80.0	0.0	0.0	0.0
22	23.00	5.581	9.60	0.0	0.2	0.7	2.1	30.1	20.0	0.0	80.0	0.0	0.0	0.0
23	23.00	5.581	9.60	0.0	0.2	0.7	2.1	30.1	20.0	0.0	80.0	0.0	0.0	0.0
24	23.00	5.581	9.60	0.0	0.2	0.7	2.1	30.1	20.0	0.0	80.0	0.0	0.0	0.0

Table 4–15
Long-Term/Short-Term Asset Allocation: Optimal Residual Strategy (48-month period)

Strategy	Annual Expected Return	Annual Standard Deviation	Annual Expected Yield	Probability of Annual Return Less than					Minimum Risk Asset Mix					
				0.0 Percent	8.0 Percent	10.0 Percent	12.0 Percent	20.0 Percent	KLGA	KLII	KLLC	S&P500	AMEX	USTB
1	6.80%	2.023%	6.80%	0.0%	88.5%	99.8%	100.0%	100.0%	40.0%	0.0%	0.0%	0.0%	0.0%	60.0%
2	6.86	2.031	6.78	0.0	87.2	99.8	100.0	100.0	39.2	0.0	0.0	0.6	0.1	60.0
3	6.91	2.042	6.76	0.0	86.1	99.8	100.0	100.0	38.8	0.0	0.0	0.8	0.4	60.0
4	6.95	2.056	6.75	0.0	85.0	99.8	100.0	100.0	38.3	0.0	0.0	1.0	0.7	60.0
5	6.99	2.072	6.74	0.0	83.8	99.8	100.0	100.0	37.9	0.0	0.0	1.2	0.9	60.0
6	7.03	2.091	6.73	0.0	82.7	99.8	100.0	100.0	37.5	0.0	0.0	1.4	1.1	60.0
7	7.26	2.246	6.66	0.0	75.2	99.3	100.0	100.0	35.2	0.0	0.0	2.4	2.4	60.0
8	7.58	2.589	6.56	0.0	63.6	97.0	100.0	100.0	31.9	0.0	0.0	3.8	4.3	60.0
9	8.19	3.415	6.72	0.0	46.9	86.1	98.7	100.0	41.7	0.0	0.0	5.3	6.2	46.7
10	8.80	4.266	6.99	0.0	36.8	72.6	93.6	100.0	56.8	0.0	0.0	6.5	7.7	29.0
11	9.41	5.125	7.27	0.0	30.6	60.9	85.3	100.0	71.9	0.0	0.0	7.7	9.1	11.3
12	10.02	5.997	7.38	0.0	26.6	51.9	76.1	99.9	79.2	0.0	0.0	9.5	11.3	0.0
13	10.63	6.951	7.24	0.1	24.1	45.3	67.5	99.6	69.6	3.7	0.0	12.1	14.5	0.0
14	11.24	7.946	7.36	0.2	22.4	40.4	60.3	98.6	41.2	28.2	0.0	14.4	16.3	0.0
15	11.85	8.956	7.39	0.3	21.3	36.8	54.5	96.7	20.0	44.7	0.0	16.5	18.8	0.0
16	12.47	10.018	7.14	0.5	20.5	34.1	49.8	93.9	20.0	38.5	0.0	18.0	23.5	0.0
17	13.08	11.134	6.89	0.8	20.1	32.1	46.1	90.4	20.0	32.2	0.0	19.6	28.3	0.0
18	13.70	12.290	6.63	1.1	19.9	30.7	43.2	86.6	20.0	25.9	0.0	21.1	33.0	0.0
19	14.31	13.474	6.38	1.5	19.8	29.5	40.9	82.7	20.0	19.6	0.0	22.7	37.7	0.0
20	14.93	14.682	6.13	2.0	19.8	28.7	39.0	79.0	20.0	13.2	0.0	24.3	42.5	0.0
21	15.55	15.917	6.00	2.4	19.8	28.1	37.5	75.5	20.0	10.0	0.0	19.1	50.9	0.0
22	16.16	17.217	6.00	3.0	20.0	27.7	36.4	72.2	20.0	0.0	8.0	12.7	59.3	0.0
23	16.78	18.573	6.00	3.6	20.3	27.5	35.5	69.2	20.0	0.0	8.0	0.4	71.6	0.0
24	16.80	18.613	6.00	3.6	20.3	27.5	35.5	69.1	20.0	0.0	8.0	0.0	72.0	0.0

Table 4–16
Long-Term/Short-Term Asset Allocation Optimal Composite Statistics (60-months horizon)

Strategy	Annual Expected Return	Annual Standard Deviation	Annual Expected Yield	Probability of Annual Return Less Than				
				0.0 percent	8.0 percent	10.0 percent	12.0 percent	20.0 percent
1	7.17%	1.848%	6.87%	0.0%	84.7%	100.0%	100.0%	100.0%
2	7.50	1.903	6.89	0.0	72.8	99.8	100.0	100.0
3	8.00	2.024	6.94	0.0	50.8	98.6	100.0	100.0
4	8.50	2.182	7.00	0.0	31.2	93.9	100.0	100.0
5	9.00	2.368	7.05	0.0	17.7	83.3	99.8	100.0
6	9.50	2.573	7.11	0.0	9.9	67.7	98.5	100.0
7	10.00	2.847	7.16	0.0	6.0	51.2	94.4	100.0
8	10.50	3.268	7.17	0.0	4.5	37.8	85.4	100.0
9	11.00	3.859	7.30	0.0	4.2	29.3	73.1	100.0
10	11.50	4.518	7.52	0.0	4.3	24.1	61.5	100.0
11	12.00	5.214	7.74	0.0	4.5	20.8	52.1	100.0
12	12.50	5.941	7.82	0.0	4.7	18.6	44.8	99.7
13	13.00	6.751	7.71	0.0	5.2	17.3	39.5	99.0
14	13.50	7.607	7.81	0.0	5.7	16.6	35.6	97.4
15	14.00	8.484	7.83	0.0	6.1	16.1	32.7	94.8
16	14.50	9.412	7.63	0.0	6.7	15.8	30.5	91.5
17	15.00	10.390	7.43	0.0	7.3	15.8	29.0	87.6
18	15.50	11.405	7.23	0.1	7.9	15.9	27.8	83.6
19	16.00	12.448	7.03	0.1	8.5	16.1	27.0	79.6
20	16.50	13.511	6.82	0.2	9.1	16.3	26.3	75.9
21	17.00	14.599	6.72	0.4	9.7	16.6	25.9	72.4
22	17.50	15.744	6.72	0.5	10.3	16.9	25.6	69.2
23	18.00	16.937	6.72	0.8	11.0	17.4	25.5	66.4
24	18.01	16.973	6.72	0.8	11.0	17.4	25.5	66.3

2. The investment horizon is 60 months.

3. The investor has expectations for a 12-month horizon that differs from the 60-month horizon.

4. The basic expectational values for the 60-month (long-term) and 12-month (short-term) horizons are shown in Tables 4–12 and 4–13, respectively.

5. Minimum and maximum concentration constraints are imposed for each subperiod as shown in Tables 4–12 and 4–13.

6. The minimum yield for both subperiods is set at 6 percent.

Table 4–14 displays the optimal strategies for the 12-month horizon. Table 4–15 shows the optimal strategies for the residual term horizon of 48 months. The optimal composite statistics for the 60-month horizon based on the optimal strategies shown in Tables 4–14 and 4–15 are displayed in Table 4–16.

■ Applications of the Asset Allocation Model

Application for Pension Funds

Asset allocation can serve the function of setting the investment policy for pension funds. A rational policy is desirable to ensure that the objective is achieved. The objective is typically to control risk in general or, more specifically, to maximize the likelihood that a minimum return will be achieved.

The user's estimates concerning the capital markets can be transformed into an analysis suitable for insuring that the predefined objective is achieved. Asset allocation is the focal point for integrating a number of information sources.

The time dimension is of primary importance since the longer-term orientation of pension funds permits an assumption of higher risk and higher return profiles. Short-term portfolio value variations are usually not critical. Therefore, horizons typically will range from a minimum of three years to as long as ten years or more. Because of a possible intuitive aversion to short-term variation, however, some consideration of the implications of a long-term policy over the short term may be appropriate. This consideration may temper assuming the higher risk/return allocations. In summary, the long-term perspective is of paramount interest, but short-term considerations may be important based upon the particular end user.

Using the risk-of-loss analysis, the relevant return benchmark can be evaluated. By observing the behavior of the risk-of-loss return benchmarks over the expected return levels available, a basis for understanding the implications of risk and return is established. By contrasting the long-term desired result with the short-term implications, the time dimension trade-offs will become apparent.

The entire process results in a range of optimal portfolio mixes and a framework for evaluating the alternatives. The objective is to provide assistance to the user in establishing a rational investment policy where the implications of the best return/risk portfolios can be evaluated.

Once the initial allocation is made, periodic reevaluation is necessary. As capital market expectations change, modifications of the portfolio mix can be made to maintain the proper policy relative to the objectives that have been set.

In the situation where short-run deviations put the portfolio well below its long-term target range, corrective action is appropriate. The nature of the action should depend on the controlling criterion of the analysis. If control of risk is of paramount importance, lower risk exposure should be followed; if a target return is the important objective, assuming more risk is indicated to try to make up the return.

Asset allocation should be a dynamic and responsive process that must integrate expectations and reconcile past performance with the investment objectives. Success requires more than a mechanical application of a model: the promised reward is the enhanced perspective provided through a man-machine interface with the ability to evaluate the sensitivity of judgment to investment implication.

Application for Investment Strategy

Implicit in the use of the model in making strategy decisions is the capability of providing capital market expectations with greater precision than using a historical average. Along with expected return judgments, it is assumed that the risk estimates are also capable of refinement.

For example, over periods of less than a year the normal relationship between return and risk for the highest expected return assets will be masked by the magnitude of their expected risk (variance). Hence, unless this risk can be specified to be much lower than the historical average, the model will consistently choose the lowest return, lowest risk asset mixes for the short horizons. This is intuitively proper, since, if a short-term perspective is important and there is no insight as to expected return and risk other than a historical average, the lower return and risk allocation would be most appropriate for this time horizon from a risk-of-loss standpoint.

Multioutlook analysis is especially important concerning capital market expectations. While the individual scenario distributions of return may narrow, the prospect of alternative cases may become apparent and even compelling.

Over the short run, confident return projections are extremely difficult, especially for the high expected return assets. On the other hand, if the projection is not expressed with strong conviction in the form of a relatively small expected risk, the allocation process will consistently call for low risk allocations. Therefore, a multiscenario projection allows a range of outcomes to be evaluated, and the probability-weighted composite provides a consensus outcome. The important result is the sensitivity of the outcome under alternative assumptions. A more effective perspective for decision-making is consequently achieved.

In the context of setting strategy for a pension fund that already has a long-term policy established, the value of the probability of loss for the desired return benchmark over the long-term horizon can be used as the maximum value for the short term. For example, if the long-term policy has a 15 percent probability of loss for 0 percent return, the mix may be changed over the short run, as long as the probability of loss of the new mix has a maximum of 15 percent. Therefore, by taking advantage of short-term expectations to maximize return, the integrity of the long-term policy is retained.

A floor or base probability of loss is therefore established that can provide boundaries within which strategic return/risk decisions may be made. As long as the alteration of the portfolio mix does not violate the probability of loss, increased return through strategic judgment can be pursued. Ultimately, the value of the judgment must be reviewed, but the mechanism for translating the judgment into decision-making boundaries is served through an asset allocation framework. □

5

Passive Strategies

In this chapter and the two that follow we describe three types of portfolio strategies—passive, semiactive and active strategies. Let us first differentiate between the two extreme strategies—active and passive. Active strategies basically attempt to achieve the maximum return for a given level of risk. In other words, this approach pursues the highest possible return while controlling risk. This is different from a passive strategy, in which risk aversion is more important and a less than maximum return is acceptable.

Managers who pursue an active strategy use expectations to achieve higher returns. Basic to all passive strategies, on the other hand, is the minimal expectational input required. In fact, this difference in the role of expectations is the main distinction between passive and active management. Therefore, the selection of active versus passive strategies may turn on the efficiency of the bond market. Other considerations may include preferences of the client for risk control over return maximization.

The purpose of this chapter is to discuss passive bond portfolio management strategies. First, however, we shall discuss the concept of market efficiency and the findings of several studies concerning the efficiency of the bond market since it underlies the philosophy of passive strategies.

93

■ Efficiency of the Bond Market

The term *efficient capital market* has been used in several contexts to describe the operating characteristics of a capital market. Richard West draws a distinction between an *operationally* (or *internally*) efficient capital market and a *pricing* (or *externally*) efficient capital market.[1]

In an *operationally* efficient market, market agents can obtain transaction services as cheaply as possible given the costs associated with furnishing those services. Transactions costs consist of commissions and spreads. Historically, the equity exchange markets receive a poor grade with respect to operational efficiency.[2] The elimination of fixed commissions in 1975 and the establishment of a national market system are steps to improve operational efficiency for equities. With respect to the bond market, West concludes: "Although the operational efficiency of the markets for non-equity securities such as corporate and municipal bonds has received relatively little formal analysis, casual empiricism suggests that it is quite good."[3]

Pricing efficiency refers to a market in which prices at any given point in time fully reflect all available information that is relevant to the value of the security. In an efficient capital market, active strategies based on the analysis of relevant information available today cannot be exploited to realize abnormal risk-adjusted returns. This is the context in which we mean an "efficient" market in this book.

There are three forms of market efficiency—weak, semistrong and strong. The distinction between these three forms is the relevant set of information that is believed to be impounded into the price of the security at any given point in time. *Weak efficiency* means that the price of the security fully reflects price and trading history of the security. *Semistrong efficiency* means that the price of the security fully reflects all public information (which, of course, includes historical price and trading behavior). *Strong efficiency* exists in a market in which the price of a security fully reflects all information regardless of whether or not it is publicly available.

There is no shortage of empirical studies dealing with the efficiency of the equity market. A fair conclusion of these is that the market is efficient in the weak and semistrong forms but the jury is still out on whether the

---

[1] Richard R. West, "Efficiency of the Securities Markets," Chapter 2 in *The Handbook of Securities Markets: Securities, Options, and Futures,* ed. F. J. Fabozzi and F. G. Zarb (Homewood, Ill.: Dow Jones-Irwin, 1981).

[2] One observer of the New York Stock Exchange referred to this market as: "one of the most resilient and effective long-run monopolies in the history of the United States." (R. W. Doede, "The Monopoly Power of the New York Stock Exchange," Ph.D. diss., University of Chicago, 1967, p. 20.)

[3] West, "Efficiency of the Securities Markets," p. 21.

market is efficient in the strong form. There are empirical studies, however, that have found market inefficiency in the semistrong form. These findings are often discounted by the contention that the model used to specify the equity returns may be misspecified and that the results may be due to this misspecification rather than to a market inefficiency.

Research on the pricing efficiency of the bond market has not been nearly as extensive as it has been for the equity market. Studies of weak form efficiency focus on the ability of market participants to forecast interest rates. As will be discussed in Chapter 7, interest rate forecasts are a key input in most active strategies. Most studies concluded that interest rate movements can not be predicted with a degree of consistency and accuracy sufficient to garner abnormal risk-adjusted returns.[4]

Recently, however, Michael J. Brennan and Eduardo S. Schwartz formulated a model to detect underpriced and overpriced bonds. Applying the model to U.S. government securities, they found a strong relationship between the price prediction errors produced from their model and subsequent bonds returns.[5] They conclude that "Whether or not this is interpreted as evidence of market inefficiency and a profit opportunity will depend upon one's belief in the adequacy of the underlying equilibrium model and the accuracy of the price data."[6] However, they do go on to say that "It does not seem that the results can be easily explained in terms of model misspecification."[7]

One test of the semistrong form of bond market efficiency deals with the impact of bond rating changes on bond prices or yields. In an efficient market, rating changes should be anticipated by market participants since the data employed by the commercial rating agencies to assign their rating

---

[4] See Richard Roll, *The Behavior of Interest Rates* (New York: Basic Books, 1970); Thomas J. Sargent, "Rational Expectations and the Term Structure of Interest Rates," *Journal of Money, Credit, and Banking*, February 1972, pp. 74–97; Michael J. Prell, "How Well Do the Experts Forecast Interest Rates?" Federal Reserve Bank of Kansas City *Monthly Review*, September–October 1973, pp. 3–13; Oswald D. Bowlin and John D. Martin, "Extrapolations of Yields Over the Short Run: Forecast or Folly?" *Journal of Monetary Economics*, 1975, pp. 275–88; J. Walter Elliott and Jerome R. Baier, "Econometric Models and Current Interest Rates: How Well Do They Predict Future Rates?" *Journal of Finance*, September 1979, pp. 975–86. Weak form efficiency has also been concluded for the Canadian bond market. See James E. Pesando, "On the Efficiency of the Bond Market: Some Canadian Evidence," *Journal of Political Economy*, December 1978, pp. 1057–76, and James E. Pesando, "Forecasting Interest Rates: An Efficient Market Perspective." University of Toronto, August 1979. Mimco.

[5] Michael J. Brennan and Eduardo Schwartz, "An Equilibrium Model of Bond Pricing and a Test of Market Efficiency," *Journal of Financial and Quantitative Analysis*, September 1982, pp. 301–30.

[6] Ibid., p. 302.

[7] Ibid., p. 315.

is all based on public information. Consequently, there should be no reaction to any change in bond rating. For a sample of public utility bonds, Steven Katz found that there was no anticipation of a rating change.[8] In fact, his results suggest that there may be a 6- to 10-week lag subsequent to the rating change before a complete adjustment to the new rating is realized. However, a study by George Hettenhouse and William Sartoris using public utility bond issues reached different conclusions for issues that were downgraded.[9] They find that the lower ratings were anticipated. Yet, they did not find that an upgrading of a public utility issue was anticipated. In a study focusing on the impact of a bond rating downgrade on bond prices, Paul Grier and Steven Katz find that the anticipation of rating reclassifications was not the same for both public utility and industrial issuers.[10] For public utility issues, rating downgrades were not anticipated—just as in the earlier study by Katz. However, for the industrial bonds in their sample, a downgrading of the issuer's rating was anticipated.

Assuming that the ratings by the commercial rating agencies are a proper gauge of the creditworthiness of an issuer, these three studies suggest that there may be an inefficiency in the bond market and that the degree of inefficiency varies with the segment of the bond market. In particular, the Grier and Katz study suggests that the public utility bond market may be less efficient than the industrial bond market. However, Mark I. Weinstein found for a sample of public utility and industrial bonds that bond prices reflected rating changes 6 to 18 months prior to a change with no adjustment in the 5 months prior to a change.[11] His findings, therefore, support the hypothesis that the bond market is efficient in the semistrong form.

The studies of the weak and semistrong forms of market efficiency cited above do not provide conclusive evidence about the efficiency of the bond market. Those who believe that the bond market is efficient enough that active strategies will not produce incremental returns, after considering additional risks, transaction costs, and management fees, may wish to pursue a passive bond portfolio strategy. The balance of this chapter explains how to do so.

---

[8] Steven Katz, "The Price Adjustment Process of Bonds to Rating Reclassifications: A Test of Bond Market Efficiency," *Journal of Finance*, May 1974, pp. 551–59.

[9] George W. Hettenhouse and William L. Sartoris, "An Analysis of the Informational Value of Bond Rating Changes," *Quarterly Review of Economics and Business*, Summer 1976, pp. 65–78.

[10] Paul Grier and Steven Katz, "The Differential Effects of Bond Rating Changes among Industrial and Public Utility Bonds by Maturity," *Journal of Business*, April 1976, pp. 226–39.

[11] Mark I. Weinstein, "The Effect of a Rating Change Announcement on Bond Price," *Journal of Financial Economics*, 1977, pp. 329–50.

■ Passive or Buy-and-Hold Strategy

The implication of bond market efficiency is that investors can not earn incremental returns after adjusting for additional transaction costs and management fees without incurring additional risks. The strategy that follows is that of buy-and-hold. Essentially this means purchasing and holding a security to maturity or redemption (e.g., by the issuer via a call provision) and then reinvesting cash proceeds in similar securities.

As noted earlier, the emphasis is on minimizing the expectational inputs, that is, the assumptions of the future level and direction of interest rates. By holding securities to maturity, any capital change resulting from interest rate change is neutralized or ignored because, by holding to maturity, the par amount of the bond will be received. Portfolio return, therefore, is controlled by coupon payments and reinvestment proceeds. While interest rate forecasting is largely ignored, analysis is important to minimize the risk of default on the securities held.

The buy-and-hold strategy is employed primarily by income-maximizing investors who are interested in the largest coupon income over a desired horizon. These types of investors include endowment funds, bond mutual funds, insurance companies that are seeking the maximum yield over an extended period of time, and other large pools of money where the size of the fund and large cash inflow make portfolio turnover difficult because of possible market impact. The buy-and-hold strategy was justifiable for many investors because fixed income securities were traditionally characterized as safe assets with predictable cash flows and low price volatility. By assuming a long-term perspective, a return in excess of inflation with interest rate risk minimized is the objective. This is a classic example of seeking less than the maximum return to avoid the inherent risk associated with the highest return strategy.

■ Index Fund as a Technique for a Passive Strategy

Another type of passive strategy is the index fund approach. The objective is to duplicate the performance of the bond market using a proxy which is frequently a designated index.[12] Typically, either the Salomon Brothers Bond Index or the Lehman Brothers Kuhn Loeb Bond Index is used.

---

[12] For a thorough discussion of indexing for equities, see James R. Vertin, "Passive Equity Management Strategies," Chapter 8 in *Investment Manager's Handbook*, ed. S. Levine (Homewood, Ill.: Dow Jones-Irwin, 1980). The principles of constructing a corporate bond index fund are discussed in Jane Tripp Howe, "A Corporate Bond Index Fund," Chapter 41 in *The Handbook of Fixed Income Securities*, ed. F. J. Fabozzi and I. M. Pollack (Homewood, Ill.: Dow Jones-Irwin, 1983).

The index fund approach is supported by the work of Harry M. Markowitz in 1952 on the construction of optimal (efficient) portfolios, and capital market theory as developed by William F. Sharpe, John Lintner, and Jan Mossin.[13] As explained in Chapter 3, Markowitz demonstrated how portfolios can be constructed so as to maximize return for a given level of risk. Such portfolios are called efficient or optimal portfolios. The Sharpe-Lintner-Mossin analysis demonstrated that a "market" portfolio offers the highest level of return per unit of risk in an *efficient* market. By combining securities in a portfolio with characteristics similar to the market, the efficiency of the market would be captured. The theoretical market portfolio consists of all risky assets. The weight of each risky asset in the market portfolio is equal to the ratio of its market value to the aggregate market value of all risky assets. That is, the market portfolio is a capitalization-weighted portfolio of all risky assets.

According to a survey by *Pension and Investments Age*, equity index fund assets were $9.6 billion as of May 1980.[14] This amount probably underestimates the funds actually indexed because there were probably a great number of "closet" indexers whose assets were not reported in the survey.[15] In part because of the emergence of index funds for stocks, some interest in index funds for bonds has emerged.

For the equity market, the Standard & Poor's 500 has generally been considered the most useful proxy of stock market performance. It is not representative of the entire market of equities, but does reflect the performance of the usual universe of stocks held by institutional investors.

As with equities, a fundamental issue in constructing a bond index fund is the identification of the appropriate index, which should be representative of the overall market and have a well-defined and stable composition. The broader the representation, the closer the replication of the market and, consequently, the greater the opportunity for efficiency. At the extreme, holding every security outstanding in the portfolio in proportion to its market value would be ideal, but in deference to the number of issues

---

[13] Harry M. Markowitz, "Portfolio Selection," *The Journal of Finance*, March 1952, pp. 77–91 and *Portfolio Selection: Efficient Diversification of Investment* (New York: John Wiley & Sons, 1959); William F. Sharpe, "Capital Asset Prices: A Theory of Market Equilibrium under Conditions of Risk," *The Journal of Finance*, September 1964, pp. 425–42; John Lintner, "Security Prices, Risk, and Maximal Gains from Diversification," *The Journal of Finance*, December 1965, pp. 587–616; and Jan Mossin, "Equilibrium in a Capital Asset Market," *Econometrica*, October 1966, pp. 768–83.

[14] Cathy Capozzoli, "Indexed Assets up to $9 Billion as of May 1980," *Pension and Investments Age*, July 7, 1980, p. 41.

[15] Nancy Belliveau, "The Pension Funds vs. The Closet Indexers," *Institutional Investor*, March 1978. A "closet" indexer is a fund manager whose portfolio, by accident or design, is constructed to resemble some market index, but the fund manager does not state he follows an indexing policy.

necessary, a sampling technique is sensible. This may take the form of a statistical selection which provides a representative cross section of securities, or perhaps, be based upon defined market characteristics which are achieved in the portfolio. Alternatively, segmenting the market can be pursued. As in the case for equities, there can be an emphasis on that part of the market representative of institutionally oriented securities. Use of the Salomon Brothers or Lehman Brothers Kuhn Loeb indices is an example.[16] However, this segmentation has potential problems.

There will be a trade-off between desired practical considerations and the ability to replicate the market as a whole. Because the fixed income market is both larger and broader in security type than the equity market, an all-inclusive index tends to be unwieldy. For example, the Kuhn Loeb Corporate Bond Index has over 4,000 securities and still represents only fairly high quality corporate bond issues. The breadth of the fixed income market is such that manageable indices with comprehensive coverage are a significant problem. Without the ability to represent all relevant segments of the market, the risk/return efficiency theoretically achieved among stocks cannot be achieved in the bond market. In effect, by not capturing all the relevant segments of the market, considerable residual risk (unsystematic or diversifiable risk which investors should not be compensated for bearing in an efficient market) may be assumed to frustrate one of the basic rationales of indexing. However, indices can be selected on the basis of maturity, coupon, issuing sector, quality, or combinations thereof. Table 5–1 lists 65 bond market sectors, each of which is a potential ingredient for the indexed portfolio. From the variation in return for various market cycles, it can be seen that the correct selection of the sector to index for a particular time period can make a sizable difference. However, broad replication of the market is not difficult. While more diverse than the stock market in types and number of issues, the dominance of the systematic risk component for institutional-grade fixed income securities provides a fairly homogeneous universe from a return-risk standpoint.

The implication is that total indexing may not be practical. However, there may be value in identifying a particular segment or segments as the desired index or *bogey*. Again, the basic assumption is that the segments or segment are efficient and will provide the return with minimum risk. Just as the S&P 500 does not represent the entire stock market, but is still valuable, a narrower bond index may serve a similar function.

---

[16] For a description of the following major bond indices: (1) corporates, (2) U.S. governments, (3) U.S. governments/agencies, (4) U.S. governments/agencies/corporates and U.S. governments/corporates, (5) municipal bonds, (6) Yankee bonds, and (7) Eurodollar and foreign bonds, see Arthur Williams III and Noreen Conwell, "Fixed Income Indices," Chapter 7 in *The Handbook of Fixed Income Securities*, ed. F. J. Fabozzi and I. M. Pollack (Homewood, Ill.: Dow Jones-Irwin, 1983).

Table 5–1
Sector Trend—Absolute Total Return

Sector Name	Bear Cycle (12/72–8/74)	Rank	Bull Cycle (8/74–12/76)	Rank	Full Cycle (12/72–12/76)	Rank	Bear Cycle (12/76–6/30/81)	Rank
1. LBKL Index	−10.93%	40	49.42%	21	33.09%	44	−0.36%	37
2. Government/Agency Index	1.75	3	31.47	58	33.77	32	18.12	9
3. Government/Corporate Index	−4.80	20	39.68	46	32.98	46	10.63	22
4. GNMA Index	−4.64	19	44.75	35	38.07	4	0.29	36
5. Yankee Index	n.a.		n.a.		n.a.		18.69	8
6. Eurobond Index	n.a.		n.a.		n.a.		n.a.	
7. Intermediate LBKL Index	−2.65	13	40.18	45	36.47	14	17.54	11
8. Intermediate Government/Agency Index	2.82	1	30.24	59	33.91	28	22.78	3
9. Intermediate Government/Corporate Index	1.78	2	32.20	57	34.55	22	21.88	4
10. Intermediate Yankee Index	n.a.		n.a.		n.a.		24.80	2
11. Intermediate Eurobond Index	n.a.		n.a.		n.a.		n.a.	
12. Long-Term LBKL Index	−12.94	49	52.63	13	32.88	47	−6.89	52
13. Long-Term Government/Agency Index	−6.31	22	42.58	41	33.58	35	−6.69	51
14. Long-Term Government/Corporate Index	−12.14	46	51.23	16	32.87	48	−6.67	50
15. Long-Term Yankee Index	n.a.		n.a.		n.a.		Insuff. data	
16. Long-Term Eurobond Index	n.a.		n.a.		n.a.		n.a.	
17. Industrials	−7.90	25	44.88	34	33.43	38	0.47	34
18. Utilities	−12.69	48	52.62	14	33.25	42	−2.91	41
19. Finance	−8.23	28	45.83	31	33.83	31	5.93	25
20. AAA Rated	−8.91	31	46.94	27	33.85	30	−3.38	42

#									
21.	AA Rated	−10.24	39	47.15	26	32.08	51	−0.55	39
22.	A Rated	−11.39	44	48.30	24	31.41	54	0.78	38
23.	BAA Rated	−17.42	57	64.24	3	35.63	17	3.26	29
24.	AAA Industrials	−6.54	23	42.70	40	33.37	39	−2.22	40
25.	AA Industrials	−7.11	24	43.66	39	33.45	37	0.42	35
26.	A Industrials	−8.28	29	45.14	33	33.12	43	1.04	32
27.	BAA Industrials	−9.83	35	53.03	12	37.99	5	4.39	28
28.	AAA Utilities	−9.98	36	49.26	22	34.36	24	−7.23	54
29.	AA Utilities	−11.72	45	49.46	20	31.94	52	−4.15	45
30.	A Utilities	−13.54	51	51.05	18	30.60	56	−1.34	38
31.	BAA Utilities	−23.65	58	70.57	2	30.23	58	2.73	30
32.	AAA Finance	−5.92	21	42.17	42	33.75	33	4.52	27
33.	AA Finance	−8.11	27	46.15	30	34.30	26	5.03	26
34.	A Finance	−10.04	37	47.70	25	32.87	49	8.35	23
35.	BAA Finance	−11.29	42	55.64	7	38.07	3	5.97	24
36.	Intermediate Industrials	−0.83	5	38.17	51	37.02	10	16.77	16
37.	Intermediate Utilities	−3.22	16	41.81	43	37.24	7	20.08	7
38.	Intermediate Finance	−2.82	14	39.16	48	35.24	20	15.57	18
39.	Intermediate AAA Industrials	−0.83	6	36.63	56	35.50	19	17.15	12
40.	Intermediate AA Industrials	−0.10	4	36.76	55	36.62	13	15.98	17
41.	Intermediate A Industrials	−1.28	11	38.94	50	37.16	9	17.07	13
42.	Intermediate BAA Industrials	−0.92	7	44.67	36	43.34	1	20.19	6
43.	Intermediate AAA Utilities	−1.38	10	38.10	52	36.19	15	16.88	15
44.	Intermediate AA Utilities	−1.88	12	39.25	47	36.63	12	17.07	14
45.	Intermediate A Utilities	−3.38	17	39.73	49	35.01	21	20.52	5
46.	Intermediate BAA Utilities	−9.72	34	50.31	19	37.20	8	24.82	1
47.	Intermediate AAA Finance	−3.20	15	37.72	53	33.31	41	15.28	19
48.	Intermediate AA Finance	−1.18	9	37.53	54	35.91	16	14.21	20
49.	Intermediate A Finance	−4.02	18	41.19	44	35.51	18	17.81	10
50.	Intermediate BAA Finance	−1.05	8	44.00	38	42.49	2	11.66	21

Table 5–1 (Concluded)

	Sector Name	Bear Cycle (12/72–8/74)	Rank	Bull Cycle (8/74–12/76)	Rank	Full Cycle (12/72–12/76)	Rank	Bear Cycle (12/76–6/30/81)	Rank
51.	Long-Term Industrials	−9.08	32	46.80	29	33.47	36	−5.09	46
52.	Long-Term Utilities	−14.43	53	55.43	8	33.00	45	−7.99	58
53.	Long-Term Finance	−13.12	50	53.88	6	33.69	34	−6.28	48
54.	Long-Term AAA Industrials	−8.42	30	44.66	37	32.48	50	−7.60	56
55.	Long-Term AA Industrials	−8.02	26	45.73	32	34.04	27	−6.41	49
56.	Long-Term A Industrials	−9.19	33	46.81	28	33.32	40	−3.79	43
57.	Long-Term BAA Industrials	−11.33	43	55.31	9	37.71	6	−1.43	39
58.	Long-Term AAA Utilities	−11.17	41	51.22	17	34.33	25	−10.02	61
59.	Long-Term AA Utilities	−13.73	52	51.98	15	31.11	55	−8.38	59
60.	Long-Term A Utilities	−15.34	55	54.19	10	30.54	57	−7.04	53
61.	Long-Term BAA Utilities	−28.19	59	80.03	1	29.28	59	−5.56	47
62.	Long-Term AAA Finance	−10.17	38	49.05	23	33.89	29	−8.65	60
63.	Long-Term AA Finance	−12.24	47	53.20	11	34.45	23	−7.58	55
64.	Long-Term A Finance	−16.72	56	58.31	5	31.84	53	−3.91	44
65.	Long-Term BAA Finance	−15.32	54	61.49	4	36.75	11	2.32	31

n.a. = Not available.
Source: Lehman Brothers Kuhn Loeb Inc., Fixed Income Research Department, August 19, 1981.

How Many Securities Are Necessary to Obtain Diversification?

Once the desired index is selected, a sampling approach must be used to select those securities to include in the representative portfolio. One of the key considerations is how many bond issues are necessary to obtain adequate diversification. A study by Richard W. McEnally and Calvin M. Boardman examined how diversification of bonds varies with portfolio size.[17] Their sample consisted of 515 corporate bonds with quality ratings ranging from Aaa to Baa. For all the bonds in their sample and for each quality rating, they constructed 1,000 randomly selected portfolios for a given number of issues. They then computed the variance of monthly returns. The results of the McEnally-Boardman study are summarized in Table 5–2.

The first row of Table 5–2 shows the average variance of returns for the 515 issues. The last row presents the variance of returns for a portfolio consisting of all bond issues. The body of the table shows the average variance for the 1,000 randomly constructed portfolios as the number of issues in the portfolio increases. As can be seen, as the number of issues in the portfolio increases, the average variance of the portfolio return decreases and approaches the variance of returns of the portfolio consisting of all issues. Also shown in Table 5–2 is the nondiversifiable return variation (that is, the variance of the return for the all-bond portfolio) as a proportion of the total return variation (that is, the average variation of return) for the random portfolios.

Viewing the entire sample of bonds as the universe of all fixed income securities and the quality ratings as a sector, the McEnally-Boardman results have several interesting implications for the index approach.

First, the following theoretical relationship between portfolio size and the variance of return of a portfolio consisting of n-issues is supported by their analysis:

$$\text{Var}(P_n) = \text{Var}(M) + (1/n)\,\text{Var}(R_1)$$

where

n = number of securities in the portfolio

$\text{Var}(P_n)$ = the expected value of the variance of returns of portfolios constructed by investing $1/n$ of the portfolio in each of n randomly selected securities

$\text{Var}(M)$ = the average systematic or market related variance of returns from the universe from which the n securities are drawn

---

[17] Richard W. McEnally and Calvin M. Boardman, "Aspects of Corporate Bond Portfolio Diversification," *Journal of Financial Research*, Spring 1979, pp. 27–36.

Table 5-2
Monthly Return Variance of Corporate Bond Portfolios, January 1973 to June 1976 ($\times 10^4$)

	All Issues	Aaa	Aa	A	Baa
All bonds in universe, individually [Var(P_1)]	9.257	7.756	8.419	9.912	10.977
Random portfolios of bonds [Var(P_n)]*					
1 bond	9.367 (1.85)†	7.737 (1.21)	8.308 (1.47)	9.721 (2.10)	10.974 (2.52)
2 bonds	7.469 (1.48)	7.175 (1.20)	7.234 (1.28)	7.316 (1.58)	7.557 (1.73)
4 bonds	6.004 (1.19)	6.777 (1.06)	6.298 (1.11)	5.827 (1.26)	6.100 (1.40)
6 bonds	5.782 (1.15)	6.630 (1.03)	6.096 (1.08)	5.503 (1.19)	5.446 (1.25)
8 bonds	5.591 (1.11)	6.644 (1.04)	6.075 (1.07)	5.309 (1.15)	5.229 (1.20)
10 bonds	5.376 (1.07)	6.482 (1.01)	5.965 (1.05)	5.133 (1.11)	4.982 (1.14)
12 bonds	5.401 (1.07)	6.537 (1.02)	5.894 (1.04)	5.050 (1.09)	4.912 (1.13)
14 bonds	5.341 (1.06)	6.549 (1.02)	5.871 (1.04)	5.003 (1.08)	4.845 (1.11)
16 bonds	5.299 (1.05)	6.484 (1.02)	5.876 (1.04)	4.940 (1.07)	4.768 (1.09)
18 bonds	5.266 (1.05)	6.524 (1.02)	5.784 (1.02)	4.917 (1.06)	4.760 (1.09)
20 bonds	5.274 (1.05)	6.410 (1.00)	5.809 (1.03)	4.928 (1.06)	4.699 (1.07)
40 bonds	5.155 (1.02)	6.449 (1.00)	5.767 (1.02)	4.776 (1.03)	4.513 (1.03)
All bond portfolio [Var(M)]	5.039	6.416	5.661	4.633	4.362

Key: Var(P_1) = mean variance of individual issues
Var(P_n) = mean variance of portfolios constructed by investing $1/n$ of the portfolio in each of n randomly selected securities
Var(M) = mean systematic or market related variance for the universe

* Based on 1,000 portfolios in each cell.
† Var(P_n)/Var(M) = ratio of mean variance of portfolio to mean market related variance. (Computed by authors)
Source: Richard W. McEnally and Calvin M. Boardman, "Aspects of Corporate Bond Portfolio Diversification," *Journal of Financial Research*, Spring 1979, p. 31.

$Var(R_1)$ = the average nonsystematic (diversifiable or residual) variance of the one-security portfolios from which the n securities are drawn

Thus, as an additional security is added to the portfolio, the variance of the portfolio can be expected to decrease by $1/n$ times the average nonsystematic risk of the one-security portfolios. This can be seen in Table 5–3 which repeats the results for all corporate bonds in Table 5–2 and

Table 5–3
Monthly Return Variance of Randomly Generated Portfolios of Corporate Bonds of All Quality Classes, January 1973 to June 1976 *(× 10^4)*

Number of Bonds in Portfolio	Mean Var(P_n)*	Theoretical Var(P_n)*
1	9.367	9.257
2	7.469	7.148
4	6.004	6.094
6	5.782	5.742
8	5.591	5.566
10	5.376	5.461
12	5.401	5.391
14	5.341	5.340
16	5.299	5.303
18	5.266	5.273
20	5.274	5.250
40	5.155	5.144

* $Var(P_n)$ = mean (expected value in case of theoretical) variance of portfolios constructed by investing $1/n$ of the portfolio in each of n randomly selected securities.
Source: Richard W. McEnally and Calvin M. Boardman, "Aspects of Corporate Bond Portfolio Diversification," *Journal of Financial Research*, Spring 1979, p. 34.

also shows the theoretical expected value of the variance for a portfolio of size n. There is no statistically significant difference between the theoretical expected value and the observed average value for the variance for any of the portfolios.

Second, it appears that the effect of portfolio size on diversification closely parallels the relationship found in common stocks.[18] This suggests that once a desired target is selected it can be replicated with a manageable number of securities, probably less than 40 issues.

_____

[18] See John L. Evans and Stephen H. Archer, "Diversification and the Reduction of Dispersion: An Empirical Analysis," *The Journal of Finance*, December 1968, pp. 761–767.

Finally, when constructing portfolios from different segments of the market, the number of securities necessary to diversify away nonsystematic risk in that segment may differ. For the segments represented by the quality rating of the issue, for example, the results in Table 5–2 indicate that it takes fewer issues to eliminate systematic risk for higher quality bonds than for the lower quality bonds. For example, a four-bond portfolio consisting of Aaa issues had an average variance that is 6 percent greater than a completely diversified portfolio of Aaa issues. On the other hand, a four-bond portfolio consisting of Baa issues had an average variance that is 40 percent larger than a completely diversified portfolio of Baa issues.

The Role of the Portfolio Manager in a Bond Index Fund

As can be seen from the foregoing discussion, when applying the concept of an index fund to a bond portfolio, the manager of the fund cannot be totally passive. The first decision that must be made is the selection of the target bond market index or bogey. Once a target is selected, the portfolio manager must decide whether to replicate the target market index exactly (full capitalization-weighted approach), or to select only a sample of issues from the target index (stratified sampling approach). With either approach, there will be transaction costs associated with (1) the purchase of the issues held to construct the index, (2) the reinvestment of cash proceeds from coupon interest payments and principal repayment (at maturity or early redemption), and (3) the rebalancing of the portfolio if the composition of the issues in the target index changes. Although the full capitalization approach will track the index better, practical considerations generally preclude this approach. If the stratified or segmented approach is adopted, the cost of the initial construction of the index fund is reduced. However, transaction costs will be incurred to rebalance the index fund over time in order to mirror the target index. Even with the stratified approach, the number of issues to be included must be determined. The manager must evaluate the costs and benefits associated with portfolios of different sizes. The McEnally-Boardman study will be helpful in evaluating this trade-off.

Transaction costs and management fees will result in a divergence between the return on the target index and the constructed index fund. The role of the portfolio manager in an index fund is to minimize this discrepancy.

A Methodology for Tracking a Bond Index

If it were possible to buy the whole universe of bonds that is used in the calculation of the index to be duplicated, in amounts proportional to the amount outstanding of each bond, then the performance of the index can be replicated exactly, at least before transactions costs. In reality this is not feasible. Even small indices, such as the Lehman Treasury Index, contain hundreds of securities, and some indices may actually be based on universes of several thousand bonds. An actual portfolio has to be limited to a much smaller number of securities. Moreover, the portfolio needs to be rebalanced each month to reinvest interest income and to reflect changes in the index composition, and that cannot be accomplished in practice if the portfolio were as large as to contain the whole universe.

The question then arises as to the construction and maintenance of an actual portfolio that would replicate the given index as closely as possible in actual operating conditions. Specifically, the following are typical conditions for a feasible strategy:

1. The portfolio should not contain more than a given number of securities (for example, 50).
2. The portfolio should not be rebalanced more often than monthly.
3. Any interest income should be kept as cash until the next rebalancing date or reinvested at a specified rate.
4. There should be a minimum amount for any purchase or sale (for example, $100,000 of face value).
5. All purchases or sales should be in round lots of a given size (for example, $10,000 of face value).
6. Transaction costs should be included in the portfolio returns.

In addition to these requirements, there are two desiderata that make the investment strategy practical. First, the strategy should be flexible enough to allow the portfolio manager to be involved in the selection of the securities for the portfolio. Second, the strategy should include a quantitative algorithm that determines exactly the holdings in each security selected for the portfolio, as well as the transactions necessary to maintain the portfolio.

Recently, Gifford Fong Associates developed a methodology to track the returns of an index as closely as possible, subject to the requirements discussed above.[19] The extent of the tracking accuracy can be assessed by historical simulations. The methodology consists of three steps.

The first step is to define the classes into which the index universe is to be divided. The number of classes should be made equal to the number of securities to be held in the portfolio. The classes should be as homogeneous as possible. This could be accomplished by dividing the universe into issuing sector/quality, maturity range, and coupon range. For instance, suppose that the objective is to track the Lehman Brothers Government Index with a portfolio of at most 40 bonds. The classes can be defined by distinguishing treasuries and agencies, breaking the maturity range into ten intervals (for example, 1–2, 2–3, 3–4, 4–6, 6–8, 8–10, 10–12, 15–20, and 20–30 years to maturity), and separating the securi-

---

[19] The system is called BONDTRAC.

ties with coupons of 10 percent or less from those with coupons over 10 percent. The total number of classes will then be 40 (2 × 10 × 2). Each class is reasonably homogeneous, since it contains only one type of security in a narrow maturity range and with similar coupon levels.

The second step is the selection of securities. On the initial date, as well as on each rebalancing date (typically monthly), one security is chosen from each class for inclusion in the investment portfolio. The methodology places no requirements on the selection of the security from the class. This gives the portfolio manager complete freedom to exercise personal judgment. The portfolio manager may review the list of bonds in the class and select the one which has the most appeal in terms of availability, liquidity, etc. To keep turnover down, the portfolio manager will probably choose a security that is already held in the portfolio (if any), unless there are reasons to prefer a new security within the class. As will be discussed in the next section, it is even possible to base the selection on a valuation model that ranks the securities in the class from the most underpriced to the most overpriced.

The third and final step is the determination of the amount held in each security selection. This step does not involve any judgmental input and is done completely by quadratic programming. This mathematical programming technique, which was used to solve the asset allocation problem discussed in Chapter 4, constructs the portfolio to be as representative of the index as possible. The quadratic programming technique accomplishes the following:

1. Ensures that the duration of the portfolio is equal to that of the index.[20]
2. Ensures that the distribution of maturities of the portfolio is equal to that of the index.[21]
3. The amount held in each of the selected securities is as close to being proportional to the total weight of that class in the index as is possible given the above constraints.[22]

After the quadratic programming solution is obtained, the solution can be modified to satisfy the round lot requirements and the minimum trade requirements. The residual amount of cash at the rebalancing date can also be minimized.

---

[20] Duration is explained in Chapter 2.

[21] In the next chapter we define this measure of distribution of maturities as an immunization risk measure. The measure evaluates the extent to which the payments on the portfolio are dispersed in time. For instance, if the maturities in the index are more or less laddered, matching this measure of the portfolio to that of the index would avoid ending up with a portfolio (of the same duration) that is of a bullet type, or one which is a barbell type, etc.

[22] The first two conditions are the constraints in the quadratic program. The objective function is to minimize the sum of the square of the difference between the relative weights in the portfolio and the weights in the class.

As an illustration of the methodology, a portfolio was constructed and simulated to replicate the Lehman Treasury Index. The classes were defined by 10 maturity intervals with breakpoints (in years to maturity) of 1, 2, 3, 4, 6, 8, 10, 12, 15, 20, and 30, and by coupon rates of 10 percent and less, and more than 10 percent. Within each class the security with the largest amount outstanding was selected for the portfolio. The simulation period was the 12-month period from January to December 1982. The other specifications were as follows:

a. An initial investment amount of $50 million.
b. A portfolio size not exceeding 20 securities.
c. Monthly rebalancing.
d. Interest income reinvested at the 90-day Treasury bill rate until the next rebalancing date.
e. Round lots of $100,000.
f. Minimum transaction amount of $100,000.
g. Transaction costs calculated at the rate of 30 basis points per round trip of the transaction amount (i.e., 15 basis points each for a sale and purchase).

A summary of the results before and after transaction costs are given in Table 5–4 under the column headed "Naive Strategy." As is apparent from the results, the methodology performed remarkably well. The naive strategy allowed tracking the index return within −11 basis points a year

Table 5–4
Tracking the Lehman Treasury Index: Simulated Monthly Returns before and after Transaction Costs

Month/ Year	Lehman Treasury Index	Naive Strategy Before Transaction Costs	Naive Strategy After Transaction Costs	Return-Enhancement Strategy Before Transaction Costs	Return-Enhancement Strategy After Transaction Costs
1/82	.64%	.62%	.62%	1.15%	1.15%
2/82	1.43	1.54	1.50	1.56	1.43
3/82	1.13	1.02	.90	1.29	1.24
4/82	2.44	2.45	2.38	2.46	2.41
5/82	1.46	1.36	1.31	1.36	1.35
6/82	−1.24	−1.13	−1.15	−1.07	−1.12
7/82	3.96	3.87	3.87	3.93	3.87
8/82	4.41	4.48	4.47	4.59	4.55
9/82	3.54	3.48	3.45	3.65	3.50
10/82	4.58	4.55	4.54	4.50	4.49
11/82	.68	.71	.68	.95	.80
12/82	1.95	1.93	1.86	2.14	2.04
1982	27.84%	27.73%	27.16%	29.79%	28.80%

before transaction costs, although after transaction costs the difference was −68 basis points. This is a very good tracking accuracy, considering the severe requirements placed on the portfolio size and on the minimum transaction amounts.

Tables 5–5, 5–6 and 5–7 present useful summary information for the portfolio manager. Table 5–5 is a cash account activity report that shows, for each month of the simulation period, the available cash before portfolio rebalancing, the amount of purchases and sales, transaction costs, cash after rebalancing, interest received during the month, interest on interest, and ending cash balance. The market value of the portfolio (bonds and cash) at the beginning of the month, the amount of transaction costs, capital gains during the month, interest accrued on coupon income, and the month-end portfolio value are summarized in Table 5–6. It also provides the percentage of portfolio turnover for that month, the total monthly percentage return, and the total cumulative return from the beginning of the simulation period. Table 5–7 furnishes information on the portfolio each month in terms of the number of securities held, the portfolio duration, the average yield, and maturity distribution among cash, short, intermediate, and long bonds.

Is Return Enhancement Possible?

At the beginning of this chapter, we reviewed the results of empirical studies that suggest that the bond market is efficient. The evidence was based on the inability to forecast interest rates, a key ingredient in active management, and the ability of the market to anticipate rating changes. All of this supports the position for a pure passive strategy.

In spite of these findings, however, we investigated the possibility of enhancing the return of an indexed portfolio based on a naive strategy. Since the selection of a security from a class is an independent step in the methodology described in the previous section (i.e., the second step), it is possible to combine the bond index tracking procedure with an approach that identifies securities that may be mispriced with respect to a valuation model, and choose the most underpriced securities for purchases and the most overpriced securities for sales. The result, if the valuation model is correct in pricing securities, would be an increase in the portfolio return. Two possible return-enhancement procedures are term structure analysis, described in Chapter 2 and illustrated in Appendix D, and the bond valuation model that will be described in Chapter 7.

To illustrate the combination of this return-enhancement strategy with bond index tracking, the methodology will be applied to duplicate the Lehman Treasury Index. To compare the results with the naive strategy given in the previous section, the same specifications, (a) through (g), are imposed. The return-enhancement procedure employed to select securities within a class is the term structure analysis.

Table 5-5
Cash Activity Account for Naive Strategy ($000)

Month/Year	Cash before Rebalancing	− Purchases	+ Sales	− Transaction Costs	= Cash after Rebalancing	+ Interest Received	+ Reinvestment of Cash and Income	= Ending Cash Balance
1/82	$50,000.0	$49,999.9	$ 0.0	$ 0.0	$0.2	$ 0.0	$0.0	$ 0.2
2/82	0.2	6,348.9	6,375.6	19.1	7.7	578.9	0.2	586.8
3/82	586.8	19,612.3	19,095.3	60.8	9.0	308.0	0.0	317.0
4/82	317.0	12,765.7	12,488.3	38.1	1.5	0.0	0.0	1.5
5/82	1.5	9,090.5	9,116.4	26.4	1.0	1,184.4	0.5	1,185.9
6/82	1,185.9	3,975.0	2,803.0	12.9	1.0	71.0	0.0	72.0
7/82	72.0	1,058.7	991.1	3.2	1.2	0.0	0.0	1.2
8/82	1.2	2,225.2	2,240.3	7.0	9.3	1,932.3	0.4	1,942.0
9/82	1,942.0	4,529.5	2,610.8	14.1	9.3	314.3	0.0	323.6
10/82	323.6	2,614.5	2,301.0	7.0	3.2	0.0	0.0	3.2
11/82	3.2	6,629.7	6,650.6	18.9	5.2	1,442.6	0.4	1,448.2
12/82	1,448.2	14,328.7	12,920.4	38.8	1.2	0.0	0.0	1.2

Table 5-6
Portfolio Market Value for Naive Strategy*

Month-End	Beginning Market Value	− Transaction Costs	+ Capital Gains	+ Accrued Interest	Reinvestment of Cash and Income	= Ending Market Value	Turnover (percent)	Before Transaction Costs		After Transaction Costs	
								Monthly Return (percent)	Cumulative Return (percent)	Monthly Return (percent)	Cumulative Return (percent)
1/82	$50,000.0	$ 0.0	$ −187.1	$495.5	$0.0	$50,308.4	50.0%	0.62%	0.62%	0.62%	0.62%
2/82	50,308.4	19.1	293.4	481.8	0.2	51,064.7	12.6	1.54	2.17	1.50	2.13
3/82	51,064.7	60.8	−80.0	600.6	0.0	51,524.5	37.9	1.02	3.21	0.90	3.05
4/82	51,524.5	38.1	709.6	553.9	0.0	52,750.0	24.5	2.45	5.74	2.38	5.50
5/82	52,750.0	26.4	199.5	519.4	0.5	53,442.9	17.3	1.36	7.19	1.31	6.89
6/82	53,442.9	12.9	−1,229.8	628.1	0.0	52,828.3	6.3	−1.13	5.98	−1.15	5.66
7/82	52,828.3	3.2	1,475.5	571.1	0.0	54,871.6	1.9	3.87	10.08	3.87	9.74
8/82	54,871.7	7.0	1,845.9	610.9	0.4	57,322.0	4.1	4.48	15.02	4.47	14.64
9/82	57,322.1	14.1	1,403.2	591.1	0.0	59,302.3	6.2	3.48	19.02	3.45	18.60
10/82	59,302.4	7.0	2,121.7	576.4	0.0	61,993.4	4.1	4.55	24.43	4.54	23.99
11/82	61,993.4	18.9	−186.5	627.2	0.4	62,415.6	10.7	0.71	25.32	0.68	24.83
12/82	62,414.6	38.8	590.7	611.9	0.0	63,579.5	21.8	1.93	27.73	1.86	27.16

* Dollar figures are in thousands of dollars.

Table 5–7
Beginning-of-Month Portfolio Composition for Naive Strategy

Month/Year	Bond Market Value Weighted					Cash	Maturity Composition (Percentage Bonds and Cash)		
	Number Issues	Average Coupon (percent)	Average Maturity (years)	Portfolio Duration (years)	Average Yield (percent)		Short 0–5 Years	Intermediate 5–10 Years	Long 10– Years
1/82	19	12.1%	6.5	3.5	14.0%	0.0	69.4%	13.4%	17.2%
2/82	19	12.4	6.6	3.5	14.2	0.0	68.3	14.3	17.4
3/82	19	12.9	7.0	3.5	14.1	0.0	70.8	10.1	19.1
4/82	19	12.8	7.0	3.5	14.3	0.0	70.6	10.8	18.6
5/82	19	12.9	7.0	3.6	13.8	0.0	71.9	8.9	19.2
6/82	18	13.0	6.8	3.5	13.6	0.0	70.7	10.9	18.3
7/82	18	13.0	6.7	3.5	14.5	0.0	71.0	11.0	18.0
8/82	18	13.1	6.6	3.5	13.4	0.0	70.1	12.0	17.9
9/82	18	13.1	6.7	3.6	12.3	0.0	67.7	14.7	17.6
10/82	18	13.1	6.8	3.7	11.6	0.0	65.9	15.9	18.1
11/82	18	12.8	6.9	3.8	10.5	0.0	65.8	15.6	18.6
12/82	19	12.6	6.9	3.9	10.4	0.0	66.1	16.1	17.7

A summary of the results is presented in Table 5–4. The return-enhanced portfolio outperformed the Lehman Treasury Index by 195 basis points per year before transaction costs, and by 94 basis points after transaction costs. The results were consistent from month to month. The return-enhanced strategy outperformed the Lehman Treasury Index in 9 out of the 12 monthly periods, that is, 75 percent of the time. It is important to stress that these extra returns were achieved without changing the character of the investment portfolio. The return-enhancement strategy was limited to the Treasury universe and maintained the same requirements that were imposed on the naive strategy. Therefore, no increase in risk accompanied the increase in return.

Although the simulation period is short, a proprietary study by Gifford Fong Associates found that the return-enhancement strategy consistently outperformed the Lehman Treasury Index for considerably longer simulation periods. These findings suggest that extra returns can be expected when the return-enhancement procedure is applied to any other investment strategy, whether passive or active. This is because the return-enhancement strategy is accomplished by a selection of securities identified as relatively underpriced, which could be done within the context of any investment strategy. The return-enhancement procedure should therefore be considered a management tool of potential general value.

■ *Summary*

In this chapter we discussed the philosophy behind passive bond portfolio management strategies and the empirical evidence concerning the efficiency of the bond market. The index fund approach to passive management was then discussed.

To date, bond portfolio indexing has not taken hold to the degree stock index funds have. Part of the reason can be attributed to the different circumstances between stocks and bonds from a theoretical standpoint. This and the procedural difficulties of choosing the proper index and the ability to effectively duplicate its return characteristics have created obstacles for those interested in pursuing this strategy. More work is necessary to discover whether there is a market portfolio which can be defined, which has the performance efficiency assumed among stock index funds, and which has a composition that can be replicated through time. If, indeed, this exists, then indexing represents a viable alternative for committing significant sums in a passive way. One methodology that appears to perform well for tracking a bond index is explained and illustrated in this chapter. Moreover, the possibility of a return-enhancement strategy based on term structure analysis that would be appropriate within a passive or active framework is demonstrated. □

6

Immunization and Cash Flow Matching Strategies

In this chapter we will explain two management strategies: immunization and cash flow matching. Immunization is a hybrid strategy having elements of both active and passive strategies. It is used to minimize the risk of reinvestment over a specified investment horizon. Immunization can be employed to structure a portfolio designed to fund a single terminal period liability ("bullet" immunization). Where there are a number of liabilities to fund, recent advances in immunization theory provide a strategy to construct a dedicated portfolio. This is a portfolio designed to fund a schedule of liabilities from portfolio return and asset value, with the portfolio's value diminishing to zero after payment of the last liability. Cash flow matching is an alternative strategy for designing a dedicated portfolio.

Immunization is appropriate for accumulation-maximizing investors who require a high degree of assurance of compounded return over a specified investment horizon. By accepting a more modest return than the highest that can be expected, they are more likely to realize the desired return. This is another example of the classic trade-off between return and risk. Potential users of immunization include life insurance companies, pension funds, and some banks for their own investment portfolios. Life insurance companies can employ immunization to invest the proceeds

115

from their guaranteed investment contracts (GICs) and fixed annuities. GICs provide for a lump-sum payment at a specific time in the future and at a rate of return guaranteed by the insurance company. Annuities provide for a series of payments for a predetermined time frame (sometimes to death). In both contracts, the specific terms are important, especially the premature redemption and reinvestment terms. These are investment vehicles that have a specific required payment at a defined future date. The difference between the promised return on the contract or annuity and the realized return would be revenue available for expenses and profit. It is the ability to fund specified liabilities on a timely basis that makes immunization attractive. Its use among banks and other savings institutions involves structuring the assets of the investment portfolio to match the liabilities of the balance sheet.

Pension funds seeking to fund the retired lives liability or seeking an alternative to a GIC vehicle for the funding of such liabilities have also used immunization strategies. The latter application represents an asset alternative that can fill an investment need customized for the fund sponsor.

Recently, greater interest in immunization and cash flow matching has been expressed by corporate pension sponsors because of the accounting treatment of liabilities funded by these two strategies. Because of the funding risks associated with a pension fund plan, the actuarial profession has been very conservative in its actuarial cost determinations and investment return assumptions. Consequently, while interest rates soared to 15 and 16 percent in 1982, many pension funds were laboring under low actuarial investment return assumptions in the 6 to 8 percent range. Since the actuarial rate is the rate used to obtain the present value of the liability of the firm, and the firm's contributions to the pension plan depend on the difference between that liability and the size of the fund's assets, raising the actuarial rate would reduce the firm's contributions. Locking in a portfolio rate that is higher than the current actuarial rate will reduce pension contributions and could possibly result in overfunding of the current liability with existing assets. The acceptance by actuaries of an actuarial rate closer to the expected rate of return for a dedicated portfolio has provided the incentive for corporate pension sponsors to employ a dedicated strategy. As long as there is a disparity between the available dedication rate and the actuarial rate, the incentive for a distressed firm to use this strategy that can provide some excess funding for its pension fund, and thereby lower pension fund contributions, is very compelling.

■ Immunization

Classical immunization can be defined as the process by which a fixed income portfolio is created having an assured return for a specific time horizon irrespective of interest rate changes.[1] In a concise form, the following are the important characteristics:

1. Specified time horizon.
2. Assured rate of return during the holding period to a fixed horizon date.
3. Insulation from the effects of potential adverse interest rate change on the portfolio value at the horizon date.

The fundamental mechanism underlying immunization is a portfolio structure that balances the change in the value of the portfolio at the end of the investment horizon with the return from the reinvestment of portfolio cash flows (coupon payments and maturing securities). That is, immunization requires offsetting interest-rate risk and reinvestment risk. To accomplish this balancing requires the use of the concept of duration.

Duration, as explained in Chapter 2, is a measure of the average life of a bond or, more precisely, the average time (in years) necessary to recover the price (plus accrued interest) of the bond in present value terms where each cash flow is discounted by the bond's yield-to-maturity. The specific definition of duration presented in Chapter 2 is the duration measure suggested by Macaulay. This is the most commonly used measure for immunization purposes.[2] By setting the duration of the portfolio equal to the desired portfolio time horizon, the offsetting of positive and negative incremental return sources can be assured. This is a necessary condition for effectively immunized portfolios.

Illustration: Immunization of a Single Bond

To demonstrate the principle of immunization we shall first use a single bond rather than a bond portfolio. Consider the total return for a 9 percent bond with 10 years remaining to maturity and selling for par ($1,000). The duration for this hypothetical bond was computed in Table 2–6 and was shown to be equal to 6.79 years.

Table 6–1 shows the total dollar return and realized compound yield for this bond from all three sources of return for six different holding periods and four possible changes in the interest rate immediately following the purchase of this bond. The target yield is 9 percent, which is the yield on the hypothetical bond. As can be seen from Table 6–1, if interest

---

[1] The classical theory of immunization is set forth in F. M. Reddington, "Review of the Principles of Life Insurance Valuations," *Journal of the Institute of Actuaries*, 1952; and Lawrence Fisher and Roman Weil, "Coping with Risk of Interest Rate Fluctuations: Returns to Bondholders from Naive and Optimal Strategies," *Journal of Business*, October 1971, pp. 408–31.

[2] See Fisher and Weil, "Coping with Risk."

Table 6-1
Total Return on a 9 Percent, $1,000 Bond Due in 10 Years and Held through Various Holding Periods

	Interest Rate at Time of Reinvestment	Holding Period in Years					
Income Source		1	3	5	6.79*	9	10
Coupon income	5%	$ 90	$270	$450	$611	$ 810	$ 900
Capital gain or loss		287	234	175	100	39	-0-
Interest on interest		1	17	54	105	191	241
Total return		$378	$521	$679	$816	$1,040	$1,141
(Total yield)		(37.0%)	(15.0%)	(11.0%)	(9.0%)	(8.5%)	(8.2%)
Coupon income	7%	$ 90	$270	$450	$611	$ 810	$ 900
Capital gain or loss		132	109	83	56	19	-0-
Interest on interest		2	25	78	149	279	355
Total return		$224	$404	$611	$816	$1,108	$1,255
(Total yield)		(22.0%)	(12.0%)	(10.0%)	(9.0%)	(8.6%)	(8.5%)
Coupon income	9%	$ 90	$270	$450	$611	$ 810	$ 900
Capital gain or loss		-0-	-0-	-0-	-0-	-0-	-0-
Interest on interest		2	32	103	205	387	495
Total return		$ 92	$302	$553	$816	$1,197	$1,395
(Total yield)		(9.0%)	(9.0%)	(9.0%)	(9.0%)	(9.0%)	(9.0%)
Coupon income	11%	$ 90	$270	$450	$611	$ 810	$ 900
Capital gain or loss		-112	-95	-75	-56	-18	-0-
Interest on interest		2	40	129	261	502	647
Total return		$ 20	$215	$504	$816	$1,294	$1,547
(Total yield)		(2.0%)	(6.7%)	(8.5%)	(9.0%)	(9.7%)	(9.8%)

* Duration of a 9 percent bond bought at par and due in 10 years.

rates remain at 9 percent, then, regardless of the holding period, the total return will produce a yield equal to the target yield of 9 percent. However, if interest rates decrease below 9 percent, for example, to 5 or 7 percent, the total return and realized compound yield will be less than the target yield of 9 percent if the bond is held to maturity. The reason is that even though interest rates decline, the investor does not realize a capital gain since the bond is held to maturity. The target yield is not achieved since the interest-on-interest component is less than the amount necessary to produce a 9 percent yield ($495). This, of course, is due to the reinvestment of the coupon payments at a lower rate. In fact, even if the bond is held for 9 years instead of 10, the capital gain realized is insufficient to offset the required interest-on-interest needed to produce the target yield. The opposite results if the bond is held for 1, 3, or 5 years. Although the interest-on-interest component is adversely affected by the lower reinvestment rate, the capital gain is large enough to produce a yield greater than the target yield. However, if the holding period is 6.79 years, which is equal to the duration of our hypothetical bond, the capital gain realized will exactly offset the lower interest-on-interest income due to the lower reinvestment rate, leaving the investor with the target yield of 9 percent.

If interest rates rise above the target yield, for example, to 11 percent as shown in Table 6–1, the opposite of what occurs if interest rates fall is true for holding periods above and below 6.79 years. That is, if a bond is held for more than 6.79 years, the interest-on-interest component more than compensates for the capital loss, resulting in a yield greater than the target yield. The capital loss dominates the higher interest-on-interest income from reinvesting at a higher rate producing a yield lower than the target yield for holding periods less than 6.79 years. Again, for a holding period of 6.79 years, the target yield is achieved, because the lower interest-on-interest income exactly offsets the capital loss from an increase in interest rates.

As can be seen from this illustration, to immunize a bond from a change in interest rates over a given investment horizon, a bond should be purchased for its duration, not its maturity. Therefore, if an investor has a 10-year investment horizon, a bond with a duration of 10 years, not a maturity of 10 years,[3] should be purchased to immunize against a change in interest rates.

Illustration: Immunization of a Portfolio

To immunize a bond portfolio, the portfolio must be initially constructed so that its duration is equal to the investment horizon. However, the duration

---

[3] Unless, of course, it is a zero coupon bond since for such bonds maturity is equal to duration and the bond will be immunized against any interest rate changes.

of a portfolio will change due to two factors; (1) the mere passage of time and (2) changes in interest rates.

With respect to the first factor, as time passes, the duration of the portfolio will decline. The change in the duration of the portfolio with the passage of time, however, will generally not equal the amount of time that has passed. For example, suppose a portfolio is initially created with a duration of 8 years which is equal to the investment horizon. After 1 year, the duration of the portfolio may decline to 7.3 years, or by 0.7 years which is less than the passage of time of 1 year. Consequently, the portfolio manager must rebalance the portfolio so that the duration of the portfolio is equal to the *remaining* investment horizon. If a portfolio manager does not rebalance the portfolio, duration wandering will affect the performance of the immunized portfolio.

The second factor, changes in interest rates, will also change the duration of the portfolio. As explained in Chapter 2, a property of duration is that it changes in the opposite direction as the change in market yields. Periodic rebalancing will allow a portfolio to be immunized against multiple shifts in interest rates.

For purposes of illustrating the rebalancing mechanics, a simulated example using only U.S. Treasury obligations will be presented.[4] In the simulated illustration the following assumptions are made:[5]

1. The initial investment is $18 million on September 1, 1982.
2. The investment horizon is five years.
3. The portfolio will consist of U.S. Treasury bonds in maximum initial denominations of $1 million.
4. The target rate of return established on September 1, 1982, was 14 percent. Since the initial investment is $18 million, the target terminal value of the portfolio is $34,565,737.[6]
5. The portfolio will be rebalanced each year on September 1.
6. The rate at which cash flows are reinvested between the date that they are received and the date the portfolio is rebalanced is shown on Table 6–2.
7. Transaction costs are a quarter point on bond sales and no transaction costs on bond purchases.

---

[4] For an illustration of immunization for a portfolio of municipal bonds, see: Sylvan G. Feldstein, Peter E. Christensen, and Frank J. Fabozzi, "Checking Interest Rate Volatility by Immunizing a Municipal Bond Portfolio," Chapter 34 in *The Municipal Bond Handbook: Volume I*, ed. Frank J. Fabozzi, Sylvan G. Feldstein, Irving M. Pollack and Frank G. Zarb (Homewood, Ill.: Dow Jones-Irwin, 1983).

[5] This illustration is taken from Peter E. Christensen, Sylvan G. Feldstein, and Frank J. Fabozzi, "Bond Portfolio Immunization," Chapter 36 in *The Handbook of Fixed Income Securities*, ed. Frank J. Fabozzi and Irving M. Pollack (Homewood, Ill.: Dow Jones-Irwin, 1983).

[6] The target terminal value is found as follows: $18,000,000 (1.14)^5 = $34,565,737.

Table 6–2
Assumed Yield Curves: 1982–1987

	Year 1— 9/1/82	Year 2— 9/1/83	Year 3— 9/1/84	Year 4— 9/1/85	Year 5— 9/1/86	At Termination— 9/1/87
Rate on cash flow between rebalancing		12%	9%	9%	10%	9%
1982	14	—	—	—	—	—
1983	14	10	—	—	—	—
1984	14	10	8.00	—	—	—
1985	14	10	8.13	10.00	—	—
1986	14	10	8.27	10.13	10	—
1987	14	10	8.40	10.27	10	8.00
1988	14	10	8.53	10.40	10	8.13
1989	14	10	8.67	10.53	10	8.27
1990	14	10	8.80	10.67	10	8.40
1991	14	10	8.93	10.80	10	8.53
1992	14	10	9.07	10.93	10	8.67
1993	14	10	9.20	11.07	10	8.80
1994	14	10	9.33	11.20	10	8.93
1995	14	10	9.47	11.33	10	9.07
1996	14	10	9.60	11.47	10	9.20
1997	14	10	9.73	11.60	10	9.33
1998	14	10	9.87	11.73	10	9.47
1999	14	10	10.00	11.87	10	9.60
2000	14	10	10.13	12.00	10	9.73

The simulation also requires that yield curves for the initial year and the following five years on September 1 be assumed. The yield curve assumptions are shown in Table 6–2. These are *not* interest rate projections. They are used here merely to subject an immunized portfolio to a wide variety of interest rate fluctuations over the five-year investment horizon. Notice that a flat yield curve is assumed in the initial year (year 1) and in years 2 and 5. For the other three years, an upward sloping yield curve is assumed.

Table 6–3 shows the composition of the portfolio and summary information for the portfolio on September 1 of each year. Notice that at the beginning of each year, the duration of the rebalanced portfolio is approximately equal to the remaining investment horizon.

Tables 6–4 through 6–8 summarize the actual portfolio transactions each year. The terminal value of the portfolio is $35,082,338, which exceeds the target terminal value of the portfolio of $34,565,757 by $516,581. The realized yield for the simulated immunized portfolio is 14.33 percent or 33 basis points greater than the target rate of return.

Table 6-3
Portfolio Status on September 1 of Each Year

September 1, 1982

Par (000)	Issue	Coupon	Maturity	Price	Yield	Market Value
1000	Tsy	12.375	1/15/88	93.96	14.00	$ 955,454
1000	Tsy	13.250	4/15/88	97.10	14.00	1,021,107
1000	Tsy	8.250	5/15/88	77.87	14.00	803,013
1000	Tsy	14.000	7/15/88	100.00	14.00	1,017,891
1000	Tsy	15.375	10/15/88	105.48	14.00	1,112,926
1000	Tsy	14.625	1/15/89	102.53	14.00	1,044,010
1000	Tsy	14.375	4/15/89	101.54	14.00	1,069,108
1000	Tsy	9.250	5/15/89	79.72	14.00	824,498
1000	Tsy	14.500	7/15/89	102.11	14.00	1,039,690
1000	Tsy	10.750	11/15/89	85.49	14.00	886,625
1000	Tsy	8.250	5/15/90	73.37	14.00	758,023
1000	Tsy	10.750	8/15/90	84.68	14.00	851,610
1000	Tsy	13.000	11/15/90	95.15	14.00	989,850
1000	Tsy	14.50	5/15/91	102.41	14.00	1,066,817
1000	Tsy	14.250	11/15/91	101.21	14.00	1,054,091
1000	Tsy	14.625	2/15/92	103.20	14.00	1,038,533
1000	Tsy	13.75	5/15/92	98.630	14.00	1,026,869
1000	Tsy	7.250	8/15/92	64.31	14.00	646,334
1000	Tsy	6.750	2/15/93	60.78	14.00	610.881
200	Tsy	7.875	2/15/93	66.87	14.00	134,440

Total market value:	$17,952,371	Average maturity:	4/7/90
Total par value:	$19,200,000	Average coupon:	12.055 percent
Duration:	4.963 years	Average yield:	14.000 percent

September 1, 1983

Par (000)	Issue	Coupon	Maturity	Price	Yield	Market Value
5500	Tsy	13.750	8/15/87	111.995	10.00	$6,193,351
2000	Tsy	7.625	11/15/87	91.983	10.00	1,884,566
1000	Tsy	12.375	1/15/88	108.220	10.00	1,098,014
1000	Tsy	13.250	4/15/88	111.769	10.00	1,167,747
1000	Tsy	8.250	5/15/88	93.532	10.00	959,613
1000	Tsy	14.000	7/15/88	115.103	10.00	1,168,921
1000	Tsy	15.375	10/15/88	121.109	10.00	1,269,176
1000	Tsy	14.625	1/15/89	118.835	10.00	1,207,040
1000	Tsy	14.375	4/15/89	118.441	10.00	1,238,718
1000	Tsy	9.250	5/15/89	96.771	10.00	994,948
1000	Tsy	14.500	7/15/89	119.594	10.00	1,214,470
1000	Tsy	10.750	11/15/89	103.375	10.00	1,065,405
1000	Tsy	8.250	5/15/90	91.572	10.00	940,013
1000	Tsy	10.750	8/15/90	103.685	10.00	1,041,630
1000	Tsy	13.000	11/15/90	115.110	10.00	1,189,380
1000	Tsy	14.500	5/15/91	123.741	10.00	1,280,107

Total market value:	$23,913,099	Average maturity:	11/1/88
Total par value:	$21,500,000	Average coupon:	12.285 percent
Duration:	4.007 years	Average yield:	10.000 percent

Table 6-3 (concluded)

September 1, 1984

11800	Tsy	13.750	8/15/87	113.738	8.40	$13,493,227
2000	Tsy	7.625	11/15/87	97.788	8.42	2,000,666
1000	Tsy	12.375	1/15/88	111.318	8.44	1,128,994
1000	Tsy	13.250	4/15/88	114.622	8.47	1,196,277
1000	Tsy	8.250	5/15/88	99.261	8.48	1,016,903
1000	Tsy	14.000	7/15/88	117.766	8.51	1,195,551
1000	Tsy	15.375	10/15/88	123.268	8.55	1,290,766
1000	Tsy	14.625	1/15/89	121.629	8.58	1,234,980
1000	Tsy	14.375	4/15/89	121.536	8.62	1,269,668
1000	Tsy	9.250	5/15/89	102.333	8.63	1,050,568
1000	Tsy	14.500	7/15/89	122.789	8.66	1,246,420
1000	Tsy	10.750	11/15/89	108.453	8.69	1,116,185

Total market value:	$27,240,204	Average maturity:	3/8/88
Total par value:	$23,800,000	Average coupon:	12.784 percent
Duration:	2.974 years	Average yield:	8.470 percent

September 1, 1985

17800	Tsy	13.750	8/15/87	106.014	10.27	$18,979,318
2000	Tsy	7.625	11/15/87	94.835	10.29	1,941,606
1000	Tsy	12.375	1/15/88	104.220	10.31	1,058,014
1000	Tsy	13.250	4/15/88	106.507	10.34	1,115,127
1000	Tsy	8.250	5/15/88	95.127	10.35	975,563
1000	Tsy	14.000	7/15/88	108.763	10.38	1,105,521
1000	Tsy	15.375	10/15/88	112.888	10.42	1,186,966
1000	Tsy	14.625	1/15/89	111.579	10.45	1,134,480
1000	Tsy	14.375	4/15/89	111.429	10.49	1,168,598

Total market value:	$28,665,193	Average maturity:	11/25/87
Total par value:	$26,800,000	Average coupon:	13.144 percent
Duration:	2.012 years	Average yield:	10.300 percent

September 1, 1986

23700	Tsy	13.750	8/15/87	103.326	10.00	$24,633,159
4000	Tsy	7.625	11/15/87	97.342	10.00	3,983,492
1000	Tsy	12.375	1/15/88	102.948	10.00	1,045,294
1000	Tsy	13.250	4/15/88	104.728	10.00	1,097,337
1000	Tsy	8.250	5/15/88	97.293	10.00	997,223

Total market value:	$31,756,506	Average maturity:	9/17/87
Total par value:	$30,700,000	Average coupon:	12.712 percent
Duration:	1.013 years	Average yield:	10.000 percent

Termination of Portfolio September 1, 1987

4000	Tsy	7.625	11/15/87	99.882	8.02	$ 4,083,393
1000	Tsy	12.375	1/15/88	101.542	8.05	1,030,545
1000	Tsy	13.250	4/15/88	103.073	8.09	1,080,050
1000	Tsy	8.250	5/15/88	100.082	8.10	1,024,654

Total market value:	$ 7,218,641	Average maturity:	1/10/88
Total par value:	$ 7,000,000	Average coupon:	9.196 percent
Duration:	0.368 years	Average yield:	8.050 percent

Table 6–4
Bond Immunization Year-End Transactions Report (year 1982—August 31, 1983)

	Coupon Income		Interest on Coupon		Matured Principal	
1. Income received during year:	$2,314,500	+	134,471	+	0	

			Cash Carry Forward		Interest on Cash Carry Forward		Total Cash Received
		+	47,629	+	5,715	=	$2,502,315

2. Sell:

Par (000)	Issue	Coupon	Maturity	Yield	Price	Market Value
200	Tsy	7.875	2/15/93	10.00	87.189	$ 175,078
1000	Tsy	6.750	2/15/93	10.00	80.411	807,111
1000	Tsy	7.250	8/15/92	10.00	83.970	842,924
1000	Tsy	13.750	5/15/92	10.00	121.423	1,254,719
1000	Tsy	14.625	2/15/92	10.00	125.970	1,266,203
1000	Tsy	14.250	11/15/91	10.00	123.375	1,275,711
			Less transaction fee:			$ 13,000
						$8,111,061

3. Available to reinvest: $5,608,746

4. Buy:

Par (000)	Issue	Coupon	Maturity	Yield	Price	Market Value
5500	Tsy	13.750	8/15/87	10.00	111.995	$6,193,351
2000	Tsy	7.625	11/15/87	10.00	91.983	1,884,566
						$8,077,917

5. Cash carry forward:

$8,077,917
$ 33,144

Table 6–5
Bond Immunization Year-End Transactions Report (year 1983—August 31, 1984)

	Coupon Income		Interest on Coupon		Matured Principal		
1. Income received during year:	$2,641,250	+	106,127	+	0		
							Total Cash Received
			Cash Carry Forward		Interest on Cash Carry Forward	=	$2,783,504
		+	33,144	+	2,983		

2. Sell:	Par (000)	Issue	Coupon	Maturity	Yield	Price	Market Value
	1000	Tsy	14.50	5/15/91	8.90	127.790	$1,320,597
	1000	Tsy	13.00	11/15/90	8.84	119.513	1,233,410
	1000	Tsy	10.75	8/15/90	8.80	108.882	1,093,600
	1000	Tsy	8.25	5/15/90	8.76	97.726	1,001,553
					Less transaction fee:		$ 10,000

3. Available to reinvest:							$4,639,160

4. Buy:	Par (000)	Issue	Coupon	Maturity	Yield	Price	Market Value
	5400	Tsy	13.750	8/15/87	8.40	113.738	$7,318,360

5. Cash carry forward:							$7,318,360
							$ 104,304

$7,422,664

Table 6–6
Bond Immunization Year-End Transactions Report (year 1984—August 31, 1985)

	Coupon Income	Interest on Coupon	Matured Principal
1. Income received during year:	$3,042,500 +	108,952 +	0

			Cash Carry Forward		Interest on Cash Carry Forward	=	Total Cash Received
		+	104,304	+	9,387		$3,265,143

2. Sell:

Par (000)	Issue	Coupon	Maturity	Yield	Price	Market Value
1000	Tsy	10.750	11/15/89	10.56	100.599	$1,037,645
1000	Tsy	14.500	7/15/89	10.53	112.328	1,141,810
1000	Tsy	9.250	5/15/89	10.50	96.214	989,378

	Less transaction fee:	$ 7,500

3. Available to reinvest:	$3,161,333	$6,426,476

4. Buy:

Par (000)	Issue	Coupon	Maturity	Yield	Price	Market Value
6000	Tsy	13.750	8/15/87	10.27	106.014	$6,397,523

5. Cash carry forward:	$6,397,523	$6,397,523
		$ 28,953

Table 6–7
Bond Immunization Year-End Transactions Report (year 1985—August 31, 1986)

	Coupon Income		Interest on Coupon		Matured Principal		
1. Income received during year:	$3,522,500	+	129,016	+	0		
			Cash Carry Forward 28,953	+	Interest on Cash Carry Forward 2,895	=	Total Cash Received $3,683,364

2. Sell:

Par (000)	Issue	Coupon	Maturity	Yield	Price	Market Value
1000	Tsy	14.375	4/15/89	10.00	109.845	$1,152,758
1000	Tsy	14.625	1/15/89	10.00	109.523	1,113,920
1000	Tsy	15.375	10/15/88	10.00	110.019	1,158,276
1000	Tsy	14.000	7/18/88	10.00	106.647	1,084,361

Less transaction fee: $ 10,000

3. Available to reinvest: $4,499,315

4. Buy:

Par (000)	Issue	Coupon	Maturity	Yield	Price	Market Value
5900	Tsy	3.750	8/15/87	10.00	103.326	$6,132,305
2000	Tsy	7.625	11/15/87	10.00	97.342	1,991,746

5. Cash carry forward: $8,124,051

$8,124,051

$8,182,679

$ 58,628

Table 6-8
Bond Immunization Year-End Transactions Report (year 1986–August 31, 1987)

	Coupon Income		Interest on Coupon		Matured Principal		
1. Income received during year:	$3,902,500	+	214,792	+	23,700,000		
			Cash Carry Forward 58,628	+	Interest on Cash Carry Forward 5,276	=	Total Cash Received $27,881,197

2. Sell:	Par (000)	Issue	Coupon	Maturity	Yield	Price	Market Value
	1000	Tsy	8.250	5/15/88	8.10	100.082	$1,024,654
	1000	Tsy	13.250	4/15/88	8.09	103.073	1,080,050
	1000	Tsy	12.375	1/15/88	8.05	101.542	1,030,545
	4000	Tsy	7.625	11/15/87	8.02	99.882	4,083,393
					Less transaction fee:		$ 17,500
							$ 7,201,141

| 3. Terminal value: | | | | | | | $35,082,338 |

Extensions of Classical Immunization Theory

The sufficient condition for classical immunization is that the duration of the portfolio is equal to the length of the investment horizon. Classical theory is based on the following assumptions:

1. Any changes in the yield curve are parallel changes, i.e., interest rates move either up or down by the same amount for all maturities.
2. The portfolio is valued at a fixed horizon date and there are no cash inflows or outflows during the horizon.
3. The target value of the investment is defined as the portfolio value at the horizon date if the interest rate structure does not change (i.e., no change in forward rates).

Perhaps the most critical assumption of classical immunization techniques concerns the first assumption—the type of interest rate change anticipated. A property of a classically immunized portfolio is that the target value of the investment is the lower limit of the value of the portfolio at the horizon date if there are parallel interest rate changes.[7] This would appear to be an unrealistic assumption, since such interest rate behavior is rarely, if ever, experienced in reality. According to the theory, if there is a change in interest rates that does not correspond to this *shape preserving shift*, matching the duration to the investment horizon no longer assures immunization.[8]

Figure 6–1 illustrates the nature of the portfolio value given an immunized portfolio and parallel shifts in rates. The curve *ab* represents the behavior of the portfolio value for various changes in rates, ranging from a decline to an increase as shown on the horizontal axis. Point V_o on line *tt'* is the level of the portfolio value assuming no change in rates. As noted above, an immunized portfolio subjected to parallel shifts in the yield curve will provide at least as great a portfolio value at the horizon date as the assured target value, which therefore becomes the minimum value. Thus, if the assumptions of classical theory hold, immunization provides a minimum risk strategy.

Figure 6–2 illustrates the relationship when interest rates do not shift in a parallel fashion and indicates the possibility of a portfolio value less than the target. Depending on the shape of the nonparallel shift, either the (a) or (b) relationship will occur. *The important point is that merely matching the duration of the portfolio to the investment horizon as the condition for immunization may not prevent significant deviations from the target rate of return.*

---

[7] Fisher and Weil.

[8] For a more complete discussion of these issues, see John C. Cox, Jonathan E. Ingersoll, Jr., and Stephen A. Ross, "Duration and the Measurement of Basis Risk," *Journal of Business*, January 1979, pp. 51–61.

Figure 6–1
Changes in Portfolio Value Caused by Parallel Interest Rate
Changes for an Immunized Portfolio

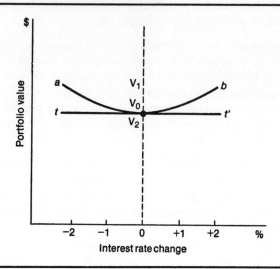

Figure 6–2
Two Patterns of Changes in Portfolio Value Caused by
Nonparallel Interest Rate Shifts for an Immunized Portfolio

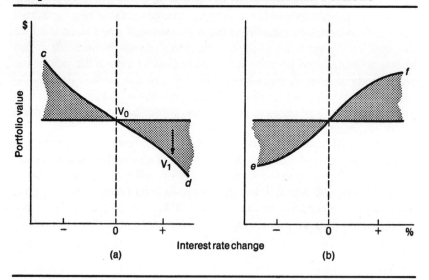

Simulated studies on the effectiveness of an immunization strategy based on Macaulay's duration measure have clearly demonstrated that immunization does not work perfectly in the real world. However, for planning horizons of 5, 10, and 20 years, Fisher and Weil find that the duration-based strategy would have come closer to the target rate or exceeded the target rate more often than the naive-maturity-based strategy for the period 1925 through 1968 even when transaction costs were considered. Leibowitz and Weinberger's findings for five-year planning horizons from January 1958 through January 1975 are shown in Figure 6–3.[9] Over the simulated period, the divergence from the target rate did not

Figure 6–3
Historical Immunization Returns over Yield-To-Maturity
Target—Actual Sequence of Yield Curves

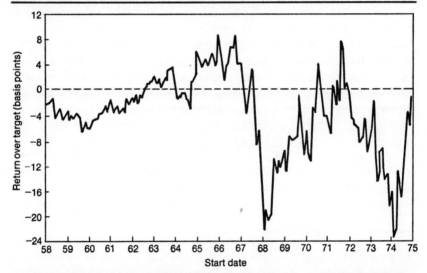

Source: Martin L. Leibowitz and Alfred Weinberger, "Contingent Immunization—Part II: Problem Areas," *Financial Analysts Journal*, January–February 1983, p. 37

exceed 25 basis points. Although there has been considerably greater volatility in market yields in recent years than in the periods investigated by Fisher and Weil and Leibowitz and Weinberger, the results do suggest that there is a high likelihood that immunization will come close to the designated target.

---

[9] Martin L. Leibowitz and Alfred Weinberger, "Contingent Immunization—Part II: Problem Areas," *Financial Analysts Journal*, January–February 1983, pp. 35–50.

A natural extension of classical immunization theory is a technique for modifying the assumption of parallel shifts in interest rates. Two approaches have been taken. The first approach has been to modify the definition of duration. Researchers have postulated alternative models of interest rate behavior and derive a measure of duration corresponding to the assumed interest rate process.[10] This approach, however, is limited since it immunizes a portfolio only against the assumed form of interest rate change. To be effective, it is necessary for the portfolio manager to predict the type of interest rate change that will occur. Moreover, simulated studies on the effectiveness of immunization based on different duration measures have generally not found that these measures would have outperformed an immunization strategy based on the simple Macaulay duration measure.[11]

Instead, what the portfolio manager requires is a strategy that can handle any arbitrary interest rate change so that it is not necessary to assume a specific type of interest rate shock. The second approach for coping with nonparallel interest rate changes does precisely that. The approach, developed by Fong and Vasicek, establishes a measure of immunization risk against any arbitrary interest rate change.[12] The immunization risk measure can then be minimized subject to the constraint that the duration of the portfolio be equal to the investment horizon resulting in a portfolio with minimum exposure to any interest rate movements. This approach will be discussed in the next section.

The second area where classical immunization theory has been extended is in overcoming the limitations of a fixed horizon (the second assumption noted earlier). Marshall and Yawitz demonstrate that under the assumption of parallel rate changes, a lower bound exists on the value of

---

[10] For duration measures based on alternative assumptions of the type of interest rate shock, see G. O. Bierwag, George G. Kaufman, Robert Schweitzer, and Alden Toevs, "The Art of Risk Management in Bond Portfolios," *The Journal of Portfolio Management*, Spring 1981, pp. 27–36; Jonathan E. Ingersoll, Jeffrey Skelton, and Roman Weil, "Duration Forty Years Later," *Journal of Financial and Quantitative Analysis*, November 1978, pp. 627–50; Chulsoon Khang, "Bond Immunization When Short-Term Rates Fluctuate More than Long-Term Rates," *Journal of Financial and Quantitative Analysis*, December 1979, pp. 1085–1090, and Cox, Ingersoll, and Ross, "Duration and the Measurement of Basis Risk." For a summary of these measures of duration, see G. O. Bierwag, George G. Kaufman, and Alden Toevs, Appendix C of "Recent Developments in Bond Portfolio Immunization Strategies," in *Innovations in Bond Portfolio Management: Duration Analysis and Immunization*, ed. G. O. Bierwag, George C. Kaufman, and Alden Toevs (Greenwich, Conn.: JAI Press, 1983).

[11] One duration measure based on a random shock assuming a generalized additive stochastic process did consistently outperform Macaulay's duration. For a summary of these studies see Bierwag, Kaufman, and Toevs, "Recent Developments in Bond Portfolio Immunization Strategies."

[12] H. Gifford Fong and Oldrich A. Vasicek, "A Risk Minimizing Strategy for Multiple Liability Immunization," paper presented at the Institute for Quantitative Research in Finance, 1980, revised February 1982.

an investment portfolio at any point in time, although this lower bound may be below the value realized if interest rates did not change.[13] Fong and Vasicek, and Bierwag, Kaufman, and Toevs extended immunization to the case of multiple liabilities.[14] Multiple liability immunization involves an investment strategy that guarantees meeting a specified schedule of future liabilities regardless of any parallel shift interest rate changes. The Fong and Vasicek study provides a generalization of the risk immunization measure for the multiple liability case. Moreover, their study extends the theory further to the general case of arbitrary cash flows (contributions as well as liabilities). Multiple liability immunization and the general case of arbitrary cash flows will be discussed later in this chapter.

In some situations, the objective of immunization as strict risk minimization may be too restrictive. The third extension of classical immunization theory is the analysis of the risk and return tradeoff for immunized portfolios. Fong and Vasicek demonstrate how this trade-off can be analyzed. Their approach, called *return maximization*, is explained later in this chapter.[15]

The fourth extension of classical immunization theory has been integrating immunization strategies with elements of active bond portfolio management strategies. The classical objective of immunization has been risk protection, with little consideration of possible returns. Leibowitz and Weinberger have proposed a technique called *contingent immunization* which provides a degree of flexibility in pursuing active strategies while ensuring a certain minimum return in the case of a parallel rate shift.[16] In this approach, immunization serves as a fall-back strategy if the actively managed portfolio does not grow at a certain rate. An alternative approach has been suggested by Gifford Fong Associates. Both this approach and contingent immunization are discussed later in this chapter.

Risk Minimization Strategy for Immunization

As noted earlier, one extension of classical immunization theory is a strategy of constructing an immunized portfolio with a minimum exposure to

---

[13] William J. Marshall and Jess B. Yawitz, "Lower Bounds on Portfolio Performance: An Extension of the Immunization Strategy," *Journal of Financial and Quantitative Analysis,* March 1982, pp. 101–14.

[14] Fong and Vasicek, "A Risk Minimizing Strategy for Multiple Liability Immunization;" G. O. Bierwag, George G. Kaufman, and Alden Toevs, "Immunization for Multiple Planning Periods," unpublished paper, Center for Capital Market Research, University of Oregon, October 1979.

[15] H. Gifford Fong and Oldrich Vasicek, "Return Maximization for Immunized Portfolios."

[16] Martin L. Leibowitz and Alfred Weinberger, "The Uses of Contingent Immunization," *The Journal of Portfolio Management,* Fall 1981, pp. 51–55.

any arbitrary interest rate change subject to the duration constraint. One way of minimizing immunization risk is shown in Figure 6–4.

The spikes in the two panels of Figure 6–4 represent actual portfolio cash flows. The taller spikes depict the actual cash flows generated by matured securities while the smaller spikes represent coupon payments. Both portfolio A and portfolio B are composed of two bonds with a duration equal to the investment horizon. Portfolio A is, in effect, a "barbell" portfolio—a portfolio comprised of short and long maturities and interim coupon payments. For portfolio B, the two bonds mature very close to the investment horizon and the coupon payments are nominal over the investment horizon. When a portfolio has the characteristic of portfolio B it is called a "bullet" portfolio.

It is not difficult to see why the barbell portfolio should be riskier than the bullet portfolio. Assume that both portfolios have durations equal to the horizon length, so that both portfolios are immune to parallel rate changes. This immunity is attained as a consequence of balancing the effect of changes in reinvestment rates on payments received during the investment horizon against the effect of changes in capital value of the portion of the portfolio still outstanding at the end of the investment horizon. When interest rates change in an arbitrary nonparallel way, however, the effect in the two portfolios is very different. Suppose, for instance, that short rates decline while long rates go up. Both portfolios would realize a decline of the portfolio value at the end of the investment horizon below the target investment value, since they experience a capital loss in addition to lower reinvestment rates. The decline, however, would be substantially higher for the barbell portfolio for two reasons. First, the lower reinvestment rates are experienced on the barbell portfolio for longer time intervals than on the bullet portfolio, so that the opportunity loss is much greater. Second, the portion of the barbell portfolio still outstanding at the end of the investment horizon is much longer than that of the bullet portfolio, which means that the same rate increase would result in a much steeper capital loss. Thus the bullet portfolio has less exposure to whatever the change in the interest rate structure may be than the barbell portfolio.

It should be clear from the foregoing discussion that immunization risk is the risk of reinvestment. The portfolio that has the least reinvestment risk will have the least immunization risk. When there is a high dispersion of cash flows around the horizon date, as in the barbell portfolio, the portfolio is exposed to higher reinvestment risk. On the other hand, when the cash flows are concentrated around the horizon date, as in the bullet portfolio, the portfolio is subject to minimum reinvestment risk.

An extreme example of a zero immunization risk portfolio is a portfolio consisting of a pure discount instrument maturing at the investment horizon. This is because there is no reinvestment risk. Moving from pure discount instruments to coupon payment instruments, the portfolio man-

Figure 6–4
Illustration of Immunization Risk Measure

A. High risk immunized portfolio

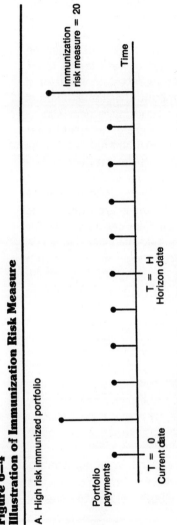

Immunization risk measure = 20

Portfolio payments

T = 0
Current date

T = H
Horizon date

Time

● Portfolio duration matches horizon length
● Payments dispersed

B. Low risk immunized portfolio

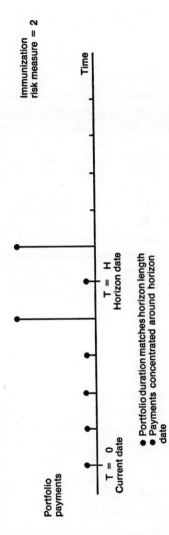

Immunization risk measure = 2

Portfolio payments

T = 0
Current date

T = H
Horizon date

Time

● Portfolio duration matches horizon length
● Payments concentrated around horizon date

ager encounters the problem of how to select coupon-paying securities that provide the best risk immunization. The foregoing discussion indicates that the portfolio manager should select securities which have most of their cash flow payments around the horizon date. Therefore, if the portfolio manager can construct a portfolio that replicates a pure discount instrument that matures at the investment horizon, that portfolio will be the lowest immunization risk portfolio.

Now let us formalize the measure of immunization risk. As explained earlier, the target investment value of an immunized portfolio is a lower bound on the terminal value of the portfolio at the investment horizon if yields on all maturities change by the same amount. If yields of different maturities change by different amounts, then the target investment value is not necessarily the lower bound on the investment value. Fong and Vasicek demonstrate that if forward rates change by any arbitrary function, the relative change in the portfolio value depends on the product of two terms.[17] The first term depends solely on the structure of the investment portfolio while the second term is a function of interest rate movement only. The second term characterizes the nature of the interest rate shock. Since the rate change can be arbitrary, this term is an uncertain quantity and therefore outside of the control of the portfolio manager. However, the first term is under the control of the portfolio manager since it depends solely on the composition of the portfolio. This first term, which is a multiplier of the unknown rate change as given by the second term, is thus a measure of risk for immunized portfolios and defined as follows:[18]

$$\frac{[PVCF_1(1 - H)^2 + PVFC_2(2 - H)^2 + \ldots + PVCF(n - H)^2]}{\text{Initial investment value}} \qquad (6-1)$$

where

$\quad PVCF_t =$ the present value of the cash flow in period t discounted at the prevailing yield-to-maturity
$\quad\quad H =$ length of the investment horizon
$\quad\quad n =$ the time to receipt of the last portfolio cash flow

It is interesting to compare this measure of immunization risk with the definition of duration given in Chapter 2. The denominator of both is the current value of the portfolio. The numerator of both includes the present

---

[17] Fong and Vasicek, "A Risk Minimizing Strategy for Multiple Liability Immunization." This result is derived by expansion of the terminal value function into the first three terms of a Taylor series.

[18] The only assumption about the interest rate changes necessary to justify this measure of risk is that the interest rate change is a sufficiently smooth function of maturity so that the Taylor series expansion is valid. Beyond that, no assumptions are necessary about the nature or dimensionality of the stochastic process that governs the behavior of the term structure of interest rates.

value of cash flows. In the case of duration, the present value of the cash flow is weighted by the time it will be received. However, for the immunization risk measure the present value of the cash flow is weighted by the square of the difference between the time it will be received and the investment horizon. Consequently, while duration is a weighted average of time to payments on the portfolio, immunization risk is a similarly weighted variance of times to payment around the horizon date.

The immunization risk measure agrees with the intuitive interpretation of risk discussed at the beginning of this section. For portfolio A in Figure 6–4, the barbell portfolio, the portfolio payments are widely dispersed in time and the immunization risk measure would be high. The portfolio payments occur close to the investment horizon for portfolio B in Figure 6–4, the bullet portfolio, so that the immunization risk measure is low.

Given the measure of immunization risk that is to be minimized and the constraint that the duration of the portfolio equal the investment horizon, as well as any other applicable investment constraints, the optimal immunized portfolio can be found using linear programming. Linear programming can be employed because the risk measure is linear in the portfolio payments.

The immunization risk measure can be used to construct approximate confidence intervals for the target rate of return over the horizon and the target end-of-period portfolio value. A confidence interval represents an uncertainty band around the target return within which the realized return can be expected with a given probability. The general expression for a confidence interval is:

Target return $\pm$ k (standard deviation of target return)

where k is the number of standard deviations around the expected target return. The confidence level determines k. The higher the probability, the smaller the k and the smaller the band around the expected target return.

Fong and Vasicek demonstrate that the standard deviation of the expected target return can be approximated by the product of the following three terms:[19] (1) the immunization risk measure; (2) the standard deviation of the variance of the one-period change in the slope of the yield curve;[20] and (3) an expression that is a function of the horizon length only.[21]

---

[19] Fong and Vasicek, "Return Maximization for Immunized Portfolios." The derivation is based on the assumption that the immunization risk measure of an optimally immunized portfolio, periodically rebalanced, decreases in time in approximate proportion to the third power of the remaining horizon length.

[20] This term can be estimated empirically from historical yield changes.

[21] The expression for the third term for the standard deviation of the expected target return of a single period liability immunized portfolio is $(7H)^{-1/2}$ where H is the length of the horizon.

The upper panel of Table 6–9 shows the optimal immunized portfolio using risk minimization as the optimality criterion based on the set of assumptions given at the bottom of the table. Table 6–10 summarizes the characteristics of the optimal portfolio.

Multiple Liability Immunization

Immunization with respect to a single investment horizon is applicable to situations where the objective of the investment is to preserve the value of the investment at the horizon date. This may be the case when a single given liability is payable at the horizon date, or a target investment value is to be attained at that date. More often, however, there would be a number of liabilities to be paid from the investment funds, and no single horizon would correspond to the schedule of liabilities. A portfolio is said to be immunized with respect to a given liability stream if there are enough funds to pay all of the liabilities when due even if interest rates change by a parallel shift.

Bierwag, Kaufman, and Toevs demonstrate that matching the duration of the portfolio to the duration of the liabilities is not a sufficient condition for immunization in the presence of multiple liabilities.[22] It is necessary that the portfolio payment stream be decomposed in such a way that each liability is separately immunized by one of the component streams. The key notion here is that it is the payment stream on the portfolio, not the portfolio itself, that can be decomposed in this manner. There may be no actual securities that would give the component payment streams.

Fong and Vasicek demonstrate the conditions that must be satisfied to assure multiple liability immunization *in the case of parallel rate shifts.*[23] The necessary and sufficient conditions are:

1. The (composite) duration of the portfolio must equal the (composite) duration of the liabilities.[24]

---

[22] Bierwag, Kaufman, and Toevs, "Immunization for Multiple Planning Periods."

[23] Fong and Vasicek, "A Risk Minimizing Strategy for Multiple Liability Immunization."

[24] The duration of the liabilities is found as follows:

$$\frac{PVL_1(1) + PVL_2(2) + \ldots + PVL_m(m)}{TPVL}$$

where

PVL_t = present value of the liability at time t
$TPVL$ = total present value of the liabilities
m = time of the last liability payment

2. The distribution of durations of individual portfolio assets must have a wider range than the distribution of the liabilities.[25]

An implication of the first condition is that if there is a liability stream that extends 30 years, to immunize that liability stream it is not necessary to have a portfolio with a duration of 30 years. The condition requires that the portfolio manager construct a portfolio so that the portfolio duration matches the weighted average of the liability durations. This is important because in any reasonable interest rate environment it is unlikely that a portfolio of investment grade coupon bonds can be constructed with a duration in excess of 15 years. However, in a corporate pension fund retired lives situation, the liability stream is typically a diminishing-amount liability stream. That is, liabilities in the earlier years are the greatest and liabilities further out toward the 30-year end are generally lower. By taking a weighted average duration of the liabilities, the portfolio manager can usually bring the portfolio duration to something that is manageable, say, eight or nine years.

The second condition states that the portfolio payments be more dispersed in time than the liabilities. That is, there must be an asset with a duration equal to or less than the duration of the shortest duration liability in order to have funds to pay the liability when it is due. And there must be an asset with a duration equal to or greater than the longest duration liability in order to avoid the reinvestment rate risk that might jeopardize payment of the longest duration were the longest duration asset of shorter duration. This bracketing of shortest and longest duration liabilities with even shorter and longer duration assets ensures the balancing of changes in portfolio value with changes in reinvestment return.[26] This means that in selecting securities to be included in the portfolio, the portfolio manager not only has to keep track of the matching of duration between assets and liabilities, but also must have the specified distribution for the assets in the portfolio.

The two conditions for multiple liability immunization assure immunity against parallel rate shifts only. To address the question of the exposure of an immunized portfolio to an arbitrary interest rate change, Fong and Vasicek generalize the immunization risk measure to the multiple liability

---

[25] More specifically, the mean absolute deviation of the portfolio payments must be greater than or equal to the mean absolute deviation of the liabilities at each payment date.

[26] To understand why the portfolio payments have to be more spread out in time than the liabilities to assure immunity, consider the single investment horizon case. There, immunization was achieved by balancing changes in reinvestment return on portfolio payments maturing prior to the investment horizon date against changes in the value at the investment horizon date of the portfolio portion still outstanding. The same bracketing of each liability by the portfolio payments is necessary in the multiple liability case, which implies that the payments have to be more dispersed in time than the liabilities.

Table 6–9
Optimally Immunized Portfolio: Risk Minimization and Return Maximization

Issuer	Coupon Rate (%)	Maturity	Rating
			Optimality Criterion:
Federal National Marketing Association	10.500	6/10/88	AAA
IB Credit Corp.	0.000	7/15/88	AAA
Ford Motor Co.	9.450	6/15/89	BAA2
Campbell Soup Co.	9.875	6/15/90	AAA
R. J. Reynolds Industries, Inc.	10.450	5/15/90	AA1
J. C. Penney Company, Inc.	10.750	6/15/90	A1
AT&T	2.875	6/1/87	AAA
AT&T	10.375	6/1/90	AAA
Southern California Edison Co.	4.375	5/15/88	AA2
Southwestern Public Service Co.	10.900	6/1/90	AA2
Cleveland Electric Illuminating Co.	7.125	1/15/90	A2
Short-term asset	0.000	12/31/83	
Total portfolio			
		Optimality Criterion: Target Return	
Ford Motor Credit Co.	12.600	6/1/87	BAA2
Ford Motor Credit Co.	9.450	6/15/89	BAA2
Amax Inc.	8.000	1/1/86	BAA
Figgie International Inc.	9.375	11/15/86	BAA3
American Stores Co. New	12,000	6/1/90	BAA3
Inland Steel Co.	11.250	6/1/90	BAA2
Walter Jim Corp.	9,500	2/1/96	BAA3
Phelps Dodge Corp.	8,100	6/15/96	BAA2
Commonwealth Edison Co.	15.375	3/15/00	A3
Philadelphia Electric Co.	13.750	10/15/92	BAA2
Alabama Power Co.	15.250	9/1/10	BAA1
Short-term asset	0.000	12/31/83	
Total portfolio			

* Because of the round lot requirement, rounding results in a concentration that

Assumptions:
1. The portfolio was constructed on December 31, 1982.
2. The initial investment is $10 million.
3. The horizon is five years.
4. Round lot size requirement of $10,000 par value.
5. Transaction cost of .025 percent of par value.
6. The short-term reinvestment rate is 5 percent.
7. No restrictions on the bond universe from which securities may be selected.
8. Maximum concentration in any one issue is 10 percent.

Optimal Value* ($000 par)	Price (Percentage of Par)	Yield-to-Maturity	Duration (years)	Market Value ($000)
Risk Minimization				
$ 810	99.313	10.666%	4.25	$ 809.328
1,760	56.500	10.577	5.54	994.400
1,180	83.832	13.251	4.80	994.105
1,030	96.069	10.650	5.38	993.969
1,000	97.979	10.850	5.23	993.079
1,020	97.266	11.300	5.26	996.919
1,270	78.522	8.854	4.13	1,000.230
1,020	97.356	10.900	5.28	1,001.729
1,310	75.820	10.353	4.72	1,000.530
190	97.750	11.353	5.20	187.427
1,200	79.669	11.401	5.24	995.400
4	95.238	4.939	1.00	3.410
$11,794		10.890%	5.00	$9,970.525
Maximization minus One Standard Deviation				
$ 1,010	97.850	13.250%	3.47	$ 998.744
1,180	83.832	13.251	4.80	994.105
1,100	86.500	13.630	2.58	995.399
960	89.000	13.075	3.26	865.845
1,050	94.182	13.250	4.99	999.267
1,140	86.299	14.301	4.99	994.349
1,290	73.375	13.985	6.50	997.459
1,660	59.750	15.209	6.85	997.744
890	108.000	14.116	6.51	1,001.407
950	102.250	13.322	5.56	998.871
110	105.250	14.465	6.91	121.347
7	95.238	4.939	1.00	7.112
$11,347		13.750%	5.00	$9,971.650

may exceed 10 percent.

9. Yield curve on December 31, 1982 as shown below.

Years to Maturity	Yield-to-Maturity
.25	8.505%
.50	8.709
1.00	8.958
2.00	9.594
3.00	10.011
5.00	10.487
10.00	10.710
20.00	10.803
30.00	10.817

case.[27] Just as in the single investment horizon case, they find that the relative change in the portfolio value, if forward rates change by any arbitrary function, depends on the product of two terms—a term solely dependent on the structure of the portfolio and a term solely dependent on the interest rate movement. However, the immunization risk measure in the multiple liability case is as follows:

$$\frac{[PVCF_1(1 - D)^2 + PVCF_2(2 - D)^2 + \ldots + PVCF_n(n - D)^2]}{\text{Initial investment value}}$$

$$- \frac{[PVL_1(1 - D)^2 + PVL_2(2 - D)^2 + \ldots + PVL_m(m - D)^2]}{\text{Initial investment value}} \quad (6\text{--}2)$$

where

PVL_t = present value of the liability at time t
m = time of the last liability payment
D = duration of the portfolio (which by the first condition is equal to the weighted average duration of the liabilities)

and $PVCF_t$ and n are as defined earlier.[28]

An optimal immunization strategy is to minimize the immunization risk measure subject to the constraints imposed by the two conditions and any other applicable constraints on the investment portfolio. Constructing minimum risk immunized portfolios can be accomplished by the use of linear programming.

Approximate confidence intervals can also be constructed in the multiple liability case. The standard deviation of the expected target return is the product of the three terms indicated in the section on risk minimization.[29]

General Cash Flows

In both the single investment horizon and multiple liability cases we have assumed that the investment funds are initially available in full. Suppose that there is a given schedule of liabilities to be covered by an immunized investment, but all the investment funds are not available at the time the portfolio is to be constructed. Some of the funds will become available in the form of cash contributions. To consider a specific example, suppose that a portfolio manager has a given obligation to be paid at the end of a

---

[27] Fong and Vasicek, "A Risk Minimizing Strategy for Multiple Liability Immunization."

[28] Note that this risk measure attains its extreme value of zero if and only if the portfolio payments coincide exactly in amount and timing with the liabilities.

[29] Fong and Vasicek, "Return Maximization for Immunized Portfolios." The expression for the third term in the multiple liability case is a function of the dates and relative sizes of the liabilities, in addition to the horizon length.

Table 6–10
Characteristics of an Optimal Portfolio: Risk Minimization and Return Maximization

	Optimality Criterion	
	Risk Minimization	Target Return Maximization minus One Standard Deviation
Number of issues	12	12
Par value	$11,794,000	$11,347,000
Market value	$ 9,971,000	$ 9,972,000
Accrued interest	$ 92,000	$ 222,000
Principal value*	$ 9,878,000	$ 9,750,000
Yield-to-maturity		
Market value weighted	10.890%	13.750%
Duration weighted	10.923%	13.870%
Average coupon	7.581%	11.009%
Average quality rating	AA2	BAA2
Average duration	4.998	4.996
Estimated standard deviation of:		
Terminal value	$121,000	$361,000
Target return	15 basis points per year	43 basis points per year
Estimated return at confidence level of:		
90%	10.74%	13.32%
95%	10.68%	13.16%
99%	10.59%	12.86%

* Market value minus principal value.

two-year horizon. Only one half of the necessary funds, however, is now available, the rest being expected at the end of the first year. This cash inflow will have to be invested at the end of the first year at whatever rates are then in effect. The question that arises is whether there is an investment strategy that would guarantee the end-of-horizon value of the investment regardless of the development of interest rates.

Under certain conditions, this is indeed possible. The expected cash contributions can be considered the payments on hypothetical securities that are part of the initial holdings. The actual initial investment can then be invested in such a way that the real and hypothetical holdings taken together represent an immunized portfolio.

We can illustrate this for the single-investment horizon using the example above. The initial investment should be constructed with a three-year duration. With half of the funds in an actual portfolio with a duration of three years, and the other half in a hypothetical portfolio with a duration of one year, the total stream of cash inflow payments for the portfolio has a duration of two years, matching the horizon length. This is a sufficient condition for immunization with respect to a single horizon. At the end of the first year, any possible decline in the interest rates at which the cash contribution is invested will be compensated for by a corresponding increase in the value of the initial holdings. The portfolio is, at that time, rebalanced by selling the actual holdings and investing the proceeds, together with the new cash, in a portfolio with a duration of one year to match the horizon date. It should be noted that the rate of return guaranteed on the future contributions is not the current spot rate, but rather the forward rate corresponding to the date of contribution.

This strategy can be extended to apply to multiple contributions and liabilities. This produces a general immunization technique that is applicable to the case of arbitrary cash flows during a horizon. Fong and Vasicek have derived the conditions for the general cash flow case.[30] The construction of an optimal immunized portfolio can then be achieved by minimizing the immunization risk measure which is equal to:

$$\frac{[PVCF_1(1 - D)^2 + PVCF_2(2 - D)^2 + \ldots + PVCF_n(n - D)^2]}{\text{Present value of the liabilities}}$$

$$+ \frac{[PVCC_1(1 - D)^2 + PVCC_2(2 - D)^2 + \ldots + PVCC_k(n - D)^2]}{\text{Present value of the liabilities}}$$

$$- \frac{[PVL_1(1 - D)^2 + PVL_2(2 - D)^2 + \ldots + PVL_m(m - D)^2]}{\text{Present value of the liabilities}} \qquad (6\text{--}3)$$

where

$PVCF_t$ = present value of the cash flow payments from the securities held in the portfolio
$PVCC_t$ = present value of the cash contribution at time t
PVL_t = present value of the liability at time t
n = the time of the last cash flow payment from the securities held in the portfolio
m = the time of the last liability payment
k = the time of the last cash contribution
D = duration of the *liability* stream

Once again, linear programming methods can be employed to obtain the optimal portfolio.

Return Maximization

The objective of risk minimization for an immunized portfolio may be too restrictive in certain situations. If a substantial increase in the expected

---

[30] Fong and Vasicek, "A Risk Minimizing Strategy for Multiple Liability Immunization."

return can be accomplished with little effect on immunization risk, the higher yielding portfolio may be preferred in spite of its higher risk. For example, suppose that an optimally immunized portfolio has a target return of 13 percent over the horizon, with a 95 percent confidence interval at ±.20 percent. This means that the minimum risk portfolio would have a 1 in 40 chance of a realized return less than 12.8 percent. Suppose that another portfolio, less well immunized, can produce a target return of 13.3 percent with a 95 percent confidence interval of ±.30 percent. In all but one case out of 40, this portfolio would realize a return above 13 percent, compared to 12.8 percent on the minimum risk portfolio. For many investors, this may be the preferred trade-off.

Fong and Vasicek develop an approach for exploring the risk/return trade-off for immunized portfolios.[31] Their strategy maintains the duration of the portfolio at all times equal to the horizon length.[32] Thus, the portfolio stays fully immunized in the classical sense. Instead of minimizing the immunization risk against nonparallel rate changes, however, a trade-off between risk and return is considered. The immunization risk measure can be relaxed if the compensation, in terms of expected return, warrants it. Specifically, the strategy maximizes a *lower bound* on the portfolio return. The lower bound is defined as a confidence interval on the realized return for a given probability level.

Linear programming can be used to solve for the optimal portfolio when return maximization is the objective. In fact, parametric linear programming can be employed to determine an efficient frontier for immunized portfolios, analogous to those in the mean/variance framework.

Using the same set of assumptions as in the risk minimization illustration, the lower panel of Table 6–9 gives the optimal portfolio when the optimality criterion is maximize the expected return minus one standard deviation. Table 6–10 summarizes the characteristics of that optimal portfolio.

Contingent Immunization

Contingent immunization consists of the identification of both the available immunization target rate and a lower safety net level return with which the investor would be minimally satisfied. The manager can continue to pursue an active strategy until an adverse investment experience drives the then available potential return—combined active return (from actual past experience) and immunized return (from expected future experience)— down to the safety net level; at such time, the manager would be obligated

---

[31] Fong and Vasicek, "Return Maximization for Immunized Portfolios."

[32] In the multiple period liability case, the two conditions for immunization are maintained.

to completely immunize the portfolio and lock in the safety net level return. As long as this safety net is not violated, the manager can continue to actively manage the portfolio. Once the immunization mode is activated because the safety net is violated, the manager can no longer return to the active mode unless, of course, the contingent immunization plan is abandoned.

The key considerations in implementing a contingent immunization strategy are: (1) establishing accurate immunized initial and ongoing available target returns, (2) identifying a suitable and immunizable safety net, and (3) implementing an effective monitoring procedure to ensure that the safety net is not violated.

To illustrate the contingent immunization strategy, suppose that a sponsor is willing to accept a 14 percent return over a five-year planning horizon at a time when a possible immunized rate of return is 15 percent.[33] The 14 percent rate of return is called the safety net (or minimum target or floor) return. The difference between the possible immunized rate of 15 percent and the safety net rate is called the *cushion spread* or *excess achievable return*. As we shall see, it is this cushion spread, 100 basis points in our example, that offers the manager latitude in pursuing an active strategy. The greater the cushion spread, the more scope the manager has for an active management policy.

Assuming an initial portfolio of $100 million, the required terminal asset value when the safety net return is 14 percent is $196 million.[34] Since the current available return is assumed to be 15 percent, the assets required *at the inception of the plan* in order to generate the required terminal value of $196 million is $95 million.[35] Therefore, the safety cushion

---

[33] This illustration is from Martin L. Leibowitz and Alfred Weinberger, "Contingent Immunization—Part I: Risk Control Procedures," *Financial Analysts Journal*, November–December 1982, pp. 17–31.

[34] Assuming semiannual compounding, the general formula for the required terminal value is:

$$\text{Required terminal value} = I(1 + s/2)^{2H}$$

where

I = initial portfolio value
s = safety net or floor rate
H = number of years in the planning horizon

In our example, the initial portfolio value is $100 million, s is 14 percent (.14) and H is 5 years. Therefore, the required terminal value is:

$$\$100(1.07)^{10} = \$196$$

[35] Assuming semiannual compounding, the required assets at any given point in time t necessary to achieve the required terminal value is:

of 100 basis points translates into an initial *dollar safety margin* of $5 million.

Now suppose that the portfolio manager placed the initial $100 million in a portfolio of 30-year par bonds with a coupon of 15 percent. Let us look at what happens if there is a change in the yield level *immediately* following the purchase of these bonds.

First, suppose the yield level decreases to 10 percent from the 15 percent level. The value of the portfolio of 30-year bonds would increase to $147 million. However, the asset value required to achieve the required terminal value if the portfolio is immunized at a 10 percent rate is $120 million.[36] The asset value above and beyond the required asset value, or dollar safety margin, is now $27 million. This amount is $22 million greater than the initial dollar safety margin and, therefore, allows the manager more freedom to pursue active management.

Suppose instead of a decline in yield levels, the immediate change is an increase in yield levels to 18.5 percent. At that yield level, the portfolio of 30-year bonds would decline in value to $81 million. The required asset value to achieve the terminal value of $196 million is $81 million. Consequently, an immediate rise in the yield by 350 basis points to 18.5 percent will decrease the dollar safety margin to zero. At this yield level, the immunization mode would be triggered with an immunization target rate of 18.5 percent to ensure that the required terminal value will be realized. If this were not followed, further adverse movements of interest rates would not ensure the required terminal value or floor portfolio of $196 million. The yield level at which the immunization mode becomes operational is called the *trigger point.*

Figure 6–5 graphically portrays the safety margin for a portfolio of 30-year bonds for an immediate change in the yield level.

$$\text{Required assets at time } t = \frac{\text{Required terminal value}}{(1 + i_t/2)^{2(H-t)}}$$

where

i_t = the market yield at time t

The other variables are as defined in the previous footnote.

Since in our example, the required terminal value is $196 and the market yield is 15 percent, the required assets are:

$$\frac{\$196}{(1.075)^{10}} = \$95$$

[36] Using the formula in the previous footnote, the required terminal value is $196 and the market yield (following the yield change) is 10 percent; therefore:

$$\frac{\$196}{(1.05)^{10}} = \$120$$

Figure 6–5
Safety Margin for a Portfolio of 30-Year Bonds

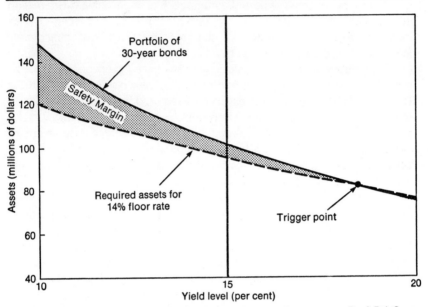

Source: Martin L. Leibowitz and Alfred Weinberger, "Contingent Immunization—Part I: Risk Control Procedures," *Financial Analysts Journal*, November–December 1982, Figure D.

For purposes of monitoring a contingent immunization plan, it is useful to recast the dollar safety margin in terms of the potential return. This return, also called the *return achievable with immunization strategy*, measures the yield that would be realized if, at any given point in time, the current value of the portfolio is immunized at the prevailing market yield. For example, suppose that there is an immediate change in the yield level to 10 percent. As indicated earlier, the value of the portfolio would increase to $147 million. Immunizing the $147 million at 10 percent would produce an achievable terminal value of $239 million. Since the initial investment is $100 million, this strategy offers a potential return of 18.25 percent[37] which exceeds the safety net or floor return. The cushion spread or achievable excess return will increase from 100 basis points at the

---

[37] The potential return at any time t can be expressed in general terms as follows:

$$\text{Potential return at time } t = 2[(M_t(1 + i_t/2)^{2(H-t)}/I)^{1/2H} - 1]$$

where

M_t = the market or actual value of the portfolio at time t

inception of the plan to 425 basis points if the yield level changed immediately to 10 percent.

If, however, there were an immediate increase in the yield level to 18.5 percent, the market value of the portfolio of 30-year bonds would decline to $81 million. Immunizing the current portfolio value at the market yield of 18.5 percent would produce a terminal value of $196. Since the initial investment is $100 million, this indicates a potential return of 14 percent which is equal to the safety net return.[38] The cushion spread is now zero and the portfolio must be placed in the immunization mode.

Figure 6–6 portrays the potential return for the portfolio of 30-year bonds that would result from an immediate change in the market yield.

Figure 6–6
The Potential Return Concept

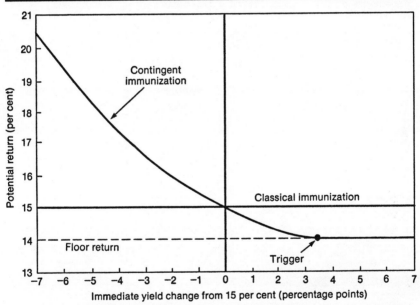

Source: Martin L. Leibowitz and Alfred Weinberger, "Contingent Immunization—Part I: Risk Control Procedures," *Financial Analysts Journal*, November–December 1982, Figure E.

The numerator of the first expression in the formula is the value of the portfolio if immunized at the prevailing market yield.

Substituting the values in our example into the above expression we have:

$$\text{Potential return} = 2[(147(1.05)^{10}/100)^{1/10} - 1] = .1825$$

[38] Using the formula for potential return in the previous footnote we have:

$$\text{Potential return} = 2[(81(1.05)^{10}/100)^{1/10} - 1] = .14$$

The *trigger yield* is the yield level at which the immunization mode becomes operational. The trigger yield is, of course, identical to the yield level at which the dollar safety margin is zero.

Since duration approximates the price sensitivity of a portfolio to changes in market yields, trigger yields can be computed for portfolios of different duration so that the manager would know how much leeway there is for a given risk position with respect to an adverse movement in the market yield; that is, how much of an adverse movement in the market yield can be tolerated before the immunization mode must be activated. In our example, the portfolio of 30-year, 15 percent par bonds has a Macaulay duration of 7 years and a trigger yield of roughly 18.5 percent. Figure 6–7 shows the trigger yield for portfolios with an initial duration of

Figure 6–7
Duration-Based Trigger Yield Contours

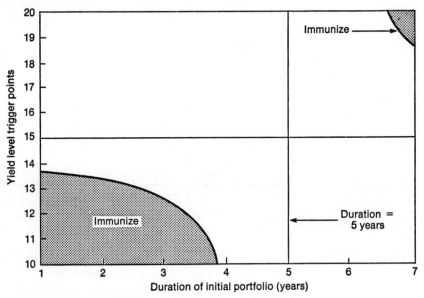

Source: Martin L. Leibowitz and Alfred Weinberger, "Contingent Immunization—Part I: Risk Control Procedures," *Financial Analysts Journal*, November–December 1982, Figure H.

from 1 to 7 years. Each point on the contours shown in the lower left and upper right corners of Figure 6–6 indicates the trigger yield on the vertical axis for the corresponding duration on the horizontal axis. The contours are called *duration-based trigger yield contours*.

As noted at the outset of this discussion, the key to a contingent immunization plan is the ability to control and monitor the performance of the portfolio over time so that the manager knows how much leeway he has to actively manage the portfolio, and when the portfolio should be immunized in order to achieve the minimum target return. An example of a monitoring analysis is shown in Tables 6–11 to 6–13.

Table 6–11
Summary Description of a Contingently Immunized Portfolio

Performance Monitoring

		Actual Asset Values ($000)	Required Asset Values ($000)
Inception date	12/1/77	$12,000	
Present date	12/1/81	16,483	$15,766
Horizon date	7/1/91		54,802
Time to horizon	9.58 yr.		
Actual portfolio duration	5.68 yr.		

Asset Value Analysis

Present actual asset value	$16,483	Achievable terminal asset value	$57,296
Present required asset value	15,766	Required terminal asset value	54,802
Present excess asset value	$ 718	Achievable excess terminal asset value	$ 2,494

Return Analysis

Return to date	8.10%/yr.	12/1/77 to 12/1/81
Present immunization target return	13.43%/yr.	12/1/81 to 7/1/91
Return achievable with immunization strategy	11.85%/yr.	12/1/77 to 7/1/91
Required return on assets	11.50%/yr.	12/1/77 to 7/1/91
Achievable excess return (cushion)	0.35%/yr.	12/1/77 to 7/1/91

Table 6–11 provides a summary description of the contingently managed portfolio and the return status of the portfolio relative to the inception date, present date, and horizon date. In the return analysis section of that table, the return to date is the return actually achieved by active management since the inception date. The present immunization target return is the return that could be earned between the present and horizon dates from immunization of the portfolio only, i.e., not including the active management component. The return achievable with immunization strategy is the combined return from active management between the inception and present dates and from immunization between the present and horizon dates. Finally, the required return on assets is the safety net return. The achievable excess return is the difference or cushion between these last two returns.

Table 6–12 evaluates the current portfolio for interest rate change

Table 6–12
Sensitivity Analysis of a Contingently Immunized Portfolio

Sensitivity of Achievable Portfolio Performance to Present Interest Rates

Interest Rate Scenario*	Asset Value Analysis			Return Analysis			
	Actual Asset Value ($000)	Required Asset Value ($000)	Excess Asset Value ($000)	Scenario Modified Return to Date (%/yr.)	Estimated Immunization Target Return† (%/yr.)	Return Achievable with Immunization Strategy (%/yr.)	Required Return (%/yr.)	Achievable Excess Return (%/yr.)
Actual	$16483	$15766	$ 718	8.10%	13.43%	11.85%	11.50%	0.35%
+200 B.P.	14895	13201	1694	5.48	15.42	12.44	11.50	0.94
+100 B.P.	15650	14424	1226	6.75	14.43	12.14	11.50	0.64
−100 B.P.	17405	17253	152	9.52	12.43	11.57	11.50	0.07
−200 B.P.	18430	19040	−609	11.02	11.34	11.25	11.50	−0.25

* Assumes parallel shifts.
† Average yield of immunized portfolio.

Table 6–13
Characteristics of Optimal Portfolio under Contingent Immunization

Selection Criterion: Risk Minimization

Portfolio	Number of Issues	Par Value ($000)	Market Value ($000) –	Accrued Interest ($000) =	Principal Value ($000)	Yield to Maturity (%) Market Value Weighted	Yield to Maturity (%) Duration Weighted	Average Coupon (%)	Average Quality Rating	Average Duration (yr.)
Current	49	$20,010	$16,483	$372	$16,111	13.776%	13.824%	10.472%	AA	5.677
Optimal	20	19,700	16,442	476	15,966	13.431	13.376	10.206	AAA	5.916
Transaction Summary										
Bought	5	11,090	9,215	333	8,882	13.081	13.045	9.653	AAA	5.933
Sold	32	11,415	9,271	229	9,042	13.693	13.843	10.112	AA	5.498
Held	19	8,610	7,227	143	7,084	13.877	13.801	10.912	AA	5.896

Estimated standard deviation of terminal value ($000): $112

Estimated standard deviation of target return: 2 B.P./yr.

Estimated return at confidence level of:

90% = 13.35%
95 = 13.34
99 = 13.32

sensitivity. The various scenarios of interest rate change are shown in the bottom panel of the page. In the upper panel, under sensitivity relative to asset value analysis, the column titled *Actual Asset Value* shows the actual market value of the bond portfolio under each interest rate assumed, diminishing (from actual) with higher rates and increasing with lower rates. The column titled *Required Asset Value* provides the amounts needed (as of the present date for each interest rate assumed) that, if immunized, would result in the achievement of the safety net return. The third column in this group indicates the excess of column 1 over column 2 for each interest rate. Note that, under the 200 basis point decrease, there is a negative excess asset value. This would mean that the safety net return could not be achieved, which is also indicated by the −0.25 percent achievable excess return (last column to the right) for this same interest rate change assumption. Finally, Table 6–13 summarizes the characteristics of the optimal portfolio.

An accurate immunization target is critical in determining not only the basis for the initial problem set-up (e.g., the safety net will usually be a certain basis point difference from the target over a specified time period), but also in determining what immunization levels are available during the management horizon. A safety net too close to the initial target return makes triggering the immunization process highly likely, while too low a safety net defeats the purpose of the process since the very low satisfactory minimum return would probably never trigger immunization. Finally, without an adequate monitoring procedure, the benefits of the strategy may be lost because of the inability to know when action is appropriate.

In spite of good control and monitoring procedures, attainment of the minimum target return may not be realized due to factors beyond the control of the portfolio manager. There are two reasons for this.[39] The first is that there is the possibility of a rapid adverse movement in market yields that is of sufficient magnitude that the portfolio manager may not have enough time to shift from the active to immunization mode at a rate needed to achieve the minimum target. Frequent jumps of market yields of several hundred basis points would hinder the effective implementation of a contingent immunization strategy. Fortunately, empirical evidence by Leibowitz and Weinberger suggests that except for portfolios of short maturities, the potential magnitude of market discontinuities is not of the order that should cause serious problems.[40] Specifically, examining the weekly movement of various maturity sectors for Treasuries for the period January 1979 to November 1981, a highly volatile period for bonds, they find that:

---

[39] Leibowitz and Weinberger, "Contingent Immunization—Part II: Problem Areas."
[40] Ibid.

1. For long maturities, as measured by 30-year maturities, the weekly movement never exceeded plus or minus 100 basis points and an absolute change of 40 basis points or less occurred in 80 percent of the weeks.
2. For intermediate maturities, as measured by 7-year maturities, the maximum weekly absolute yield change was 107 basis points and an absolute change of 40 basis points or less occurred in 80 percent of the weeks.
3. For short maturities, as measured by 1-year maturities, the maximum absolute weekly yield change was 204 basis points and an absolute change of 60 basis points or less occurred for 80 percent of the weeks.

The second reason why the minimum target return may not be attained is that, if the immunization mode becomes operational there is no guarantee that the immunized rate will be achieved even if the portfolio is reconstructed at the required rate. We discussed this problem earlier in the chapter.

Active/Immunization Strategy by Formula

Contingent immunization is not a combination or mixture strategy. The manager is either in the immunization mode by choice or because the safety net is violated, or in the active management mode. An active/immunization combination, in contrast to contingent immunization, consists of two components that prevail at the same point in time. The immunization component could be either one-period or multiperiod immunization using the techniques discussed earlier in this chapter. In the one-period situation, an assured return would be established and would serve to stabilize the total portfolio return over the planning horizon. In the multiperiod situation, the subportfolio could be immunized now, with new requirements, as they become known, taken care of through reimmunization. This would be an adaptive strategy in that the immunization component would be based on an initial set of liabilities and modified over time to take care of new retired or other new liabilities. The active portion would continue to be free to maximize expected return, given some acceptable risk level.

A procedure for allocating a portion of the initial portfolio to active management, with the balance being immunized, can be obtained from the following formula which assumes that the immunization target return is greater than either the minimum or expected worse case active returns:[41]

---

[41] Gifford Fong Associates, *The Costs of Cash Flow Matching*, 1981.

Active component

$$= \frac{\text{Immunization target rate } - \text{ Minimum return}}{\text{Immunization target rate } - \text{ Worst case active return}} \quad (6\text{--}4)$$

As an example, assuming that the available immunization target is 15 percent per year, the minimum return acceptable to the fund sponsor is 10 percent, and the worst case return for the actively managed portion of the portfolio is anticipated to be 5 percent, then the percentage in the active portion of the portfolio would be 50 percent, as shown below:

$$\text{Active component} = \frac{.15 - .10}{.15 - .05} = .50 \text{ or 50 percent}$$

An examination of the formula shows that for any given immunization target return, the smaller the minimum acceptable return and the larger the expected active return, the larger will be the percentage of the portfolio under active management. Note that the numbers assumed for the example change over time in an interactive, dynamic sense; it is the portfolio manager's responsibility to monitor these factors constantly, adjusting and rebalancing the portfolio as appropriate.

As long as the worst case is not violated—that is, as long as the actual return experienced does not drop below the minimum expected active return—the desired minimum return will be achieved. While managers may have a preference for having the entire fund actively managed at the outset, this is mitigated by portfolio constraints that are commonly associated with contingent immunization (e.g., permissible duration range). The approach described here permits the manager to pursue active management without additional portfolio constraints or external pressure.

■ Cash Flow Matching

Cash flow matching is an alternative to multiple liability immunization. It is an intuitively appealing strategy because the portfolio manager need only select securities to match liabilities. The procedure can be summarized as follows. A bond is selected with a maturity that matches the last liability. An amount of principal equal to the amount of the last liability is then invested in this bond. The remaining elements of the liability stream are then reduced by the coupon payments on this bond, and another bond is chosen for the new, reduced amount of the next-to-last liability. Going backward in time, this is continued until all liabilities have been matched by the payments on the securities in the portfolio. Notice that there are no duration match requirements as there are in multiple liability immunization. Sophisticated linear programming techniques can be employed to construct a least cost cash flow matching portfolio from a universe of securities.

With immunization, rebalancing is necessary even if interest rates do not change. No rebalancing is necessary with cash flow matching. Consequently, cash flow matching can be viewed as a buy-and-hold strategy. However, there are reasons why a portfolio manager would not want to follow a passive buy-and-hold strategy. These include the opportunity for value enhancement by rebalancing and the ongoing requirement to monitor the credit quality of the securities held. Nevertheless, a case can be made that cash flow matching is a buy-and-hold strategy compared to immunization, so if a portfolio manager wants a passive strategy, cash flow matching has an edge. Table 6–14 displays a portfolio chosen to match a sequence of liability payments shown in the second-to-last column of Table 6–14. Table 6–15 includes a number of descriptive statistics about the individual securities held and the portfolio as a whole, and also provides a cash flow analysis of sources and applications of funds. The last column in the table shows, for each time period, the remaining excess funds that are reinvested at an assumed reinvestment rate of 6 percent.

To the extent that such matching is possible, it would produce a perfectly immunized portfolio, since no interest rate change could affect a portfolio whose payments match exactly in timing and amount the liabilities to be paid. However, given typical liability schedules and bonds available for cash flow matching, perfect matching is unlikely. Under such conditions a minimum immunization risk approach would, at worst, be equal to cash flow matching and would probably be better, since an immunization strategy would require less money to fund a given liability stream.

What is worse, the portfolio obtained from cash flow matching may not be an immunized portfolio at all. The conditions for multiple liability immunity, as discussed earlier in this chapter, are much more complex than a requirement on the portfolio duration, and there is no guarantee that these conditions will be satisfied by the cash flow method. Because of the potential of overfunding in the case of cash flow matching, the portfolio duration will tend to be lower than the duration of the liabilities.

Therefore, even with the use of sophisticated linear programming techniques, cash flow matching may be technically inferior to multiple liability immunization. Using the cost of the initial portfolio as an evaluation measure, one of the authors has found that cash flow matched portfolios, using a universe of corporates rated at least double A, cost from 3 to 7 percent more, in dollars, than immunized portfolios. The reason for this is as follows. As noted above, what typically happens when applying the cash flow matching strategy is that perfect matching is not realized. This means that excess funding occurs. In the optimization process used in cash flow matching that excess funding is assumed to earn a reinvestment rate which is usually very conservative. With immunization, however, the portfolio manager is locking in all reinvestment returns at the target rate of return. Consequently, the condition that would increase the minimum cost advantage of immunization is when there is a very poor cash flow match-

Table 6–14
Characteristics of a Sample Universe for Cash Flow Matching (evaluation date 12/31/81)

Par Value	Percent of Total	Issuer Name	Coupon (Percent)	Effective Maturity Date	Price	Yield to Maturity (percent)	Duration (years)
$ 517	2.2%	Cash	0.000%	1/1/82	$100.000	0.00%	0.00
233	0.9	Federal Home Ln. Bks.	7.850	8/27/84	86.000	14.36	2.36
1199	4.6	United States Treas. Nts.	9.625	8/15/85	88.125	13.89	2.99
1215	3.8	Sears, Roebuck Accep. Corp.	8.375	12/31/86	75.500	15.61	4.04
2353	7.6	Twelve Fed. Ld. Bks.	7.600	4/20/87	75.625	14.30	4.23
2474	10.0	Northwest Bancorporation	15.350	5/1/89	94.750	16.60	4.46
4080	18.1	Federal Farm Cr. Bks.	14.700	7/22/91	100.000	14.69	5.10
1382	4.5	United States Treas. Bds.	10.125	11/15/94	77.438	13.94	6.63
6021	21.7	United States Treas. Bds.	11.500	11/15/95	84.938	13.98	6.61
1402	3.7	Caterpillar Tractor Co.	8.750	11/1/99	61.125	15.08	7.02
1357	3.7	Exxon Pipeline Co.	8.875	10/15/00	63.750	14.55	7.17
1294	5.4	United States Treas. Bds.	13.375	8/15/01	95.344	14.07	6.77
2649	6.7	Tenneco Inc.	8.375	4/1/02	58.500	14.91	7.12
1206	3.2	General Mtrs. Accep. Corp.	9.400	7/15/04	59.875	16.04	6.41
1228	4.0	RCA Corp.	12.250	5/1/05	76.000	16.24	6.46

Portfolio totals:

Average duration (years)	5.563
Average yield	14.440%
Duration weighted average yield	14.715%
Average effective maturity	1/5/94
Total par value ($000)	$28,610.000
Total market value ($000)	$24,001.990
Number of issues	15

Table 6–15
Cash Flow Analysis of a Sample Universe for Cash Flow Matching: Reinvestment Rate—6%
(evaluation date 12/31/81)

Cash Flow Analysis

Date	Previous Cash Balance	+	Interest on Balance	+	Principal Payments	+	Coupon Payments	+	Reinvestment of Payments	-	Liability Due	=	New Cash Balance
12/31/82	$ 0		$ 0		$ 517		$3128		$125		$3770		$ 0
12/31/83	0		0		0		3128		93		3104		117
12/31/84	117		7		233		3128		98		3584		0
12/31/85	0		0		1199		3110		120		4428		0
12/31/86	0		0		1215		2994		88		4298		0
12/31/87	0		0		2353		2803		185		4170		1171
12/31/88	1171		71		0		2714		82		4038		0
12/31/89	0		0		2474		2524		180		3900		1278
12/31/90	1278		78		0		2334		72		3762		0
12/31/91	0		0		4080		2334		181		3624		2971
12/31/92	2971		181		0		1734		47		3474		1460
12/31/93	1460		89		0		1734		47		3330		0
12/31/94	0		0		1382		1734		57		3174		0
12/31/95	0		0		6021		1594		89		3012		4692
12/31/96	4692		286		0		902		28		2850		3059
12/31/97	3059		186		0		902		28		2682		1493
12/31/98	1493		91		0		902		28		2514		0
12/31/99	0		0		1402		902		42		2346		0
12/31/00	0		0		1357		779		42		2178		0
12/31/01	0		0		1294		659		51		2004		0
12/31/02	0		0		2649		375		134		1836		1321
12/31/03	1321		80		0		264		9		1674		0
12/31/04	0		0		1206		264		42		1512		0
12/31/05	0		0		1228		75		53		1356		0

ing. Despite the potential cost advantage of immunization, cash flow matching is more popular because it is easier to understand and therefore intuitively appealing.

■ Application Considerations

Selection of Universe

Probably the greatest impact on the cost of an immunized and cash flow matched portfolio is the universe selected to construct the portfolio. The selection of the universe of securities in terms of acceptable credit quality, sectors, and other investment characteristics is ultimately the decision of the client. The fewer restrictions on the universe, the lower the initial cost. For example, the lower the credit quality the client is willing to accept in consultation with the manager, the lower the cost of an immunized portfolio.

Often, pension fund sponsors receive proposals from different organizations for dedicating a pension fund. Differences in the costs proposed by organizations frequently result from differences in the universe selected.

Transaction Costs

Transaction costs are important in meeting the target rate for an immunized portfolio. Transaction costs must be considered not only in the initial immunization (i.e., when the immunized portfolio is first created) but also in the periodic rebalancing necessary to avoid duration wandering. The portfolio manager does not want to get into a situation where the portfolio will incur a substantial number of trades and enjoy only marginal benefits from risk minimization. Fortunately, transaction costs can be included into the optimization framework such that a trade-off between transaction costs and risk minimization can take place.

Default Risk

The optimization process reduces the risk that the target rate will not be achieved because of arbitrary interest rates changes. However, the target rate may not be achieved due to a default of any of the issues in the immunized portfolio. Restricting the universe to only high quality issues reduces the likelihood of failing to realize the target rate due to defaults but lowers the potential return. Nevertheless, the monitoring of the portfolio for potential issues whose quality rating may be lowered is necessary. Issues whose quality ratings have been reduced while in the portfolio will increase the likelihood of realizing a rate below the target rate. The problem of default is also applicable for the cash flow matching strategy.

Call Risk

Call risk is the risk that the issuer will call in the issue before the stated maturity date. Call risk can be avoided by restricting the universe of securities to noncallable bonds and deep discount callable bonds. This procedure does not come without a cost. Because noncallable bonds and deep discount callable bonds sell at a large premium in a high interest rate environment, restricting the universe to these securities increases the cost of an immunization and cash flow matching strategy.[42]

Reinvestment Rate Assumption

Between the time a portfolio cash flow is to be received and the portfolio is to be rebalanced and/or a liability is to be paid, the proceeds must be reinvested for a short-term period. The reinvestment rate assumption specifies the rate that will be earned on those proceeds.

The reinvestment rate is applicable to cash flow matching not immunization. The reason is that in immunization the reinvestment rate is the same as the target rate of return so that there is no assumption that is necessary in an immunization strategy. Cash flow matching, on the other hand, does require a reinvestment rate specification. Typically, in cash flow matching a conservative rate is assumed; that is, the assumed reinvestment rate is significantly less than the currently available short-term rate. If the reinvestment rate is too high for the time frame of the analysis, then there is a risk of underfunding the liabilities. At the other extreme, too conservative an assumption will result in overfunding of the liabilities.

Execution Prices

Pricing is critical in implementing a semiactive strategy. Consequently, it is important for the portfolio manager to work closely with a dealer. There are dealers who will actually provide executable prices. □

---

[42] In addition, deep discount bonds trade at a premium because of the tax advantage.

7
Active
Strategies

In a general sense, active management is an approach that will achieve the maximum return for a given level of risk. That is, the emphasis is on return maximization—seeking the highest return possible while not exceeding the desired risk posture. This can be differentiated from a passive strategy, as discussed in Chapter 5, in which risk aversion dominates and a less than maximum return objective is acceptable. When investment horizons are long or risk tolerances are high, active management is the preferred strategy. Most pension funds and some closed-end mutual funds fit into this category. When this emphasis on expected return emerges, so does the key role of expectations in the process. More precisely, expectations are the prime driving force from which the return sought will be achieved. How a portfolio manager harnesses these expectations is the theme of this chapter.

The uncertainty associated with expectations is also the source of risk in the active management process. How the manager should best make use of expectations in the face of uncertainty can be interpreted as the risk-minimizing dimension of the active strategy. This is where we focus our attention in this chapter.

It is assumed that the manager has a set of expectations, however derived; the next step is to transform them effectively into managerial action. After reviewing a number of ways in which expectations may be formulated, some useful tools for implementing the expectations will be discussed. This does not minimize the importance of how the expectations themselves are arrived at, but it does suggest that if a manager classifies expectations properly and fortifies them with the appropriate techniques, better decision making and, hence, better investment results will emerge.

■ Overview of Active Management Process

Figure 7–1 describes, in a macro sense, what the active management process is all about. Typically, the manager would begin on the left side of the figure, starting with a portfolio plus a potential purchase list.

Figure 7–1
Active Management Framework

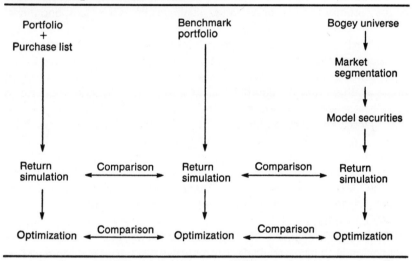

The key to this overall process resides in the step identified next: return simulation. Return simulation is the process by which a manager takes a set of expectations and transforms them into expected rates of return. That is the bottom-line output. These expected rates of return would capture all the expectations that go into the process, whether they are expectations about interest rate changes, credit risk changes, or spread relationship changes. These all can be finally expressed in a bottom-line number, an expected rate of return for both individual securities and the portfolio as a whole.

The results from return simulation lead directly to portfolio optimization, which can actually suggest specific changes to the portfolio by taking the expected rates of return that have been defined from the return simula-

tion process and integrating other appropriate portfolio policy considerations. So, specific client preferences, or the particular managerial style
that the manager has adopted, can all be incorporated into the optimization process.

Along with the analysis of the current portfolio, a second step is identified by the center vertical track of Figure 7–1. This is identifying a
benchmark portfolio, some "bogey" with which the manager will be comparing the portfolio. This could be any portfolio the manager and client
decide is the appropriate bogey.

By subjecting the benchmark portfolio to the return simulation process, the manager has again transformed expectations into expected rates
of return. The manager then can subject those expected rates of return to
the same policy considerations used for the actual portfolio and come up
with a portfolio optimization analysis. The manager then compares the
actual portfolio and identified bogey, evaluates the differences, and determines the potential ability of the actual portfolio to outperform the bogey.

A third active management process for portfolio comparison starts with
a bogey universe, the rightmost column of Figure 7–1. The basic difference between this third track and the second track is that, in the bogey
universe, the manager may be dealing with a much broader universe of
securities instead of those in a benchmark portfolio. For example, the
manager may be starting with an index such as the Lehman Brothers Kuhn
Loeb Corporate Bond Index. It is comprised of approximately 3,000 to
4,000 securities. That type of bogey may be appropriate, but, in order to
subject it to the same kind of expectations transformation and optimization
analysis used in the first track, the manager has to do some interim analysis
in order to turn that large universe into a manageable portfolio.

What we have identified here is a two-step process. Starting with the
3,000 or 4,000 securities, the manager can do an analysis called market
segmentation, which essentially decomposes the universe into sectors. A
bogey portfolio can be selected for each sector, to track a bond index, that
can, in effect, replicate the return behavior of the larger universe identified
at the beginning. The manager then takes the securities in the bogey portfolio, and subjects them to the return simulation process. That provides the
manager with the transformation of expectations into expected rates of
return. The manager then can subject that set of expected rates of return to
the optimization analysis.

At the optimization level, the manager can do cross comparisons to
see how the actual portfolio—before and after the portfolio changes that
will be made—compares with a benchmark portfolio or, alternatively, with
the bogey universe identified.

This is a rather simplified schematic, and it should be pointed out that
much of the essence of the technique is really captured in the return
simulation process. So, regardless of which techniques the portfolio man-

ager selects, the important step is subjecting the technique to return simulation.

■ Techniques of Active Management

Active strategies, which are dominated by interest rate anticipation and sector/security strategies, actually span a fairly wide range of possibilities. Indeed, the increased volatility of the bond market has stimulated the development of active management techniques. In this section, we will describe interest rate anticipation strategies and sector/security strategies that could be employed by a bond portfolio manager.

Interest Rate Anticipation Strategies

The philosophy in rate anticipation is to take advantage of the return implication of expected interest rate change through bond portfolio management. As we explained in Chapter 2, interest rate change is the dominant source of marginal total return—marginal in relation to the return if no rate change had occurred. As long as there is volatility in rates, this problem will exist. If one is to pursue an active management strategy, there must be an explicit recognition of the effect of interest rate change.

As an active management technique, interest rate anticipation should be concerned with three dimensions: direction of the change in rates; magnitude of the change across maturities; and the timing of the change. If interest rates drop, the price of the bond will rise to reflect the new yield level. Conversely, if rates increase, the price of the bond will decline. The increase or decrease will be directly related to the security's duration. Therefore, the maturity should be lengthened and the coupon decreased—or, equivalently, duration should be increased—when rates are expected to drop, and the opposite action taken when rates are expected to rise. Where along the maturity spectrum the portfolio is positioned should be guided by the shape of the expected yield curve change. Finally, the timing of the expected rate change will be important in evaluating the relative importance of rate change, coupon return, and reinvestment return. This subject will be discussed in more detail later in this section.

Interest rate anticipation strategies seek to recognize and assess the role of interest rate changes on the total return of a portfolio over a specified time horizon. For purposes of discussion the generation of the required interest rate forecast itself will not be covered. It is, at best, extremely difficult to forecast the future direction of rates, much less their magnitude. As discussed in Chapter 5, there are some who would assert that it is impossible. The emphasis here is on how the portfolio manager can harness the forecast once it is determined. To assess the impact and implications of interest rate change, it is useful to apply the forecasts of interest rate change to a portfolio.

Table 7–1 summarizes inputs suitable for simulating the effect of interest rate change for a portfolio of 150 bonds shown in the lower panel of the table. A framework of one year has been chosen for this illustration, but this would vary according to the portfolio manager's expectations and desires.

Three scenarios of interest rate change are shown. These have been derived from historical interest rate change tendencies over the 10 years prior to the analysis. There is a bullish scenario, a market-implicit forecast scenario, and a bearish scenario. The market-implicit forecast is based on the term structure analysis described in Chapter 2 and in Appendix D.

Multiscenario approaches recognize the uncertainty associated with interest rate forecasting and, accordingly, allow a form of sensitivity analysis. In the illustration, these forecasts take the form of the most likely (market-implicit), optimistic (declining rates), and pessimistic (rising rates) cases. The manager's own forecast would be, of course, an alternative. Each scenario is described along with a specified probability. Figures in Table 7–1 reflect the forecast yield for each senario as well as the present yield to maturity for each scenario.

To reflect the effect of quality, issuing, or coupon sectors, additional factors can be imposed which will modify the basic shift represented by the forecast Treasury yield curves in Table 7–1. For example, a single A rated bond may be expected to shift by 10 percent less than the anticipated shift of a Treasury bond of the same maturity. Assuming the Treasury bond yield was to shift 100 basis points, the modified shift for the single A bond would be 90 basis points. The additional factors of issuing sector and coupon group could further modify the primary shift. All of these factors can be termed *volatility factors*. They modify, on the margin, the anticipated change due to overall interest rates, and allow the fine tuning of the anticipated reaction to interest rate changes based on the unique characteristics of the bond.

The volatility factor for an issuing sector can be estimated from historical data using the following simple linear regression:

$$\Delta S_t = a + (1 + b)\Delta T_t + e_t \qquad (7\text{–}1)$$

where

ΔS_t = change in interest rate for the issuing sector in month t (in basis points)

ΔT_t = change in interest rate for the Treasury issue in month t (in basis points)

e_t = error term in month t

Table 7–1
Interest Rate Projection and Sample Bond Portfolio

Scenario 1 (33.33% probability): falling rates, 10-year historical volatility basis (1/73 to 1/83), reinvestment rate is calculated for each bond.
Scenario 2 (33.33% probability): market-implicit forecast (using term structure analysis), reinvestment rate is calculated for each bond.
Scenario 3 (33.33% probability): rising rates, 10-year historical volatility basis (1/73 to 1/83), reinvestment rate is calculated for each bond.
Interest rate projection (12/31/82 to 12/31/83)

Maturity (years)	Present Yield to Maturity (percent)	Forecast Yield (percent)			Maturity Date	Forecast Yield Shifts (Basis Points)			
		Scenario 1	Scenario 2	Scenario 3		Roll Effect	Scenario 1	Scenario 2	Scenario 3
0.250	8.500%	6.570%	10.400%	11.940%	4/1/83	0.0	-193.0	190.0	344.0
0.500	8.710	6.880	10.490	11.940	7/2/83	0.0	-183.0	178.0	323.0
1.000	8.960	7.270	10.290	11.850	12/31/83	-46.0	-239.0	144.0	298.0
2.000	9.590	8.140	10.620	12.130	12/31/84	-63.0	-232.0	70.0	226.0
3.000	10.010	8.610	10.860	12.310	12/31/85	-42.0	-187.0	61.0	212.0
4.000	10.310	8.910	10.980	12.470	12/31/86	-30.0	-170.0	55.0	200.0
5.000	10.490	9.130	11.020	12.590	12/31/87	-18.0	-158.0	49.0	198.0
10.000	10.710	9.370	11.030	12.380	12/31/92	-4.4	-138.8	31.8	171.2
20.000	10.800	9.700	11.040	12.500	12/31/2	-0.9	-113.3	23.9	168.8
30.000	10.820	9.730	11.030	12.530	12/31/12	-0.2	-109.3	21.1	170.7

Sample Portfolio of 150 Issues (with calls priced 12/31/82; par value for each issue $1,000)

ID No.	Percent of Total	CUSIP	Issuer Name	Quality	Coupon	Stated Maturity Date	Effective Maturity Date	Price	Yield-to-Maturity (%)	Duration (years)
1	0.7	313586KJ	Federal National Mortgage Association	AAA	11.100	8/10/84	8/10/84	101.625	9.97	1.46
2	0.7	313388HF	Federal Home Loan Banks	AAA	10.800	3/25/85	3/25/85	101.625	9.95	1.99
3	0.8	313586KT	Federal National Mortgage Association	AAA	13.000	11/12/85	11/12/85	106.000	10.51	2.46
4	0.7	313311ED	Federal Farm Credit Banks	AAA	10.000	12/ 1/86	12/ 1/86	99.375	10.19	3.31

Table 7–1 (continued)

ID No.	Percent of Total	CUSIP	Issuer Name	Quality	Coupon	Stated Maturity Date	Effective Maturity Date	Price	Yield-to-Maturity (%)	Duration (years)
5	0.7	313338HG	Federal Home Loan Banks	AAA	11.100	3/25/87	3/25/87	101.500	10.64	3.40
6	0.7	313586KK	Federal National Mortgage Association	AAA	11.150	5/11/87	5/11/87	101.500	10.70	3.53
7	0.7	313586KN	Federal National Mortgage Association	AAA	10.500	6/10/88	6/10/88	99.313	10.67	4.25
8	0.8	313311EJ	Federal Farm Credit Banks	AAA	11.700	7/20/88	7/20/88	104.125	10.69	4.06
9	0.7	313311EE	Federal Farm Credit Banks	AAA	10.400	7/23/90	7/23/90	98.375	10.72	5.16
10	0.7	313311CN	Federal Farm Credit Banks	AAA	9.100	7/22/91	7/22/91	91.375	10.66	5.75
11	0.6	313388DR	Federal Home Loan Banks	AAA	7.375	11/26/93	11/26/93	79.500	10.59	7.18
12	0.9	313311HQ	Federal Farm Credit Banks	AAA	14.250	4/20/94	4/20/94	119.875	11.11	6.24
13	0.5	313586GJ	Federal National Mortgage Association	AAA	8.200	7/10/ 2	7/10/ 2	70.875	12.12	7.97
14	0.7	313400AW	Federal Home Loan Mortgage Corporation	AAA	10.250	3/15/ 4	3/15/ 4	93.250	11.08	8.40
15	0.7	313400AY	Federal Home Loan Mortgage Corporation	AAA	12.450	9/15/ 4	9/15/ 4	99.500	12.51	7.62
16	0.7	029379AB	Federal Home Loan Mortgage Corporation	AAA	8.500	4/15/84	4/15/84	96.748	11.25	1.23
17	0.7	190349AB	American Savings and Loan Association California Coast Federal Savings and Loan Association L.A.	AAA	10.500	6/ 1/85	6/ 1/85	99.656	10.66	2.18
18	0.8	449220AA	IBM Credit Corporation	AAA	14.375	7/15/86	7/15/84	107.375	9.71	1.36
19	0.4	449220AB	IBM Credit Corporation	AAA	0.0	7/15/88	7/15/88	56.500	10.57	5.54
20	0.8	067900AA	Barclays North American CAP Corporation	AAA	14.625	6/15/91	6/15/91	109.250	12.80	5.23
21	0.6	894180AA	Travelers Corporation	AAA	8.700	8/ 1/95	8/ 1/95	81.879	11.45	7.06
22	0.5	008140AA	Aetna Life & Casualty	AAA	8.125	10/15/ 7	10/15/ 7	74.037	11.25	8.97
23	0.7	814823AC	Security Pacific Corporation	AA2	10.750	6/15/84	6/15/84	100.000	10.74	1.38

#		CUSIP	Issuer	Rating	Coupon			Price		
24	0.7	066050AH	BankAmerica Corporation	AA1	10.450	5/15/85	5/15/85	98.952	10.95	2.13
25	0.8	173034AN	Citicorp	AA1	14.375	2/ 1/86	2/ 1/86	104.750	12.46	2.48
26	0.7	441812BJ	Household Finance	AA3	12.000	4/15/87	4/15/87	101.250	11.61	3.40
27	0.7	370424CB	General Motors Acceptance Corporation	AA3	10.875	7/15/87	7/15/87	98.856	11.20	3.52
28	0.7	369622AR	General Electric Corporation	AA1	11.500	4/15/90	4/15/87	101.375	11.08	3.43
29	0.8	025818AJ	American Express Credit Corporation	AA2	12.875	1/15/91	1/15/88	106.250	11.22	3.70
30	0.6	125569AP	CIT Finance Corporation	AA3	9.500	6/ 1/95	6/ 1/95	85.759	11.70	7.08
31	0.5	370424BF	General Motors Acceptance Corporation	AA3	8.125	10/15/96	10/15/96	76.062	11.65	7.57
32	0.7	370424CC	General Motors Acceptance Corporation	AA3	11.750	7/15/ 0	7/15/ 0	95.722	12.35	7.21
33	0.6	370424BU	General Motors Acceptance Corporation	AA3	9.750	5/ 1/ 3	5/ 1/ 3	82.649	12.05	8.10
34	0.7	369622AS	General Electric Credit Corporation	AA3	11.750	6/ 1/ 5	6/ 1/ 5	98.047	12.00	8.13
35	0.7	053528AN	AVCO Financial Services Inc.	AA1	8.500	4/15/84	4/15/84	96.347	11.60	1.23
36	0.7	081721AT	Beneficial Corporation	A3	9.400	8/ 1/85	8/ 1/85	94.445	11.95	2.26
37	0.7	370424BE	General Motors Acceptance Corporation	A3	8.150	8/15/86	8/15/86	90.542	11.40	3.08
38	0.7	046003AS	Associates Corporation North America	A1	11.000	8/ 1/87	8/ 1/87	98.406	11.45	3.55
39	0.7	450680AJ	ITT Financial Corporation	A2	11.000	6/15/88	6/15/88	98.395	11.40	4.22
40	0.7	370424BZ	General Motors Acceptance Corporation	A2	11.625	6/ 1/90	6/ 1/86	101.625	11.03	2.90
41	0.6	0.53528AS	AVCO Financial Services Inc.	A1	9.125	3/ 1/98	3/ 1/98	77.259	12.50	7.31
42	0.7	450680AH	ITT Financial Corporation	A3	11.850	12/ 1/99	12/ 1/99	96.120	12.40	7.43
43	0.7	046003AQ	Associates Corporation North America	A2	12.125	2/ 1/ 0	2/ 1/ 0	94.024	13.00	6.96
44	0.6	125569AV	CIT Financial Corporation	A2	9.850	8/15/ 4	8/15/ 4	79.096	12.70	7.71
45	0.7	081721AW	Beneficial Corporation	A3	11.500	1/15/ 5	1/15/ 5	99.750	11.53	7.98
46	0.7	345397BP	Ford Motor Credit Company	BAA2	9.500	1/15/85	1/15/85	93.465	13.25	1.82
47	0.7	345397AY	Ford Motor Credit Company	BAA2	8.875	1/15/86	1/15/86	89.319	13.25	2.59
48	0.7	345397BV	Ford Motor Credit Company	BAA2	12.600	6/ 1/87	6/ 1/87	97.850	13.25	3.48
49	0.6	345397BT	Ford Motor Credit Company	BAA2	9.450	6/15/89	6/15/89	83.832	13.25	4.80

Table 7–1 (*continued*)

ID No.	Percent of Total	CUSIP	Issuer Name	Quality	Coupon	Stated Maturity Date	Effective Maturity Date	Price	Yield-to-Maturity (%)	Duration (years)
50	0.7	423326AM	Walter E Heller & Company	BAA2	11.750	7/15/90	7/15/90	93.638	13.10	4.84
51	0.7	046003AR	Associates Corporation North America	BAA1	13.125	5/15/ 0	5/15/ 0	99.454	13.20	7.09
52	0.5	345397AZ	Ford Motor Credit Company	BAA2	9.750	1/15/1	1/15/1	72.774	13.90	6.99
53	0.6	893485AC	Transamerica Corporation	BAA1	10.625	5/ 1/ 4	5/ 1/ 4	85.125	12.65	7.82
54	0.7	191216AA	Coca Cola Company	AAA	9.875	6/ 1/85	6/ 1/85	98.989	10.35	2.19
55	0.7	459200AA	International Business Machines	AAA	9.500	10/ 1/86	10/ 1/86	97.380	10.35	3.16
56	0.7	374280AA	Getty Oil Company	AAA	10.000	7/15/87	7/15/87	98.046	10.55	3.58
57	0.7	134429AA	Campbell Soup Company	AAA	9.875	6/15/90	6/15/90	96.069	10.65	5.38
58	0.6	302292AB	Exxon Pipeline Company	AAA	8.250	3/ 1/ 1	3/ 1/ 1	77.905	11.10	8.35
59	0.6	302292AC	Exxon Pipeline Company	AAA	8.875	10/15/ 0	10/15/ 0	82.527	11.15	8.26
60	0.6	459200AB	International Business Machines	AAA	9.375	10/ 1/ 4	10/ 1/ 4	89.125	10.67	8.81
61	0.7	074077AC	Beatrice Foods Company	AAA	10.875	5/ 1/10	5/ 1/10	96.393	11.30	8.76
62	0.7	048825AF	Atlantic Richfield Company	AAA	11.375	5/ 1/10	5/ 1/10	98.500	11.55	8.59
63	0.7	713448AC	Pepsico Incorporated	AA2	8.250	1/15/85	1/15/85	96.038	10.45	1.85
64	0.7	852245AA	Squibb Corporation	AA3	8.000	6/15/85	6/15/85	94.695	10.50	2.27
65	0.7	905581AD	Union Carbide Corporation	AA3	9.125	8/15/86	8/15/86	95.060	10.80	3.05
66	0.7	887360AB	Times Mirror Company	AA3	9.625	9/15/86	9/15/86	96.748	10.70	3.11
67	0.7	565845AE	Marathon Oil Company	A3	10.250	7/15/87	7/15/87	94.989	11.70	3.54
68	0.7	761753AC	Reynolds R J Industries Incorporated	AA1	10.450	5/15/90	5/15/90	97.979	10.85	5.23
69	0.7	915302AB	Upjohn Company	AA2	10.650	7/15/90	7/15/90	98.977	10.85	5.10
70	0.6	812387AD	Sears Roebuck & Company	AA2	8.625	10/ 1/95	10/ 1/95	81.547	11.40	7.25
71	0.6	406216AE	Halliburton Company	AA1	9.250	4/ 1/ 0	4/ 1/ 0	85.214	11.20	8.07
72	0.6	717081AD	Pfizer Incorporated	AA2	9.250	8/15/ 0	8/15/ 0	81.531	11.75	7.82
73	0.6	913017AG	United Technologies Corporation	AA3	9.375	1/15/ 4	1/15/ 4	81.606	11.75	8.06
74	0.6	406216AF	Halliburton Company	AA1	10.200	6/ 1/ 5	6/ 1/ 5	91.829	11.20	8.65
75	0.7	761525AC	Revlon Incorporated	AA3	10.875	7/15/10	7/15/10	92.862	11.75	8.25

76	0.7	0.7	718167AF	Philip Morris Incorporated	A2	8.500	3/15/85	3/15/85	96.218	10.45	2.01
77	0.7	0.7	761688AC	Rexnord Incorporated	BAA2	10.500	5/15/85	5/15/85	97.544	11.70	2.13
78	0.7	0.7	718167AJ	Philip Morris Incorporated	A2	9.550	6/ 1/86	6/ 1/86	96.625	10.75	2.97
79	0.7	0.7	597715AB	Midland Ross Corporation	BAA2	10.750	5/15/87	5/15/87	97.614	11.45	3.54
80	0.7	0.7	848355AG	Sperry Corporation	A3	10.500	6/15/87	6/15/87	96.742	11.45	3.64
81	0.7	0.7	708160AD	Penney J C Incorporated	A1	10.750	6/15/90	6/15/90	97.266	11.30	5.26
82	0.8	0.8	880370AQ	Tenneco Incorporated	A2	13.375	1/15/88	1/15/91	103.500	12.42	3.63
83	0.6	0.6	022249AH	Aluminum Company America	A2	9.450	5/15/ 0	5/15/ 0	82.776	11.80	7.96
84	0.6	0.6	260543AF	Dow Chemical Company	A1	8.900	11/ 1/ 0	11/ 1/ 0	77.969	11.90	8.04
85	0.4	0.4	708160AH	Penney J C Incorporated	A1	6.000	5/ 1/ 6	5/ 1/ 6	54.000	11.84	9.11
86	0.7	0.7	260543AN	Dow Chemical Company	A1	11.250	7/15/10	7/15/10	90.694	12.45	7.85
87	0.7	0.7	122781AK	Burroughs Corporation	A2	11.500	8/ 1/10	8/ 1/10	91.900	12.55	7.83
88	0.7	0.7	345370AJ	Ford Motor Company Del	BAA2	14.750	4/ 1/85	4/ 1/85	102.590	13.35	1.94
89	0.6	0.6	717265AC	Phelps Dodge Corporation	BAA2	8.500	6/ 1/85	6/ 1/85	90.506	13.20	2.21
90	0.6	0.6	023127AD	Amax Incorporated	BAA	8.000	1/ 1/86	1/ 1/86	86.500	13.62	2.59
91	0.6	0.6	316830AA	Figgie International Incorporated	BAA3	9.375	11/15/86	11/15/86	89.000	13.07	3.26
92	0.7	0.7	783549AH	Ryder Systems Incorporated	A2	12.250	12/15/86	12/15/86	101.222	11.85	3.24
93	0.8	0.8	345370AK	Ford Motor Company Del	BAA2	14.250	4/ 1/87	4/ 1/87	104.044	13.14	3.25
94	0.7	0.7	030096AA	American Stores Company New	BAA3	12.000	6/ 1/90	6/ 1/90	94.182	13.25	4.99
95	0.6	0.6	457470AL	Inland Steel Company	BAA2	11.250	6/ 1/90	6/ 1/90	86.299	14.30	4.99
96	0.5	0.5	933169AG	Walter Jim Corporation	BAA3	9.500	2/ 1/96	2/ 1/96	73.375	13.98	6.51
97	0.4	0.4	717265AB	Phelps Dodge Corporation	BAA2	8.100	6/15/96	6/15/96	59.750	15.21	6.86
98	0.7	0.7	749285AF	RCA Corporation	BAA2	12.250	5/ 1/ 5	5/ 1/ 5	92.507	13.30	6.86
99	0.6	0.6	146227AD	Carter Hawley Half Stores Incorporated	BAA2	11.875	5/15/10	5/15/10	88.264	13.50	7.48
100	0.7	0.7	912827JX	United States Treasury Notes	AAA	9.250	5/15/84	5/15/84	100.094	9.16	1.31
101	0.7	0.7	912827KP	United States Treasury Notes	AAA	10.375	5/15/85	5/15/85	101.500	9.64	2.14
102	0.7	0.7	912827HY	United States Treasury Notes	AAA	8.250	8/15/85	8/15/85	96.813	9.65	2.34
103	0.7	0.7	912827FW	United States Treasury Notes	AAA	8.000	8/15/86	8/15/86	94.188	9.94	3.11
104	0.7	0.7	912827KY	United States Treasury Notes	AAA	10.750	8/15/90	8/15/90	101.438	10.47	5.21
105	0.8	0.8	912827LF	United States Treasury Notes	AAA	13.000	11/15/90	11/15/90	111.375	10.81	5.23
106	0.7	0.7	912810CQ	United States Treasury Bonds	AAA	10.375	5/15/95	5/15/95	98.938	10.53	7.12

Table 7–1 (continued)

ID No.	Percent of Total	CUSIP	Issuer Name	Quality	Coupon	Stated Maturity Date	Effective Maturity Date	Price	Yield-to-Maturity (%)	Duration (years)
107	0.6	912810BV	United States Treasury Bonds	AAA	8.375	8/15/ 0	8/15/ 0	82.750	10.55	8.41
108	0.8	912810CM	United States Treasury Bonds	AAA	11.750	2/15/10	2/15/ 5	107.563	10.84	8.35
109	0.7	912810CP	United States Treasury Bonds	AAA	10.000	5/15/10	5/15/10	95.250	10.53	9.33
110	0.6	030177AH	American Telephone and Telegraph Company	AAA	3.250	9/15/84	9/15/84	91.214	8.90	1.66
111	0.6	0.30177AL	American Telephone and Telegraph Company	AAA	2.875	6/ 1/87	6/ 1/87	78.522	8.85	4.13
112	0.7	030177BJ	American Telephone and Telegraph Company	AAA	10.375	6/ 1/90	6/ 1/90	97.356	10.90	5.28
113	0.4	030177AV	American Telephone and Telegraph Company	AAA	6.000	8/ 1/ 0	8/ 1/ 0	61.447	11.00	8.84
114	0.5	030177BR	American Telephone and Telegraph Company	AAA	7.000	2/15/ 1	2/15/ 1	67.684	11.20	8.56
115	0.6	030177BG	American Telephone and Telegraph Company	AAA	8.625	2/ 1/ 7	2/ 1/ 7	77.655	11.35	8.60
116	0.7	882661BF	Texas Power and Light Company	AAA	11.375	5/ 1/10	5/ 1/10	93.469	12.20	8.25
117	0.5	842332AX	Southern Bell Telephone and Telegraph Company	AAA	8.250	4/15/16	4/15/16	71.460	11.65	8.89
118	0.7	451794AP	Illinois Bell Telephone Company	AAA	12.250	8/ 5/17	8/ 5/17	99.571	12.30	8.10
119	0.7	842400BL	Southern California Edison Company	AA2	7.250	7/ 1/84	7/ 1/84	95.518	10.56	1.40
120	0.6	744567AL	Public Service Electric and Gas Company	AA3	4.375	11/ 1/86	11/ 1/86	80.813	10.58	3.51

121	0.7	976656AT	Wisconsin Electric Power Company	AA1	13.750	12/ 1/86	12/ 1/86	105.798	11.85	3.15
122	0.5	842400AT	Southern California Edison Company	AA2	4.375	5/15/88	5/15/88	75.820	10.35	4.72
123	0.7	845743AS	Southwestern Public Service Company	AA2	10.900	6/ 1/90	6/ 1/90	97.750	11.35	5.20
124	0.8	842400BR	Southern California Edison Company	AA2	15.250	5/15/91	5/15/91	113.875	12.52	5.13
125	0.5	842400BC	Southern California Edison Company	AA2	7.875	12/ 1/95	12/ 1/95	73.759	11.90	7.46
126	0.5	744567BK	Public Service Electric and Gas Company	AA3	7.500	4/ 1/ 2	4/ 1/ 2	67.540	11.80	8.43
127	0.6	842400BM	Southern California Edison Company	AA2	9.625	11/ 1/ 3	11/ 1/ 3	82.571	11.90	8.22
128	0.7	842400BQ	Southern California Edison Company	AA2	13.500	11/15/10	11/15/10	102.545	13.15	7.73
129	0.8	843486AJ	Southern New England Telephone Company	AA2	14.125	3/15/20	3/15/20	106.250	13.28	7.66
130	0.7	341081BK	Florida Power and Light Company	A1	9.125	5/ 1/84	5/ 1/84	97.759	10.95	1.27
131	0.7	843452AN	Southern Natural Gas Company	A2	8.250	5/ 1/86	5/ 1/86	92.464	11.00	2.93
132	0.8	341099BA	Florida Power Corporation	A1	13.625	4/ 1/87	4/ 1/85	105.000	11.03	1.96
133	0.6	186108AF	Cleveland Electric Illum Company	A2	7.125	1/15/90	1/15/90	79.669	11.40	5.25
134	0.8	264399BJ	Duke Power Company	A1	12.000	7/ 1/90	7/ 1/87	102.500	11.28	3.42
135	0.8	744465AW	Public Service Company Industries Incorporated	A3	12.125	9/ 1/90	9/ 1/86	103.000	11.10	2.97
136	0.8	202795CA	Commonwealth Edison Company	A3	15.375	3/15/ 0	3/15/93	108.000	14.04	5.44
137	0.5	264399AO	Duke Power Company	A1	7.500	3/ 1/ 1	3/ 1/ 1	66.988	12.00	8.17
138	0.6	264399BE	Duke Power Company	A1	10.875	10/ 1/ 9	10/ 1/ 9	87.466	12.50	8.04
139	0.7	144141AX	Carolina Power and Light Company	A2	12.250	11/ 1/ 9	11/ 1/ 9	94.739	12.95	7.82
140	0.6	694886BN	Pacific Telephone and Telegraph Company	A3	9.750	7/ 1/19	7/ 1/19	80.183	12.20	8.18
141	0.8	694886BU	Pacific Telephone and Telegraph Company	A3	15.000	11/ 1/20	11/ 1/20	109.750	13.65	7.59
142	0.7	542671AY	Long Island Lighting Company	BAA2	9.875	9/ /84	9/ 1/84	96.835	12.00	1.53
143	0.7	037735AS	Appalachian Power Company	BAA1	10.500	12/ 1/84	12/ 1/84	99.875	10.56	1.78
144	0.7	649840AU	New York State Electric and Gas Corporation	BAA2	12.125	12/ 1/86	12/ 1/86	100.000	12.12	3.20

Table 7–1 (concluded)

ID No.	Percent of Total	CUSIP	Issuer Name	Quality	Coupon	Stated Maturity Date	Effective Maturity Date	Price	Yield-to-Maturity (%)	Duration (years)
145	0.7	694784BJ	Pacific Power and Light Company	BAA2	10.750	5/ 1/90	5/ 1/90	92.156	12.40	5.07
146	0.8	906548AZ	Union Electric Company	BAA2	15.375	2/ 1/91	2/ 1/88	111.000	12.39	3.58
147	0.7	717537BM	Philadelphia Electric Company	BAA2	13.750	10/15/92	10/15/92	102.250	13.32	5.56
148	0.5	010392BB	Alabama Power Company	BAA1	7.875	4/ 1/ 2	4/ 1/ 2	65.274	12.75	7.97
149	0.6	373334BS	Georgia Power Company	BAA1	11.000	4/ 1/ 9	4/ 1/ 9	86.436	12.80	7.87
150	0.8	010392BR	Alabama Power Company	BAA1	15.250	9/ 1/10	9/ 1/10	105.250	14.47	6.91

Portfolio Totals

Average duration (years)	5.108
Average yield (percent)	11.630
Duration weighted average	11.811
Average effective maturity	3/ 9/94
Total par value	$150,000,000
Total market value	$142,605,448

and *a* and *b* are the parameters of the model to be estimated. The parameter *b* is the issuing sector volatility and the parameter *a* is the issuing sector spread change.

Table 7–2 shows the estimate of *a* and *b* for 41 issuing sectors based on 10 years of monthly data. For example, if Treasuries increase by 100 basis points, AAA Industrials will, on average, increase by only 88.9 basis points, as shown below:

$$\Delta S = -3.6 + [1 + (-.075)]\Delta T$$
$$= -3.6 + .925(100)$$
$$= -3.6 + .925(100) = 88.9$$

For AA Financials, a 100 basis point increase in Treasuries would increase the interest rate on obligations in this issuing sector by 93.2 basis points, on average, as shown below:

$$\Delta S = 7.9 + [1 + (-.147)]\Delta T$$
$$= 7.9 + .853(100)$$
$$= 7.9 + .853(100) = 93.2$$

As noted previously, it is also possible to refine the procedure further by estimating different sector spreads by an issuing sector for different maturities and/or quality classifications.

Table 7–3 exemplifies the results of translating interest rate change into expected (composite) rates of return for four individual securities in the portfolio. The returns are also presented for each of the three scenarios. Returns are based on maturity unless indicated that the issue would be called under the particular scenario. The columns are largely self-explanatory, but those of particular importance are described below:

Yield curve	Return due to changes in the nominal yield curve.
Time	Return assuming the initial yield curve remains constant over the projection horizon (i.e., rolling down the yield curve).
Spread change	Return attributable to spread change and volatility effects.
Earned interest	Interest accrued over the projection period.
Maturity/call	Change in principal value for securities projected to be called or to mature. (The price change is separate from that caused by the interest rate effects.)
Reinvestment	Interest on interest earned over the projection period, as well as reinvestment from maturities, calls, puts, sinking fund payments and any other prepayments.
Total return	The sum of all components of return.
Duration	The first figure in the column is current duration: remaining figures are the duration at the end of the assumed holding period for the particular scenario.

Table 7–4 summarizes the portfolio return for each scenario and the composite return for the 150-issue portfolio for which the return simulation was performed. The foregoing analysis can be extremely helpful in execut-

Table 7–2
Issuing Sector Spread Changes and Issuing Sector Volatility*

Sector ID	Issuing Sector	Issuing Sector Spread Changes (basis points)	Issuing Sector Volatility (percent)
TR	U.S. Treasury	0.0	0.0%
AG	U.S. Agency	−6.5	6.60
PS	Passthroughs	0.0	0.00
MC	FHLMC GMC	0.0	0.00
I1	AAA Industrial	−3.6	−7.50
I2	AA Industrial	5.7	−15.60
I3	A Industria.	15.8	−27.40
I4	BAA Industrial	25.1	−31.40
O1	AAA Oil	1.4	−6.70
O2	AA Oil	6.5	−18.60
O3	A Oil	12.2	−21.40
O4	BAA Oil	42.3	−12.90
AT	American Telephone & Telegraph Company	0.0	0.00
T1	AAA Telephone	0.0	0.40
T2	AA Telephone	3.6	−7.20
T3	A Telephone	7.2	−4.90
T4	BAA Telephone	12.9	−26.30
E1	AAA Electric Utility	−8.6	9.20
E2	AA Electric Utility	5.7	−9.10
E3	A Electric Utility	6.5	−8.00
E4	BAA Electric Utility	8.6	−7.20
G1	AAA Gas Utility	0.0	0.00
G2	AA Gas Utility	2.9	−11.20
G3	A Gas Utility	1.4	−13.40
G4	BAA Gas Utility	10.0	−22.30
R1	AAA Rail	1.4	−13.30
R2	AA Rail	15.1	−37.60
R3	A Rail	12.9	−39.60
R4	BAA Rail	15.1	−32.50
B1	AAA Bank	0.0	0.00
B2	AA Bank	0.0	0.00
B3	A Bank	0.0	0.00
B4	BAA Bank	0.0	0.00
F1	AAA Finance	0.7	1.20
F2	AA Finance	7.9	−14.70
F3	A Finance	14.4	−20.30
F4	BAA Finance	24.4	−24.50
X1	AAA International	0.0	0.00
X2	AA International	0.0	0.00
X3	A International	0.0	0.00
X4	BAA International	0.0	0.00
PP	Private Placement	0.0	0.00

* Based on an estimate of the following linear regression for 10 years of monthly data:

$$\Delta S_t = a + (1 + b)\Delta T_t + e_t$$

where

ΔS_t = change in interest rate for the issuing sector in month t (in basis points)
ΔT_t = change in interest rate for the Treasury issue in month t (in basis points)
a = issuing sector spread
b = issuing sector volatility

ing an effective active management strategy. Analytical insights are achieved by partitioning a set of expected interest rate changes into implied rates of return. Each graduation provides further insight into the sources and, hence, the causes of performance. Analysis beyond the total return permits both the establishment and monitoring of policy. For example, a manager stressing rate anticipation should have the return due from overall changes in interest rates dominate the return from spread relationships. Conversely, a manager with an emphasis on spread relationship exploitation should have this component dominate.

In terms of a portfolio perspective, comparing total returns of securities in the portfolio can be the first step in screening the most desirable portfolio holdings.

Relative return value analysis. Relative return analysis is a tool that allows a manager to compare alternative securities systematically. It recognizes that choosing the highest expected return security may be inappropriate, since either it may not be the security with the highest realized return, or the level of associated risk may be undesirable. The objective here is to identify the highest expected return security for a given level of risk.

This technique is illustrated in Figure 7–2. Duration is on the horizontal axis and on the vertical axis is the composite expected return, which is the probability-weighted return of each of the three scenario returns from the return simulation process; however, any other alternative that a manager employs for defining expected return can be used. Within the diagram is a regression line (dashed line), individual security representation (asterisks), portfolio average return/duration (letter T) and bond identification number (far right hand margin). The regression line represents the average relationship between return and duration exhibited by the individual securities making up the portfolio. Using the regression line as fair value, we can conclude that bonds above the line are those with greater expected return per unit of duration than the average relationship; bonds below the line have less return per unit of duration.

For example, the best bond for the total expected return and duration optimizer appears to be bond 97, which has a duration of about 6.89 years and composite return of about 13.4 percent.

Table 7–5 indicates the individual securities from the 150-issue sample bond portfolio that lie one standard error (in this case an excess return of 1.0026 percent) above the market line. As can be seen from Table 7–5, bond 97, Phelps Dodge Corp., 8.1s of 1996, had an excess return of 2.7 percent at the time of the analysis. The worst bond, as indicated in Figure 7–2, is bond 111. An analysis similar to that in Table 7–3 would explain why bonds 97 and 111 would be expected to perform in this manner.

Table 7–3
Analysis of 5 Issues of the 150-Issue Portfolio for Each of the Three Interest Rate Forecasts and the Composite
(current date 12/31/82; projection date 12/31/83)

Face Value ($000)	Bond Description		Price (percent)	Yield to Effective Maturity	Yield Curve
	66				
1000	Times Mirror Co	Current:	96.748%	10.71mat	
	9.6250% 9/15/86 12 AA3	Scenario 1:	100.000	9.63call	0.0%
		Scenario 2:	96.302	11.25mat	−2.1
		Scenario 3:	93.592	12.48mat	−5.4
		Composite:	96.631	11.12	−2.5
	67				
1000	Marathon Oil Company	Current:	94.989	11.70mat	
	10.2500% 7/15/87 12 A3	Scenario 1:	99.620	10.38mat	4.2
		Scenario 2:	94.532	12.20mat	−2.2
		Scenario 3:	91.242	13.44mat	−6.3
		Composite:	95.131	12.01	−1.4
	68				
1000	Reynolds R J Industries	Current:	97.979	10.86mat	
	10.4500% 5/15/90 12 AA1	Scenario 1:	102.025	9.48call	4.2
		Scenario 2:	96.398	11.26mat	−2.4
		Scenario 3:	91.269	12.48mat	−8.5
		Composite:	96.564	11.07	−2.2
	69				
1000	Upjohn Co.	Current:	98.977	10.85mat	
	10.6500% 7/15/90 12 AA2	Scenario 1:	102.651	9.45call	3.9
		Scenario 2:	97.278	11.25mat	−2.4
		Scenario 3:	92.039	12.47mat	−8.6
		Composite:	97.323	11.06	−2.4
	70				
1000	Sears, Roebuck & Co.	Current:	81.547	11.40mat	
	8.6250% 10/1/95 12 AA2	Scenario 1:	88.424	10.35mat	9.4
		Scenario 2:	80.557	11.71mat	−2.2
		Scenario 3:	74.475	12.90mat	−11.0
		Composite:	81.152	11.65	−1.3

	Components of Return				Total Return (percent)	Effective Maturity Date	Duration (years)	Note
Time	Spread Change	Earned Interest	Maturity Call	Reinvestment				
						9/15/86	3.20	
0.0%	0.0%	7.6%	3.4%	1.9%	12.8%	10/6/83	0.00	called
1.6	0.1	9.9	0.0	0.3	9.8	9/15/86	2.44	
1.6	0.6	9.9	0.0	0.3	7.0	9/15/86	2.44	
1.0	0.2	9.2	1.1	0.8	9.9	9/22/85	1.63	
						7/15/87	3.72	
1.6	−1.0	10.8	0.0	0.3	16.0	7/15/87	3.06	
1.6	0.1	10.8	0.0	0.3	10.6	7/15/87	3.04	
1.6	0.7	10.8	0.0	0.3	7.2	7/15/87	3.03	
1.6	−0.1	10.8	0.0	0.3	11.3	7/15/87	3.04	
						5/15/90	5.30	
0.7	−0.7	10.7	0.0	0.3	15.1	5/15/86	2.16	
0.7	0.0	10.7	0.0	0.3	9.3	5/15/90	4.78	
0.7	1.0	10.7	0.0	0.3	4.1	5/15/90	4.73	
0.7	0.1	10.7	0.0	0.3	9.5	1/13/89	3.89	
						7/15/90	5.36	
0.6	−0.8	10.8	0.0	0.3	14.7	7/15/86	2.29	
0.6	0.0	10.8	0.0	0.3	9.3	7/15/90	4.85	
0.6	1.0	10.8	0.0	0.3	4.1	7/15/90	4.79	
0.6	0.1	10.8	0.0	0.3	9.4	3/15/89	3.98	
						10/1/95	7.43	
1.1	−2.0	10.6	0.0	0.3	19.3	10/1/95	7.33	
1.1	−0.1	10.6	0.0	0.3	9.7	10/1/95	7.10	
1.1	1.2	10.6	0.0	0.3	2.2	10/1/95	6.91	
1.1	−0.3	10.6	0.0	0.3	10.4	10/1/95	7.11	

* mat = yield to maturity
call = yield to call.

Table 7–4
Summary of Portfolio Return for Each of the Three Interest Rate Scenarios and the Composite (*portfolio return on beginning market value—12/31/82 to 12/31/83*)

	Yield Change Impact	Time (Roll) Impact	Spread Change Impact	Earned Interest	Coupon Reinvestment	Matured/ Called	Maturity/Call Reinvestment	Total	Annual Total
Scenario 1 (12/31/83)	5.68%	0.88%	−0.97%	10.96%	0.29%	0.07%	0.15%	17.06%	16.39%
Scenario 2 (12/31/83)	−1.88	0.92	−0.13	11.12	0.33	0.0	0.0	10.37	10.11
Scenario 3 (12/31/83)	−7.97	0.92	0.52	11.12	0.35	0.0	0.0	4.94	4.88
Composite (12/31/83)	−1.39	0.91	−0.19	11.07	0.32	0.02	0.05	10.79	10.51

Figure 7–2
Composite Total Return versus Duration

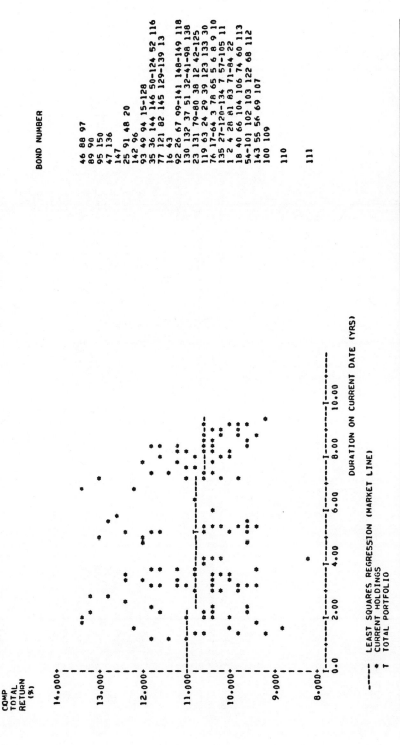

Table 7-5
Tabular Presentation of Composite Total Return versus Duration on Current Date for Bonds More than One Standard Error above the Market Line*

Bond Number	Bond Name	Coupon Rate (percent)	Stated Maturity	Quality	Composite (percent)	Duration (years)	Return minus Market Line*
97	Phelps Dodge Corp.	8.1000%	6/15/96	BAA2	13.4%	6.89	2.7
88	Ford Motor Co. Del	14.7500	4/ 1/85	BAA2	13.4	2.00	2.5
90	Amax Inc.	8.0000	1/ 1/86	BAA	13.3	2.71	2.4
46	Ford Motor Credit Co.	9.5000	1/15/85	BAA2	13.3	1.90	2.4
150	Alabama Power Co.	15.2500	9/ 1/10	BAA1	13.1	7.23	2.4
95	Inland Steel Co.	11.2500	6/ 1/90	BAA2	13.1	5.04	2.3
89	Phelps Dodge Corp.	8.5000	6/ 1/85	BAA2	13.1	2.23	2.2
136	Commonwealth Edison Co.	15.3750	6/15/ 0	A3	12.9	5.65	2.1
47	Ford Motor Credit Co.	8.8750	1/15/86	BAA2	12.9	2.71	2.0
147	Philadelphia Electric Co.	13.7500	10/15/92	BAA2	12.6	5.71	1.8
91	Figgie International Inc.	9.3750	11/15/86	BAA3	12.5	3.30	1.6
20	Barclays North American Cap Corp.	14.6250	6/15/91	AAA	12.3	5.26	1.6

48	Ford Motor Credit Co.	12.6000	6/ 1/87	BAA2	12.4	3.51	1.6
25	Citicorp	14.3750	2/ 1/86	AA1	12.3	2.61	1.5
96	Walter Jim Corp.	9.5000	2/ 1/96	BAA3	12.2	6.85	1.4
15	Federal Home Loan Mtg Corp.	12.4500	9/15/ 4	AAA	12.0	7.89	1.3
93	Ford Motor Co. Del	14.2500	4/ 1/90	BAA2	12.1	3.35	1.2
128	Southern California Edison Co.	13.5000	11/15/10	AA2	11.9	7.85	1.2
142	Long Island LTG Co.	9.8750	9/ 1/84	BAA2	12.1	1.58	1.2
49	Ford Motor Credit Co.	9.4500	6/15/89	BAA2	12.0	4.82	1.2
94	American Stores Co. New	12.0000	6/ 1/90	BAA3	12.0	5.04	1.2
116	Texas Power & Light Co.	11.3750	5/ 1/10	AAA	11.8	8.41	1.1
124	Southern California Edison Co.	15.2500	5/15/91	AA2	11.9	5.21	1.1
52	Ford Motor Credit Co.	9.7500	1/15/ 1	BAA2	11.7	7.41	1.0
	MEAN	12.0145%	5/5/93	A3	12.5%	4.75	1.7

* One standard error is 1.0026% above the estimated market line. Bonds are listed in descending order with respect to the arithmetic value, (return − market line).

The analysis should also be performed for each scenario. Figures 7–3 and 7–4 are the results for the best case (scenario 1), and worst case (scenario 3), respectively.

Given this kind of two-dimensional framework, a manager has the ability—at least a first cut—to differentiate the return characteristics of the securities in a portfolio. This form of analysis is very similar to the security market line approach, which is used fairly widely in the analysis of equity securities.[1]

It should be noted that in the fixed income market, there is no measure of risk comparable to the equity measure of market risk or beta.[2] What is used in the analysis is duration, which is not necessarily a risk measure. It is a measure of volatility. Although volatility is not the best measure of risk, duration does quantify risk to the extent that the volatility is a risk surrogate. Also, duration is a measure of the length of the security—a better measure, in many situations, than maturity. So, duration is a measure for differentiating securities. If, lacking a better summary risk measure, we can use duration (like beta is used on the equity side), we might consider the horizontal axis to be a normalization for volatility, so we can make judgments about any two securities that lie along the same vertical line projecting upward from any given duration level.

Strategic frontier analysis. Strategic frontier analysis is a tool for evaluating both the upside and the downside return characteristics of a security. It is a procedure for analyzing the return behavior of securities under alternative interest rate scenarios.

Figure 7–5 provides the display that is employed in strategic frontier analysis. Again we have a two-dimensional framework. The total expected return is shown on the vertical axis. This could be the total expected return of the most likely scenario of interest rate change, or perhaps the return of the most optimistic scenario of interest rate change. On the horizontal axis is the return of the worst case scenario. Again, these scenarios are those used in the return simulation process.

In Figure 7–5, the dots represent the individual security holdings in the portfolio we are analyzing as well as the securities on the potential purchase list. The intersection of the dashed lines in this diagram indicates the portfolio average return, and we can see that this represents a particular position within this framework. Any particular position is defined by the return under either the optimistic scenario or the most likely scenario along one axis, and the returns from the worst case scenario along the other axis.

---

[1] William F. Sharpe, *Investments* (Englewood Cliffs, N.J.: Prentice-Hall, 1981), pp. 164–65.

[2] Ibid. pp. 156–59.

Figure 7–3
Scenario 1: Total Return versus Duration

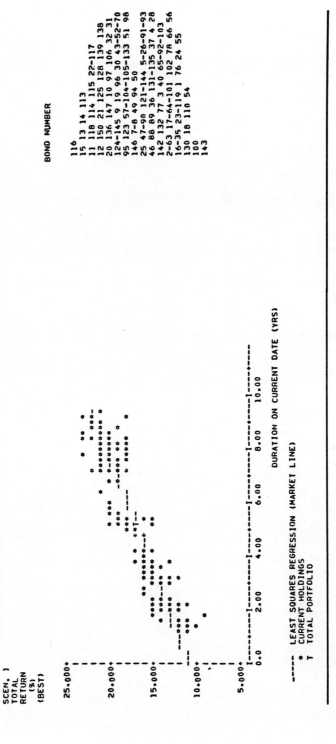

Figure 7–4
Scenario 3: Total Return versus Duration

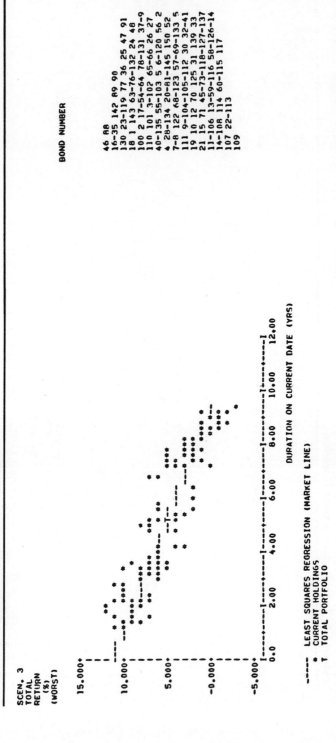

SCEN. 3
TOTAL
RETURN
(%)
(WORST)

BOND NUMBER

46 8
16-35 142 9 90
30 23-119 77 36 25 47 91
18 1 143 63-76-132 24 48
100 2 17-54 78-131 37-9
110 101 3-102 65-66 26 27
40-135 55-103 5 6-120 56 2
4 28-134 20-81-145 150 52
7-8 122 68-123 57-69-133 5
111 9-104-105-112 30 32-41
19 10 12 70 125 31 139 33
21 15 71 45-73-118-127-137
11-106 13-59-116 58-126-14
14-108 114 60-115 117
107 22-113
109

15.000+

10.000+

5.000+

-0.000+

-5.000+

0.0   2.00   4.00   6.00   8.00   10.00   12.00

DURATION ON CURRENT DATE (YRS)

----- LEAST SQUARES REGRESSION (MARKET LINE)
  * CURRENT HOLDINGS
  T TOTAL PORTFOLIO

Figure 7–5
Hypothetical Upside/Downside Trade-off

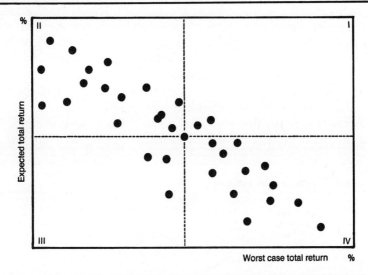

Once we have this type of framework, we can actually partition the diagram into quadrants as displayed in Figure 7–5. The portfolio average is at the origin, or center, of the quadrants. Partitioning the diagram into the four quadrants allows a manager to draw conclusions about the return behavior of the securities that fall into each of these quadrants. Let's discuss each of these quadrants.

Securities within quadrant II might be considered *aggressive* securities. They are aggressive from the standpoint that, if the most likely scenario prevails, a manager would do extremely well. If, however, the worst case scenario were to prevail, a manager would do relatively badly. So, if a manager had very high convictions about the most optimistic scenario, he would tend to choose securities from this quadrant.

In quadrant IV are what might be considered *defensive* securities. They are defensive in that, if the worst case scenario prevailed, a manager would do relatively well. But if the most likely scenario were to occur, a manager would do relatively poorly. So, if a manager wanted to posture his portfolio defensively, he would concentrate it in securities that fall within quadrant IV.

Quadrant III contains securities that might be considered *inferior*. They are inferior because, regardless of scenario outcome—either the most likely or worst case—these securities would perform relatively worse than the portfolio average. Securities falling into quadrant III are the potential sales from the existing portfolio since, by definition, they are no-win situations.

That leaves the securities falling in quadrant I. These might be considered *superior* securities because, regardless of scenario outcome, these securities would always outperform the portfolio, providing a no-loss situation. If a manager were to increase his holdings of the securities that fall in this quadrant, he would tend to move the portfolio results to the upper right portion of the quadrant. That would enhance his overall portfolio results, regardless of the scenarios being evaluated.

Figure 7–6 is another characterization of this type of analysis, and what we call a *strategic frontier*. This frontier essentially maps out the

Figure 7–6
Strategic Frontier Analysis

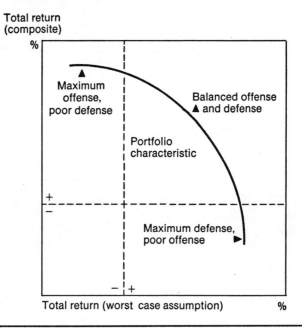

upper right region, from which a manager can choose securities that would do the best job, given his convictions. For example, if a manager wanted maximum offense or maximum aggressiveness but was willing to give up the defensive nature of some of the other securities, then he would choose securities along the strategic frontier mapped in or near the upper left quadrant. If a manager wanted a maximum defensive posture and was willing to live with the relatively poor returns should the most likely scenario prevail, then he would choose securities along the frontier in or near the lower right quadrant. Finally, the ultimate objective, especially in the face of the high uncertainty and an unsteady conviction about either scenario, would be to drive the portfolio into the upper right quadrant as far as possible.

For our sample portfolio of 150 bonds, Figure 7–7 presents a plot of the trade-off based on the total return for the best and worst case. Table 7–6 lists the bonds and provides a summary of information for the securities in quadrant I. In Table 7–7, a plot of each bond in descending order of total return is displayed. The ranking may be based on the total return from any of the scenarios or the composite. The plot in Table 7–7 is based on the total return from scenario 1 (best case). The plot, which somewhat resembles a histogram, gives a visualization of the returns. For any one bond, both its rank position and range of returns (generally analogous to variance) are seen at a glance. The return/risk characteristics of the portfolio composition are revealed by the overall wedge of the diagram.

Maturity management analysis. Table 7–8 displays a convenient asset mixing diagram that can assist a manager in maturity management. The bonds in the portfolio are first classified into the following three maturity classifications: short bonds (less than 3 years), intermediate bonds (3–12 years), and long bonds (greater than 12 years). Each cell in the table gives the upside (best case or scenario 1), downside (worst case or scenario 3), and composite total return for various allocations among the three maturity classifications. The columns indicate the percentage of the portfolio allocated to short bonds while the rows show the amount allocated to long bonds. For a given cell, the amount allocated to intermediate bonds is 100 percent minus the amount allocated to short and long bonds. For example, consider the cell representing 40 percent in short bonds and 10 percent in long bonds. Then 50 percent, of course, would be in intermediate bonds. For this allocation, the total return under the composite scenario is 10.8 percent. For the best case (denoted by "High" in the table) the total return would be 15.4 percent while for the worst case (denoted by "Low") it would be 6.7 percent.

The maturity management table is useful because it is easy for a manager to see the effect of reweighting the maturity composition of his portfolio. For example, the composition of the portfolio under analysis (as shown in the lower panel of Table 7–1) is 21.17 percent short bonds, 41.24 percent intermediate bonds and 37.59 percent long bonds. From Table 7–4, the portfolio summary, the composite total return is 10.79 percent and the best case (scenario 1) and worst case (scenario 3) total returns are 17.06 percent and 4.94 percent, respectively. If the portfolio is rebalanced to 30 percent short bonds, 40 percent intermediate bonds and 30 percent long bonds—which is essentially shifting the current portfolio

Figure 7–7
Strategic Frontier Analysis for Sample Portfolio of 150 Bonds: Best Case versus Worst Case

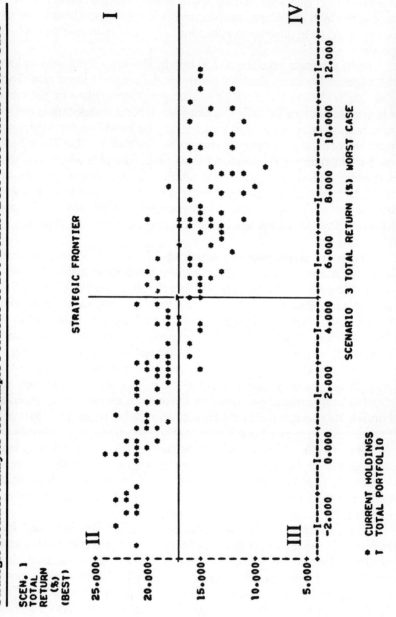

* CURRENT HOLDINGS
† TOTAL PORTFOLIO

Table 7–6
Scenario 1 Total Returns (Percent) for Quadrant I

Bond Number	Bond Name	Coupon Rate (percent)	Stated Maturity	Scenario: Probability:	1 33%	2 33%	3 33%	Composite
136	Commonwealth Edison Co.	15.3750%	3/15/00		20.2%	12.8%	5.7%	12.9%
20	Barclays North American Cap Corp.	14.6250	6/15/91		20.2	11.5	5.4	12.3
147	Philadelphia Electric Co.	13.7500	10/15/92		20.1	11.8	5.8	12.6
97	Phelps Dodge Corp.	8.1000	6/15/96		20.0	13.0	7.3	13.4
124	Southern California Edison Co.	15.2500	5/15/91		18.8	11.2	5.7	11.9
145	Pacific Power & Light Co.	10.7500	5/1/90		18.8	10.8	5.2	11.6
96	Walter Jim Corp.	9.5000	2/1/96		18.7	11.7	6.1	12.2
95	Inland Steel Co.	11.2500	6/1/90		18.2	12.5	8.5	13.1
49	Ford Motor Credit Co.	9.4500	6/15/89		17.5	11.4	7.1	12.0
50	Walter E. Heller & Co.	11.7500	7/15/90		17.5	11.2	6.7	11.8
94	American Stores Co. New	12.0000	6/1/90		17.1	11.4	7.4	12.0
	Quadrant mean	12.3608%	8/7/92		18.8%	11.7%	6.4%	12.3%

Table 7-7
Scenario 1 Rank Order and Range Plot

Total Return (percent)

Bond Number	Scenario: 1 33%	2 33%	3 33%	Composite
116	23.8	11.4	0.2	11.8
13	23.5	11.0	0.2	11.6
15	23.0	11.6	1.4	12.0
14	22.6	9.9	-1.2	10.4
113	22.5	9.1	-1.9	9.9
117	22.3	10.2	-0.9	10.5
114	22.2	9.4	-1.3	10.1
118	22.2	11.0	0.6	11.3
22	22.1	9.6	-1.6	10.0
115	22.0	9.8	-1.1	10.2
11	21.6	9.1	0.1	10.3
21	21.3	9.7	1.0	10.7
109	21.3	8.9	-2.6	9.2
150	21.3	13.1	4.9	13.1
107	21.3	8.8	-1.6	9.5
148	21.2	10.8	1.7	11.2
61	21.2	10.2	0.1	10.5
58	21.2	9.8	0.2	10.4
140	21.1	10.4	0.4	10.6
59	21.1	9.9	0.5	10.5
108	21.0	9.3	-1.4	9.6
137	21.0	10.0	0.7	10.6

Total Return (percent)

(Range plot with axis marks at 0.0, 5.0, 10.0, 15.0, 20.0; each bond plotted with markers "3", "2", "C", and "1" indicating scenario 3, scenario 2, composite, and scenario 1 returns respectively.)

ID					Dendrogram
62	21.0	10.5	0.6	10.7	3————————————C————————1
128	21.0	11.8	3.0	11.9	3—————————————C————1
139	20.9	11.4	2.5	11.6	3—————————————C————1
149	20.8	11.0	1.9	11.3	3—————————2C————1
60	20.8	9.4	-0.7	9.8	3————2C—————————1
138	20.8	10.9	1.6	11.1	3——————————C————1
126	20.7	9.9	0.4	10.4	2C————1
12	20.6	9.9	2.1	10.9	3—————2—C————1
125	20.6	10.0	1.9	10.9	3————————2—C————1
127	20.3	10.2	1.0	10.5	2C————1
136	20.2	12.8	5.7	12.9	3——————————C——1
20	20.2	11.5	5.4	12.3	3——————————2—C——1
35	12.4	11.7	11.3	11.8	3C1
24	12.4	10.5	8.9	10.6	3——C——1
55	12.4	9.5	6.4	9.4	3————C——1
76	12.4	10.0	8.8	10.4	3—2C——1
16	12.3	11.3	10.8	11.4	3C—1
23	11.9	10.6	10.1	10.8	32C—1
119	11.8	10.3	9.7	10.6	3—C——1
1	11.7	9.7	8.8	10.0	32C——1
130	11.5	10.9	10.5	11.0	3C1
18	11.1	9.5	8.7	9.8	3—2C—1
110	10.8	8.5	7.4	8.9	3——2C——1
54	10.8	9.9	8.1	9.6	3——C2—1
100	10.2	9.0	8.5	9.2	3C—1
143	8.7	10.2	9.0	9.3	13C2
Portfolio	**17.1**	**10.4**	**4.9**	**10.8**	3——————————2C————————1

Table 7–8
Maturity Management Table of Total Return Expectations for Varying Maturity Concentrations

Percent Short Bonds

Percent			0%	10%	20%	30%	40%	50%	60%	70%	80%	90%	100%
	100%	High	20.2										
		Low	1.6										
		Composite	10.7										
	90%	High	19.8	19.4									
		Low	2.0	2.4									
		Composite	10.7	10.8									
	80%	High	19.4	19.1	18.7								
		Low	2.4	2.8	3.2								
		Composite	10.7	10.8	10.8								
	70%	High	19.0	18.7	18.3	18.0							
		Low	2.8	3.2	3.6	3.9							
		Composite	10.7	10.8	10.8	10.8							
	60%	High	18.6	18.3	18.0	17.6	17.3						
		Low	3.3	3.6	4.0	4.3	4.7						
		Composite	10.7	10.8	10.8	10.8	10.8						

Long Bonds

		1	2	3	4	5	6	7	8	9	10	11
50%	High	18.3	17.9	17.6	17.2	16.9	16.5					
	Low	3.7	4.0	4.4	4.7	5.1	5.5					
	Composite	10.7	10.8	10.8	10.8	10.8	10.8					
40%	High	17.9	17.5	17.2	16.8	16.5	16.2	15.8				
	Low	4.1	4.4	4.8	5.2	5.5	5.9	6.2				
	Composite	10.7	10.8	10.8	10.8	10.8	10.8	10.9				
30%	High	17.5	17.2	16.8	16.5	16.1	15.8	15.4	15.1			
	Low	4.5	4.8	5.2	5.6	5.9	6.3	6.6	7.0			
	Composite	10.7	10.8	10.8	10.8	10.8	10.9	10.9	10.9			
20%	High	17.1	16.8	16.4	16.1	15.7	15.4	15.1	14.7	14.4		
	Low	4.9	5.3	5.6	6.0	6.3	6.7	7.1	7.4	7.8		
	Composite	10.7	10.8	10.8	10.8	10.8	10.9	10.9	10.9	10.9		
10%	High	16.7	16.4	16.0	15.7	15.4	15.0	14.7	14.3	14.0	13.6	
	Low	5.3	5.7	6.0	6.4	6.7	7.1	7.5	7.8	8.2	8.6	
	Composite	10.8	10.8	10.8	10.8	10.8	10.9	10.9	10.9	10.9	10.9	
0%	High	16.4	16.0	15.7	15.3	15.0	14.6	14.3	13.9	13.6	13.3	12.9
	Low	5.7	6.1	6.4	6.8	7.2	7.5	7.9	8.2	8.6	9.0	9.3
	Composite	10.8	10.8	10.8	10.8	10.8	10.9	10.9	10.9	10.9	10.9	11.0

holding from longs to shorts—then there will be an imperceptible change in the composite total return; however, the worst case total return is improved by 66 basis points (from 4.94 percent to 5.6 percent) while the best case declines by only 56 basis points (from 17.06 percent to 16.5 percent).

In addition to providing a useful tool to analyze the "risk/return" trade-off from portfolio rebalancing, the maturity management table allows a manager or sponsor to determine the alternative portfolio rebalancing necessary to achieve a minimum total return. For example, suppose a sponsor establishes a minimum portfolio return of 8.2 percent. By looking at the portfolio maturity composition that would produce a total return of at least 8.2 percent in the worst case, a manager could determine how the portfolio must be rebalanced. In this illustration, these are the five portfolios in the lower right hand corner of the table.

Although the foregoing analysis was performed utilizing maturities, the same could be performed using duration.

Timing. The timing of active strategies can be important. Over a given planning horizon, judgment is necessary to determine when a strategy is to be implemented. Figure 7–8 illustrates two common yield curve shapes. When the first curve (positively sloped) exists, and if it is interpreted as a forecast of higher future interest rates, the strategy taken must be carefully timed. To benefit from an ensuing rate increase, a shortening of maturity (duration) is called for. However, by moving to the left of the curve, a lower yield to maturity must be accepted. Premature rate anticipation under these circumstances would result in a lower realized return for the time frame before rates increase; if the increase never materializes, significant return give-up may be experienced.

Conversely, if the second curve (negatively sloped) prevails and rates are expected to decrease, again timing is important since a premature lengthening of maturity results in a lower yield to maturity with much riskier longer maturity (duration) portfolios. The conclusion is that effective timing of rate anticipation is a necessary and important consideration.

Moreover, rate anticipation should not be considered complete after the initial timing issue is resolved. When to reverse or modify the strategy must be continually considered. The return component interactions originally estimated will be constantly in flux, and the manager must continually balance anticipated capital changes against current yield and reinvestment return effects. This makes the "round-trip" character of successful rate anticipation apparent. That is, the rate anticipation efforts of the manager cannot be judged to be successful until the move taken in anticipation of any given rate increase (decrease) is reversed with a timely opposite move when rates are expected to decrease (increase). It should be pointed out, however, that the manager's performance is most appropriately judged

Figure 7–8
(a) Positive or Upward Sloping Yield Curves; (b) Negative or Downward Sloping Yield Curve.

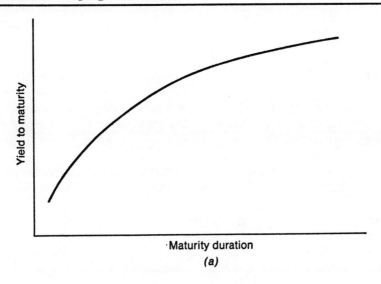

·Maturity duration
(a)

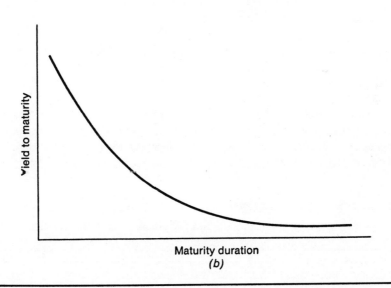

Maturity duration
(b)

over an entire interest rate cycle and in the context of the entire portfolio rather than on individual transactions.

In addition, other terms of a security should be analyzed, such as the effects of refunding terms. For example, suppose that in a scenario of rising rates the prepayment experience of GNMA securities (Ginnie Maes) is expected to decline as homeowners tend to want to hold on to lower interest rate mortgages. Conversely, if rates decline, there is an incentive to refinance; hence, higher refunding and shorter-lived Ginnie Maes can be expected. Forearmed with knowledge of the anticipated average life of a GNMA security under various interest rate scenarios, the manager can decide whether to embrace or avoid these securities with their potentially altered average maturity.

As another example, the call feature of bonds tends to be unused by issuers if rates rise because the issuer will not want to retire or refinance bonds issued at rates lower than current rates. As a result, callability is not of concern to the manager when scenarios call for rising rates. The opposite is true when rates are expected to fall. In such case, the issuer will have an incentive to retire callable bonds and refinance at lower rates.

Fortunately, all considerations can be integrated into the return simulation analysis described. This allows the manager to focus attention on the most important dimensions of direction, shape, and timing of interest rate change.

Interest rate forecasting in Canada and the United States may be thought of as a good example of an activity associated with a highly efficient market. That is, wide distribution of information, low transaction costs, and many intelligent participants contribute to the difficulty of consistently and correctly forecasting the direction of rate changes. This does not say that some people cannot do it well, but it does suggest success will be extremely difficult to achieve on a consistent basis. However, the rewards of being right are great, not only in terms of realized returns, but in the amount of investment management business one can accrue. Unfortunately the converse is also true.

Sector/Security Strategies

Beyond rate anticipation, there is the possibility of enhancing returns relative to risk by evaluating individual securities and subgroups of securities. This takes three basic forms: credit analysis, spread analysis, and bond valuation, each of which is discussed below.

Credit analysis. Credit analysis is concerned with the assessment of default risk—the probability that the issuer will be unable to meet all contractual obligations fully and in a timely manner. Default risk is important for two reasons. The first is the chance of loss due to actual acts of default. The second is the likelihood of adverse bond price changes that are precipitated by the increased probability of default, typically via downgrading of a bond's quality by the rating agencies, even though no act of default actually takes place.

Default risk has both systematic and unsystematic elements. For a variety of reasons, individual bond issuers may experience difficulty in meeting their obligations from time to time. If these are isolated acts of default, they may be diversified away or be eliminated by effective credit analysis. More worrisome is the possibility of adverse general business conditions, such as occurred during the 1930s, the mid-1970s, and in the early 1980s, which are associated with significant increases in the frequency of acts of default and widespread price declines due to concern over credit quality. This event requires more macro-oriented analysis. Default was a real concern in 1981–82 because of the steady deterioration in the coverage of interest charges by corporate earnings over the preceding decade.

Risk of default is often quantified by quality ratings provided by Duff & Phelps, Moody's, and Standard & Poor's. Historically, such ratings have proved to be valid, but they are not foolproof indicators of default risk. An excellent recent example of this is the Washington Public Power Supply System (WPPSS) bonds. In the early 1980s both Standard & Poor's and Moody's gave these bonds their highest ratings. While these ratings were in effect, WPPSS sold over $8 billion in long-term bonds. By June of 1983, they did not rate any of the issues. In July of 1983, WPPSS defaulted on its Projects 4 and 5 bonds. In fact, since 1975 all of the major municipal debt defaults initially had been given investment grade ratings.[3]

Quality ratings also appear to be closely related to other traditional measures of credit quality, such as relative debt burden, interest or fixed charges expense coverage (by earnings before deduction of interest and tax expenses), and variability in earnings streams. However, many sophisticated, fixed income investors—such as bond funds, insurance companies, investment banking firms, and bank trust departments—do not rely exclusively on the rating agencies; they also engage in their own credit analysis.[4] There are two reasons for this activity, both of which are based on the assumption that yields in the marketplace are closely correlated to agency ratings, *ceteris paribus*.

---

[3] For a further discussion, see the preface to Sylvan G. Feldstein, Frank J. Fabozzi, and Irving M. Pollack, eds., *The Municipal Bond Handbook: Volume II* (Homewood, Ill.: Dow Jones-Irwin, 1983), pp. vii–x.

[4] For a detailed discussion of credit analysis, see Jane Tripp Howe, "Credit Analysis for Corporate Bonds," Chapter 14 in *The Handbook of Fixed Income Securities*, ed. Frank J. Fabozzi and Irving M. Pollack (Homewood, Ill.: Dow Jones-Irwin, 1983), and Feldstein, Fabozzi, and Pollack, eds., *The Municipal Bond Handbook: Volume II.*, Sections 3–5.

1. The analyst's assessment of credit quality may be more accurate and/or timely than those of the rating agencies. In this case the portfolio manager can achieve added yield at relatively small cost in terms of credit risk exposure, or can avoid paying in terms of reduced yield for nonexistent incremental quality.

2. The timely review of ratings outstanding is believed to be one of the greatest difficulties facing investors and the rating companies. A commercial rating company may have as many as 20,000 ratings outstanding. Consequently, a substantial delay may occur between published reviews of ratings. With astute credit analysis it may be possible to anticipate such upgrades or downgrades and profit from the yield and price changes which may ensue.

Spread analysis. Spread analysis involves sectoral relationships. It may be possible to identify subclasses of fixed income securities that tend to behave in a highly similar manner. For example, prices and yields on lower investment-grade bonds tend to move together, as do yields on utility bonds. Such identifiable classes of securities are referred to as sectors. (In this sense maturity ranges are also sectors, but the influence of maturity on total return is so dramatic that yield/maturity analysis is usually treated separately.) Relative prices or yields among sectors may change due to (1) altered perceptions of the creditworthiness of a sector or of the market's sensitivity to default risk; (2) changes in the market's valuation of some attribute or characteristic of the securities in the sector, such as a zero coupon feature; (3) changes in supply and demand conditions.

Analysis of relative sectoral relationships coupled with appropriate management response can be rewarding in fixed income portfolio management. The objective, obviously, is to be heavily invested in the sector or sectors that will display the strongest relative price movements. In monitoring such sectoral relationships, it is customary to concentrate on spreads—i.e., the difference, usually measured in basis points, in yield between two sectors—among yield series that are broadly representative of the securities in the sector. A number of brokerage firms maintain such yield series on a historical basis so that abnormal differences can be identified. These firms are usually able to conduct specialized analyses for clients, such as measurement of the historical average, and maximum and minimum spread among sectors. Such analysis, plus consideration of other relevant factors, leads to what is, in effect, a relative valuation of a sector's worth. If the relative values are enough out of line, the results will be arbitragelike sector swapping so as to obtain the largest gain or smallest loss as sector yields return to more normal relationships.

In both credit analysis and spread analysis the potential for return enhancement, while dominated by gains from proper rate anticipation, still holds the promise of a significant contribution to portfolio objectives. The drawbacks may include the need to do many trades for the contribution to be meaningful, and the danger that overall changes in interest rates will dwarf these efforts.

Valuation analysis. Bond valuation is a relatively recent approach to active management. The essence of bond valuation is the ability to evaluate the difference between the actual yield and default-free yield that constitutes the yield premium. What a manager wants to be able to do, for example, in evaluating a corporate bond, is determine what the yield premium on that bond is; ascertain what the components of that yield premium are; define what the normal values for that yield premium are; and then compare the normal or normalized value of that bond's yield with its actual yield. The difference is the bond's over- or undervaluation, depending on whether it is a negative or positive difference.

The yield premium is basically a compensation to the investor for a number of things such as default risk, issuer options, and tax effects. So the problem in bond valuation is to attribute a value to each of these factors and any others that are significant.

One approach to bond valuation is to first estimate the term structure of default-free interest rates as of any given date from the prices on U.S. Treasury issues using the term structure analysis discussed in Chapter 2 and Appendix D. The estimated term structure can be used to price any default-free security as of that date. By pricing a security we mean determining its dollar price or market value that corresponds to the current structure of rates.

The term structure of default-free rates, however, is not sufficient to determine the market value of risky securities, such as corporate bonds. Unlike the Treasury issues, the promised payments on corporate securities are not certain to be received by the bondholder. The payments are subject to the risk of default, calls, sinking fund redemptions, and other contingencies. To value a corporate bond, these factors have to be incorporated. Using a regression model, the market value of a corporate bond that is consistent with the current structures of rates and with the market valuation of the risk elements of the instrument can be estimated. The model first determines the yield premia attributable to the quality rating of the bond, industrial classification of the issuer, call schedule and sinking fund features of the issue, and other relevant attributes.[5] This is accom-

---

[5] The explanatory variables in the regression model would be both qualitative and quantitative. Qualitative variables such as issuing sector and quality would be included by means of "dummy" or "binary" variables. The value of a call option and sinking fund feature to be included as a quantitative variable is not straightforward. What can be done is to estimate a theoretical value based on the modern theory of option pricing applied to a stochastic model of the term structure. The theoretical values of the call and sinking fund schedules, obtained by solving a partial differential equation, serve as explanatory variables in the least squares regression to determine the market valuation of these attributes. This is, in fact, the procedure employed to estimate the regression parameters shown in Table 7-9.

plished by simultaneous least-squares regression of the actual yields in excess of the default-free yields on a sample universe of corporate bonds. Once the current market valuation of the various bond attributes has been estimated, the value of any given bond can be determined by adding the yield premia corresponding to its characteristics to the appropriate default-free yield.

Table 7–9 presents the regression results for a valuation model based on 2,656 issues on July 31, 1983.[6] Dealer prices for the sample were obtained from Lehman Brothers. Overall, the 32 explanatory variables— 30 qualitative and 2 quantitative—explained 98.5 percent of the total variation in the yield premia of the sample. Only two of the explanatory variables—the qualitative variables AAA Industrials and zero coupon—are not statistically significant at any reasonable level as indicated by the t-statistic in the last column of Table 7–9. The other 30 explanatory variables are significant at the 1 percent level of significance.[7]

Notice that the sign and relative magnitude of the quality variable coefficients is that which theory would predict (i.e., it increases as the quality decreases). For example, for AAA electric utilities, the valuation model indicates that there should be a yield premium due to quality of 53.7 basis points. For AA electric utilities, the yield premium increases to 72.7 basis points. For the lowest rated electric utilities investigated by the model, BAA electric utilities, the yield premium should be 153.4 basis points.

Once the coefficients of the valuation model have been estimated, a fitted value for each bond in the universe under investigation can be computed. Table 7–10 shows the results for 15 issues under investigation. The fitted value and actual value are in terms of both price and yield. The difference between the actual value and the fitted value is the residual. When measured in terms of price (yield), a positive (negative) residual means that the issue is overvalued. A negative (positive) residual when price (yield) is used means that the issue is undervalued. To determine whether the residual is statistically significant, a t-statistic can be computed for each issue. The only two undervalued issues at any reasonable level of statistical significance of the 15 shown in Table 7–10 are Transamerica

---

[6] The original sample consisted of 2,992 issues. However, 252 issues were eliminated because of the unavailability of call data and 84 because of outliers in a first pass regression. The elimination of outliers is admittedly subjective and may, in fact, compromise one of the purposes of the exercise which is to identify mispriced issues.

[7] It is interesting to note that if the theoretical value of the call option is the same value as that assigned by market agents, the coefficient will not be statistically different from one. The estimated coefficient is .281 or 28.1 basis points. Thus, the market values the call option at much less than the theoretical value. In estimating the valuation model for other periods, the coefficient of the call option variable has ranged from .15 to 1.

Table 7–9
Regression Results for a Valuation Model Based on 2,656 Issues on July 31, 1983

Number of bonds in the universe	2,992
Number of bonds excluded	
Incorrect price data	0
Call data not available	252
Outliers	84
Number of bonds used in estimation	2,656

Average yield	12.297	Average price	83.952
Standard deviation of yield	0.953	Standard deviation of price	19.204
Average yield premium	0.678	Average price premium	−3.674
Standard deviation of yield premium	0.753	Standard deviation of price premium	4.630
Residual standard error of yield	0.516	Residual standard error of price	2.335
		R-square	0.985

Number	Variable	Coefficient	Standard Error	t-Statistic
1	Government agency	0.052	0.023	2.310
2	AAA Industrial	0.058	0.074	0.781
3	AA Industrial	0.415	0.044	9.423
4	A Industrial	0.737	0.034	21.677
5	BAA Industrial	1.206	0.063	19.206
6	AA Telephone	0.422	0.052	8.147
7	A Telephone	0.693	0.044	15.616
8	BAA Telephone	1.370	0.123	11.176
9	AAA Electric utility	0.537	0.172	3.122
10	AA Electric utility	0.727	0.058	12.521
11	A Electric utility	1.143	0.047	24.273
12	BAA Electric utility	1.534	0.047	32.769
13	AA Other utility	0.807	0.089	9.079
14	A Other utility	0.921	0.060	15.248
15	BAA Other utility	1.496	0.111	13.438
16	AAA Finance	0.371	0.143	2.590
17	AA Finance	0.274	0.040	6.892
18	A Finance	0.736	0.055	13.295
19	BAA Finance	1.192	0.093	12.795
20	AAA Transportation	1.018	0.172	5.917
21	AA Transport	0.407	0.084	4.856
22	A Transportation	0.779	0.060	13.064
23	BAA Transport	0.990	0.156	6.360
24	AAA Canadian	0.925	0.065	14.330
25	AA Canadian	1.041	0.076	13.672
26	A Canadian	1.403	0.051	27.301
27	BAA Canadian	1.918	0.143	13.396
28	AAA Foreign	0.572	0.059	9.724
29	AA Foreign	0.815	0.172	4.738
30	Current yield	0.023	0.002	11.116
31	Zero coupon	0.028	0.058	0.478
32	Call option	0.281	0.015	18.837

Table 7-10
Fitted Value and Residual on July 31, 1973, from Bond Valuation Model

		Default-Free	Issuing Sector	Quality	Current Yield	Call Effect	Fitted Value	Actual Value	Residual	t-Statistic
17 Standard Oil Co. Indiana 8.375% 6/15/5 O1 A	Price ($)	74.373	-0.354	0.0	-1.179	-2.972	69.868	70.975	1.107	-0.42
	Yield (%)	11.626	0.058	0.0	0.196	0.518	12.397	12.200	-0.197	
18 J.C. Penney Company Inc. 6.000% 5/1/6 I3 C	Price ($)	55.242	-0.281	-3.134	-0.608	0.0	51.219	50.750	-0.469	0.23
	Yield (%)	11.635	0.058	0.680	0.140	0.0	12.512	12.622	0.110	
19 British Columbia Hydro & Power 8.625% 12/1/6 X1 A	Price ($)	76.008	-3.482	0.0	-1.160	0.0	71.366	69.697	-1.669	0.63
	Yield (%)	11.626	0.572	0.0	0.201	0.0	12.400	12.700	0.300	
20 Caterpillar Tractor Co. 6.000% 5/1/7 I2 T	Price ($)	54.848	-0.280	-1.681	-0.634	0.0	52.254	50.000	-2.254	1.11
	Yield (%)	11.634	0.058	0.357	0.140	0.0	12.190	12.712	0.523	
21 Northern Indiana Public Service Co. 8.500% 11/1/7 E3 V	Price ($)	74.814	-3.248	-3.373	-1.044	-2.708	64.440	65.963	1.523	-0.65
	Yield (%)	11.626	0.537	0.606	0.198	0.542	13.509	13.200	-0.309	
22 St. Regis Paper Co. 10.625% 6/15/10 I3 U	Price ($)	91.794	-0.436	-4.871	-1.663	-5.677	79.147	78.730	-0.417	0.15
	Yield (%)	11.624	0.058	0.680	0.248	0.919	13.528	13.600	0.072	
23 St. Regis Paper Co. 10.625% 6/15/10 I3 U	Price ($)	91.794	-0.436	-4.871	-1.663	-5.677	79.147	78.730	-0.417	0.15
	Yield (%)	11.624	0.058	0.680	0.248	0.919	13.528	13.600	0.072	

Transamerica Financial Corp. 6.500% 3/15/11 F3 C	Price ($) Yield (%)	57.805 11.632	−1.838 0.371	−1.706 0.365	−0.682 0.152	0.0 0.0	53.579 12.519	53.500 12.537	−0.079 0.018	0.04
25										
General Foods Corp. 7.000% 6/15/11 I2 S	Price ($) Yield (%)	61.872 11.631	−0.310 0.058	−1.861 0.357	−0.817 0.163	−2.235 0.469	56.648 12.678	57.250 12.549	0.602 −0.130	−0.27
26										
Kerr McGee Corp. 7.000% 11/1/11 I3 U	Price ($) Yield (%)	61.795 11.630	−0.310 0.058	−3.450 0.680	−0.777 0.163	0.0 0.0	57.258 12.531	55.750 12.860	−1.508 0.329	0.70
27										
Washington D.C. Metropolitan Area Tm. 7.350% 7/1/12 AG A	Price ($) Yield (%)	64.586 11.630	−0.293 0.052	0.0 0.0	−0.942 0.172	0.0 0.0	63.351 11.854	62.834 11.950	−0.517 0.096	0.20
28										
Transamerica Financial 0.0% 9/1/12 F3 C	Price ($) Yield (%)	3.640 11.719	−0.353 0.371	−0.313 0.365	−0.023 0.028	0.0 0.0	2.952 12.483	4.086 11.299	1.134 −1.184	−2.50
29										
Southwestern Bell Telephone Co. 7.625% 10/1/13 T3 U	Price ($) Yield (%)	66.683 11.629	0.0 0.0	−3.795 0.693	−0.910 0.178	−2.537 0.523	59.442 13.023	61.478 12.600	2.036 −0.423	−0.89
30										
Bell Telephone Co. Pennsylvania 9.625% 7/15/14 T2 S	Price ($) Yield (%)	83.297 11.626	0.0 0.0	−2.881 0.422	−1.461 0.225	−4.885 0.812	74.070 13.085	77.221 12.550	3.151 −0.535	−1.13
31										
South Central Bell Telephone Co. 9.875% 9/15/18 T3 C	Price ($) Yield (%)	85.196 11.626	0.0 0.0	−4.768 0.693	−1.475 0.231	−5.414 0.923	73.539 13.473	78.329 12.650	4.790 −0.823	−1.74

Financial's zeros of 2012 and South Central Bell Telephone's 9.875s of 2018.

In addition to its usefulness in identifying mispriced issues, bond valuation is a useful tool in performance measurement, as discussed later in this chapter.

■ Portfolio Optimization

Portfolio optimization can be thought of as a strategy for quantifying the optimal integration of return and risk expectations with desired portfolio objectives and policy. It may include either a modification of an existing portfolio or the creation of an entirely new one.

Portfolio optimization serves as a focal point for much of what we have covered previously in this chapter. Moreover, it may be considered the epitome of the active portfolio management process. The portfolio manager begins with a basic set of expectations in the form of expected rates of return, and proceeds to structure a portfolio, taking into account the needs of the client in the form of desired portfolio parameters. These parameters are a direct result of identifying the preferences and requirements of the client, as well as the style and emphasis of the manager. Examples of these considerations include a minimum yield objective, minimum and/or maximum concentration constraints, desired duration range or level, and minimum portfolio return requirement.

The objective of portfolio optimization may be expressed as maximizing the return of the portfolio for a given level of acceptable risk. The expected returns come directly from the expectations that are provided. The estimate of risk is not so straightforward. Two alternative portfolio optimization approaches are suggested below. They differ primarily in their treatment of risk.

Variance/Covariance Approach

The variance/covariance approach is akin to the traditional Markowitz formulation that was discussed in Chapter 4 to assist managers in making the asset allocation decision. In most equity optimization approaches, the standard deviation or variance of portfolio returns has been used as the risk objective to be minimized. The process for equities involves creating a covariance matrix that, along with expectations of stock returns, is then optimized by a quadratic optimization program. Including such things as turnover, concentration, and dividend yield constraints, a minimum risk portfolio for a given level of return is produced. The problem is tractable since the creation of the covariance matrix can always resort to an estimate based upon historical return experience.

In bond analysis, however, no such convention is available. Because of the finite life of a fixed income security, its covariance characteristic with other bonds changes with time, if for no other reason than just because the maturity of each bond becomes shorter with time. Moreover, with a given rate change, there can be yield curve shape changes as well as direction changes. The latter can alter, and in some cases reverse, the covariance relationship between securities. The problem thus becomes one of estimation. Indeed, if a covariance matrix could be created, then the optimization process could parallel the analysis for stock.

Worst Case Approach

An alternative approach to portfolio optimization is the worst case approach. Using this approach, the estimated returns—specifically the interest rate scenario with the lowest returns—serve as the measure of risk. The portfolio is then structured by the optimization process to achieve at least the worst case scenario return while simultaneously maximizing the return of another scenario. In other words, if a manager were to do a scenario projection of expected rates of return of the portfolio, the worst case return of the scenarios being used would be the measure of risk, and the optimization process would try to enhance return over and above this identified risk level. However, one of the problems of this approach is its dependence on the particular scenarios being used.

There are four main inputs required for optimization. The first is an objective or objective function which the analysis will seek to maximize. This is expressed as the total return of any scenario or the composite return or any return components. The essence of the analysis will be to maximize this return element while conforming to the other three input classes. The second category of input is the cash flow to be invested at the beginning of the period. The third input category is concerned with constraint specifications. Constraints come from the following four sources: (1) return policy constraints, (2) portfolio duration constraints, (3) upper concentration limit on any security, and (4) individual security limits. These constraints permit the implementation of policy guidelines which seek to control portfolio characteristics. Because the analytical procedure is linear, it allows a computationally more efficient algorithm via a linear programming optimization than the variance/covariance approach.

Tables 7–11, 7–12, and 7–13 present the results of the portfolio optimization process using scenario 2 as the worst case scenario for the sample portfolio of 150 bonds used throughout this chapter. Thus, the objective is to maximize total return for scenario 2. Table 7–11 sets forth the constraint data. Although portfolio inflows or outflows can be accommodated within this approach, none are assumed in this illustration. The projected portfolio performances for the current and optimized portfolio are presented in Table 7–12. The next to the last column of Table 7–13

Table 7-11
Bond Portfolio Optimization: Constraint Data

Objective: Maximize total portfolio return for scenario 2
Current date: 12/31/82
Projection date: 12/31/83

Constraints

1. No cash contribution to current market value of total portfolio: $0.0

2. Return policy constraints

Portfolio Return Component	Scenario	Relationship	Return Requirement	Optimized Portfolio	Imputed Cost* (b.p.)
Total (unadjusted)	3	Greater than or equal to	5.00%	6.50%	0.0%
Total (unadjusted)	1	Greater than or equal to	17.06%	18.12%	0.0%

Upper concentration limit on any security: (unless individual limit is specified)   5% of total portfolio market value

3. Special security group concentration constraints (percent of total market value)

Identification Number of Issues Included in Constrained Group

46	47	48	49	50	51	52	53	77	79	88	89
90	91	93	94	95	96	97	98	99	142	143	144
145	146	147	148	149	150						

Concentration

Minimum	Maximum	Required to Optimize	Imputed Cost* (b.p.)
0.0%	25.0%	25.0%	1.72U

4. Quality rating may not be less than A

* The imputed cost (also called the shadow price) is a by-product of the linear programming solution. For small changes in a constraint, it indicates the impact on the optimal solution. The designation "U" indicates that it was the constraint's upper bound that was binding.

Table 7-12
Bond Portfolio Optimization: Projected Portfolio Performance

Objective: Maximize total portfolio return for scenario 2
Current date: 12/31/82
Projection date: 12/31/83

Projected Portfolio Performance

	Matured Bonds		Called Bonds			Portfolio Return on Beginning Market Value (percent)								
	Face Value ($000)	Reinvestment Interest ($000)	Face Value ($000)	Redemption Value ($000)	Reinvestment Interest ($000)	Yield Change Impact	Time (Roll) Impact	Spread Change Impact	Earned Interest	Coupon Reinvestment	Matured Called	Matured/Called Reinvestment	Total	Annual Total
						Current Portfolio								
Scenario 1	0	0.0	5000	5000.000	202.833	5.68	0.88	−0.97	10.96	0.29	0.07	0.15	17.06	16.39
Scenario 2	0	0.0	0	0.0	0.0	−1.88	0.92	−0.13	11.12	0.33	0.0	0.0	10.37	10.11
Scenario 3	0	0.0	0	0.0	0.0	−7.97	0.92	0.52	11.12	0.35	0.0	0.0	4.94	4.88
Composite	0	0.0	1667	1666.666	67.611	−1.39	0.91	−0.19	11.07	0.32	0.02	0.05	10.79	10.51
						Optimized Portfolio with Transactions Rounded to Nearest 100 Bonds								
Scenario 1	0	0.0	1000	1000.000	11.276	5.25	0.89	−0.77	12.35	0.38	0.02	0.01	18.12	17.36
Scenario 2	0	0.0	0	0.0	0.0	−1.59	0.90	−0.13	12.36	0.41	0.0	0.0	11.94	11.60
Scenario 3	0	0.0	0	0.0	0.0	−7.58	0.90	0.39	12.36	0.42	0.0	0.0	6.50	6.39
Composite	0	0.0	333	333.333	3.759	−1.31	0.90	−0.17	12.36	0.40	0.01	0.00	12.18	11.83

Table 7-13
Bond Portfolio Optimization: Changes Required to Optimize (purchases in order of decreasing change in market value)

Objective: Maximize total portfolio return for scenario 2
Current date: 12/31/82
Projection date: 12/31/83

Current Par Value ($000)	Current Weights (percent)	Optimal Par Value ($000)	Optimal Weights (percent)	Rounded Change In Par Value ($000)	Change In Market Value ($000)	Description of Security	Expected Return			Transaction Cost	
							Objective Component (percent)	Total Composite (percent)	Constraint Impact on Portfolio (Imputed Cost) (bp/bd)	As Return Component (percent)	Net Total Composite Return (percent)
1000.0	0.431%	11600.0	4.997%	10600.0	6333.5	Phelps Dodge Corp. 8.1000% 6/15/96 59.750 BAA2 97	13.0%	13.4%	0.000U	-0.228%	13.2%
1000.0	0.697	7200.0	5.022	6200.0	5998.4	American Savings & Loan Association California 8.5000% 4/15/84 96.748 AAA 116	11.3	11.4	0.000U	-0.215	11.2
1000.0	0.674	7400.0	4.987	6400.0	5982.0	Texas Power & Light Co. 11.3750% 5/ 1/10 93.469 AAA 46	11.4	11.8	0.000U	-0.216	11.6
1000.0	0.674	7400.0	4.986	6400.0	5981.8	Ford Motor Credit Co. 9.5000% 1/15/85 93.465 BAA2	12.9	13.3	0.000U	-0.216	13.1

1000.0	0.694	7200.0	5.001	6200.0	5973.5	AVCO Financial Services Inc. 8.5000% 4/15/84 96.347 A3 35	11.7	11.8	0.000U	−0.215	11.6
1000.0	0.717	7000.0	5.021	6000.0	5970.0	Federal Home Loan Mortgage Corp. 12.4500% 9/15/4 99.500 AAA 15 139	11.6	12.0	0.000U	−0.214	11.8
1000.0	0.683	7300.0	4.986	6300.0	5968.6	Carolina Power & Light Co. 12.2500% 11/1/9 94.739 A2 148	11.4	11.6	0.000U	−0.216	11.4
1000.0	0.470	0.0	0.0	−1000.0	−652.7	Alabama Power Co. 7.8750% 4/1/2 65.274 BAA1 113	10.8	11.2	0.001L	0.0	0.0
1000.0	0.443	0.0	0.0	−1000.0	−614.5	American Telephone & Telegraph Co. 6.0000% 8/1/0 61.447 AAA 19	9.1	9.9	0.001L	0.0	0.0
1000.0	0.407	0.0	0.0	−1000.0	−565.0	IBM Credit Corp. 0.0 % 7/15/88 56.500 AAA 85	8.6	9.7	0.001L	0.0	0.0
1000.0	0.389	0.0	0.0	−1000.0	−540.0	J.C. Penney Company Inc. 6.0000% 5/1/6 54.000 A1	9.4	9.6	0.000L	0.0	0.0
	100.000		100.000	−6700.0	−61.4	Totals for optimized portfolio	11.9	12.2		−0.393	11.8

shows the total return of the portfolios for each scenario. Notice that for each scenario and for the composite, there is an expected improvement of the total return by using the optimization process. The improvement is the result of the changes in the portfolio indicated in Table 7–13. This table shows the purchases and sales, expected returns associated for each change, and the transaction costs.[8]

■ Other Active Strategies or Tactics

In addition to the active strategies already discussed, a number of other approaches may be identified. While their potential impact on total portfolio return may not be as great, they still may make a significant contribution and for many managers represent a chosen expertise.

Total Realized Compound Yield[9]

As we explained in Chapter 2, implicit in the yield to maturity of a fixed income security is the ability to reinvest coupon payments at the same rate. If the reinvestment rate is different, then the actual realized return will diverge considerably from the promised yield. In maximizing the total return, the management of cash flow is therefore important, and increasingly so the longer the time horizon. Part of the problem is the ability to reinvest what may be relatively small amounts of funds, since transaction costs and available investment alternatives may be unfavorable. Return simulation analysis can be a useful tool for determining the optimal strategy for reinvesting bond portfolio cash flow; it requires expectations of the direction, shape, and timing of interest rate (yield curve) changes.

---

[8] A by-product of the linear programming solution to the bond portfolio optimization problem is information about how the relaxation of a constraint will impact the optimal solution. This is called the imputed cost or shadow price of a constraint and is appropriate for only very small changes of a constraint. When a constraint is binding, the imputed cost or shadow price will be nonzero. If there is a positive value, the optimization suggests relaxation of the upper bound of the constraint. Conversely, if the value is negative, that suggests the lowering of the lower bound of the constraint. For example, the limitation on the constrained group of securities shown in Table 7–11 is that it may not exceed 25 percent. In the optimal solution, this constraint is binding because the amount required to optimize is 25 percent. The imputed cost or shadow price for this constraint, as shown in Table 7–11, is 1.72 basis points. This is interpreted as follows. If the constraint is increased from 25 percent to 26 percent, the optimal solution will increase by 1.72 basis points. For a nonbinding constraint, the imputed cost or shadow price is zero because the relaxation of a nonbinding constraint will not increase the value of the optimal solution.

[9] For a further discussion of this approach, see Martin L. Leibowitz, "Total Aftertax Bond Performance and Yield Measures for Taxable Bonds held in Taxable Portfolios," Chapter 28 in *The Handbook of Fixed Income Securities,* ed. Fabozzi and Pollack, and Martin L. Leibowitz, "Total Aftertax Bond Performance and Yield Measures for Tax-Exempt Bonds Held in Taxable Portfolios" Chapter 32 in *The Municipal Bond Handbook: Volume I,* ed. Fabozzi, Feldstein, Pollack, and Zarb.

Trades or Exchanges[10]

Pure yield pickup trade or exchange. Switching to a security having a higher yield is called a pure yield trade or exchange (sometimes referred to by other writers as swaps). The transaction may be made to achieve either a higher coupon yield or a larger yield to maturity. It would appear that such transactions would always be done as long as there is no significant shift in risk level (or liquidity). However, accounting rules or regulatory mandates constrain some investors from yield pickup trades that create a loss, usually unless offset by a gain elsewhere in the portfolio, even though a portfolio benefit would result.

Substitution trade or exchange. This transaction involves substituting one security for another that has a higher yield to maturity but is otherwise identical in terms of maturity, coupon, and quality. This type of trade depends on a capital market imperfection. As such, the portfolio manager expects the yields to maturity on the two securities to reestablish a normal yield spread relationship, usually resulting in a price increase and hence capital appreciation for the holder of the higher yielding issue. The workout period (time for the expected realignment in yields to occur) can be critical, since the sooner it occurs the greater the return on an annualized basis; if the security must be held to maturity, the realized annual return may be marginal.

Intermarket or sector spread trade or exchange. Based on the expected normal yield relationship between two different sectors of the bond market, trades may be made when there is a perceived misalignment. This may involve switching to the higher yielding security when the yield spread is too wide and is expected to narrow, and to the lower yielding security when the spread is too narrow and is expected to widen. The risk, especially of the latter switch, is that the anticipated adjustment will not be made, resulting in a reduced portfolio yield.

Maturity-Spacing Strategies

Alternative portfolio maturity structures may be used. These include a balanced maturity schedule with equal spacing of maturities held; an all-short or all-long maturity strategy; or a *barbell* structure, where bond holdings are concentrated in short maturities and long maturities, with the intermediates of lesser or no importance. The rationale for an equal-maturity portfolio is to provide the portfolio with some reinvestment risk protec-

---

[10] For a further discussion, see Sidney Homer and Martin L. Leibowitz, *Inside the Yield Book* (Englewood Cliffs, N.J.: Prentice-Hall, 1972), Chapters 6 and 7; and Christina Seix, "Bond Swaps," Chapter 30 in *The Handbook of Fixed Income Securities*.

tion, spreading out reinvestment over the full interest rate cycle. That is, there will be a relatively continuous cash flow over time from maturity *laddering,* and these funds can be reinvested at the then current rates. The effects of overall interest rate change will tend to be averaged and the extremes of return and risk will be truncated. An all-short or all-long maturity portfolio strategy is frequently a temporary strategy adopted as a result of rate (change) anticipation, but it is a strategy of potentially large reinvestment rate risk. For a manager who stays with an all-short portfolio there is usually either a preference for high liquidity or an extreme aversion to principal risk. A barbell approach anticipates that the best return-risk reward is achieved by balancing the defensive qualities of short-term securities with the aggressive qualities of long-term securities and avoiding the intermediates.

There is no assurance from empirical testing of these various strategies that any one has been consistently superior over time.[11]

Consistency of Style

As a general observation, consistency of management style is important. Given the range of strategies and expertise required, it is important to identify the style that is compatible with the investment policy established for the portfolio or is most effective for the portfolio management organization. Pursuing this style with emphasis should provide the best results. This is not to say that other strategies should be neglected. In some cases there should be attempts at insulating the portfolio from the effects of interest rate change or quality effects; in other cases there might be some attempts at, say, substitution trading. The point is that consistency of management style, assuming the rationale for that style has been carefully thought through, should provide the best results over time and therefore should be stressed.

■ Bond Performance and Analysis

As this topic suggests, there are two activities to address. One is the measurement of performance. Explaining how the actual portfolio return was achieved is also an important objective of performance analysis and is the second activity of concern.

---

[11] See, for example, Russell H. Fogler and William A. Groves, "How Much Can Active Bond Management Raise Returns?" *The Journal of Portfolio Management,* Fall 1976, pp. 35–40; and Russell H. Fogler, William A. Groves, and James G. Richardson, "Managing Bonds: Are 'Dumbells' Smart?" *The Journal of Portfolio Management,* Winter 1976, pp. 54–60.

Performance measurement has evolved in response to changing information requirements of those reviewing performance. In the early versions, the issues concerned the appropriate measure of total return. Paralleling developments in the equity sector, the first measure used for bond portfolios was the *dollar-weighted rate of return* (or *internal rate of return*). This was a useful measure for determining the changes in fund size from one date to another. However, the need to evaluate relative performance by developing a measure which would allow comparisons between portfolios in the face of different cash flow patterns ushered in use of the *time-weighted rate of return* measure.[12] To date, this is probably the most widely used measure of total return performance.

Of growing interest is the partitioning of overall portfolio return into components that shed light on the genesis of performance. Understanding the sources of the return of a portfolio can help in monitoring the management process' effectiveness and in identifying its strengths and weaknesses. The manager can evaluate the consequences of the decision-making process more effectively. A framework providing sources of return may also serve as a communication aid for clients or for marketing purposes. For the portfolio sponsor, this analysis provides insight into where and how much contribution to return has been made from the various sources. This is useful again as an aid to communication and also in the selection of managers by desired skill or style.

An example of this type of analysis is risk-adjusted performance measurement of equity portfolios. By identifying that part of total return due to overall market returns and that part of total return due to stock selection, equity portfolio performance measurement has contributed to understanding the origins of performance. This type of breakdown allows a segregation of return due to the amount of market and nonmarket risk assumed, and, after sufficient history is evaluated, patterns concerning the market timing and stock selection capabilities of the manager. Professor Eugene Fama has provided a framework for an even finer breakdown of how portfolio return can be partitioned into constituent components for equity portfolios.[13] Subsequent research has provided extensions of Fama's framework for measuring the components of total return for equity portfolios.[14]

---

[12] Bank Administration Institute, *Measuring the Investment Performance of Pension Funds* (Park Ridge, Ill.: Bank Administration Institute, 1968).

[13] Eugene F. Fama, "Components of Investment Performance," *Journal of Finance,* June 1972, pp. 551–67.

[14] See, for example, Stanley J. Kon and Frank C. Jen, "The Investment Performance of Mutual Funds: An Empirical Investigation of Timing, Selectivity and Market Efficiency," April 1979, pp. 551–67; and Stanley J. Kon, "The Market Timing Performance of Mutual Fund Managers," *The Journal of Business,* July 1983, pp. 323–47.

The components analysis framework for bond portfolio performance discussed in this chapter was developed by Fong, Pearson, and Vasicek.[15] The approach is based on the recent investment technologies described earlier in this chapter—namely, security repricing based on term structure analysis and valuation analysis—which permit a more refined and precise methodology.

Desired Characteristics of a Bond Portfolio Analysis Process

There are three desired requirements of a bond portfolio analysis process. The first is that the process be accurate. For example, the typical means of measuring portfolio return is the time-weighted return recommended by the Bank Administration Institute. In this approach, time-weighted cash flows are generally averaged over a month so that cash flows are assumed to come at either the beginning or end of the month. In the process described in this chapter, the portfolio is evaluated at the time when each cash flow actually occurs, resulting in a much more accurate measure of what the actual portfolio performance was.

The second requirement is that the process be informative. It should be capable of evaluating the managerial skills that go into fixed income portfolio management. In order to be informative, the process must effectively address the key management skills, and explain how these can be expressed in terms of realized performance.

The final requirement is that the process be simple. Whatever the output of the process is, it should be understood by the portfolio manager and sponsor, or others who may be concerned with the performance of the portfolio.

As we proceed with the process for analyzing bond performance these requirements should be kept in mind.

---

[15] Gifford Fong, Charles Pearson, and Oldrich Vasicek, "Bond Performance: Analyzing Sources of Return," *The Journal of Portfolio Management*, Spring 1983, pp. 46–50. Earlier work on this topic was formulated by Peter O. Dietz, Russell Fogler, and Donald J. Hardy in "The Challenge of Analyzing Bond Portfolio Returns," *The Journal of Portfolio Management*, Spring 1980, pp. 53–58. The Dietz-Fogler-Hardy approach breaks the total bond return into yield to maturity, interest rate effect, sector/quality effect, and a residual. While this approach represents a significant development in bond performance measurement, it has several limitations. Yield to maturity is taken to represent the holding-period return under the assumption of no change in interest rates, which is not quite correct. The sector/quality component may be misleading, since the way it is calculated does not account for the differences in the maturity composition of the sectors. Most important, the return components are identified only for the portfolio as it existed at the beginning of the evaluation period. Thus, any actual management of the portfolio other than the initial portfolio selection is not included in the appropriate return components.

Fundamental Issues in the Analysis of Return

There are six fundamental issues associated with bond portfolio performance and analysis.

1. Total portfolio return measurement. Return is generally measured in terms of a rate of return over some period of time based on the average value of the funds invested during that time period. For a portfolio, the value of the funds invested changes over the period under consideration due to cash inflows representing a return on investment (dividends and interest) and new contributions to the fund, and to cash outflows due to payments to beneficiaries in the case of a pension fund or a net redemption of shares in the case of a mutual fund. The impact of cash flows that are beyond the control of the manager must be taken into consideration.

There are a number of approaches for measuring the rate of return for a portfolio. The two most common measures are the dollar-weighted rate of return and the time-weighted rate of return. The dollar-weighted rate of return, also known as the internal rate of return, is a measure equivalent to the yield-to-maturity. It measures the average growth of all funds invested during the evaluation period. The drawback of the dollar-weighted rate of return is that it measures the impact of both the managerial decisions and the timing and magnitude of contributions to, and withdrawals from, the portfolio. Consequently, if cash inflows and outflows that are beyond the control of the manager occur at propitious times, the evaluation of management's performance is difficult to assess. The time-weighted rate of return, however, has the advantage that it is not affected by the portfolio cash flow pattern during the evaluation period. The time-weighted rate of return is a weighted average of the internal rates of return for subperiods dated by the contribution or withdrawal of funds from a portfolio. It is this measure of total portfolio return that should be used in the measurement of performance.

2. External environment versus management contribution. To investigate the performance of the portfolio manager, it is necessary to first identify the macro sources of return. This requires decomposing the total portfolio return into (1) that portion which was attributable to the external environment and which was therefore not under the control of management and (2) that portion which was under the control of management and which therefore represents the manager's contribution.

3. Specific management skills. After identifying that portion of the total portfolio return that represented management contribution, it is necessary to define the micro components of return. These include maturity (or duration) management, spread/quality management, and individual security selection. For example, suppose that the manager expected that interest rates were going to decline. Based on this belief, suppose that the manager purchased long telephones. The choice of long bonds is a maturity or duration decision. The decision to purchase telephones is a sector decision. The selection of particular issues within the telephone sector is an individual security decision. Consequently, the process used to analyze performance should partition total portfolio return among these three individual management skill activities and attribute each of these components to the appropriate skill identified.

4. Individual security returns. It is also necessary to identify how each of the individual securities have performed over the security evaluation period. The security evaluation period is the period over which a particular security is held. It will differ from the portfolio evaluation period for securities purchased or sold during the portfolio evaluation period. We can look at total security returns and also the decomposition of those security returns in terms of the various components that we identified for the portfolio as a whole.

5. Effect of transactions. In evaluating transactions, the marginal impact of each purchase, sale, and swap should be examined. In evaluating a purchase or sale, it should be determined whether the transaction added to or detracted from the overall portfolio performance by comparing that security return to the portfolio return over the remainder of the portfolio evaluation period.

6. Cash account and portfolio value. The process should allow for a monitoring of the cash account balance as the result of earnings and transactions and the monitoring of the portfolio market value as the result of capital gains/losses, interest accrual, and contributions/withdrawals.

Analysis of Return[16]

In the evaluation of bond portfolio performance, the first step is the measurement of return on the portfolio over the evaluation period. The next step is an analysis of return. We can think of analysis of return as the identification of the factors that contributed to the realized performance and a quantitative assessment of the contribution of each factor to the total

---

[16] The following discussion is adapted from Fong, Pearson, and Vasicek, "Bond Performance: Analyzing Sources of Return."

return. The total portfolio return is partitioned into components, each component representing the effect of the given factor.

The first level of this decomposition aims at distinguishing between the effect of the external interest rate environment and the management contribution. If we separate the effect of circumstances that are outside the control of the portfolio manager from the effect of the portfolio management process, we can gain valuable insight into the nature of the portfolio performance. Denoting the total realized portfolio return by R, such a partition can be written as:

$$R = I + C \qquad (7-2)$$

where

I = the effect of the external interest rate environment beyond the portfolio manager's control

C = the contribution of the management process

If the portfolio had no element of management, then the return would be I, or the return due to the environment. This portfolio can be considered to be randomly selected from an available universe of fixed-income securities. As a proxy for this management-free randomly selected portfolio, we can use the total of all default-free securities, best approximated by all outstanding U.S. Treasury issues. These are the only available securities that are truly fixed-income securities in the sense that the promised payments can be expected with virtual certainty. Including corporate, municipal, or agency issues constitutes an element of the management process: It involves a decision to accept a degree of default risk in exchange for higher yields typically expected on lower quality securities. The standard for identification of the effect of the internal interest rate environment is thus a value-weighted Treasury index.[17]

We can achieve a more refined analysis of the external factor component by partitioning the actual holding-period return on the Treasury index into two sources: interest rate *level* and interest rate *change*. Higher interest rate levels mean higher holding-period returns, on which the effect of interest rate changes is then superimposed. The effect of the interest rate environment thus consists of two components: return that would be real-

---

[17] One might argue that the relevant portfolio bogey should vary according to investor preference. In the determination of the investor's investment objectives, individual preferences are certainly appropriate. The intent here, however, is to measure the interest rate effect on a universe that involves no other aspect, such as credit risk or spread relationships. That does not mean that a comparison of the portfolio return to a broader bond market index is inappropriate. Such comparison is in fact an integral part of the performance analysis. It is done by performing the return analysis for the chosen bogey as well, thus allowing a direct comparison of the resulting components of return between the actual portfolio and the specialized bogey.

ized if interest rates did not change, and the return due to the actual interest rate change.

To assign a precise meaning to the assumption of no change in interest rates, we use the term structure analysis technique, which was discussed in Chapter 2 and Appendix D. This technique provides a market implicit forecast. One can therefore define the effect of the current level of interest rates as the return on Treasury bonds under the assumption of no change in the current forward rates. The effect of the interest rate change is then defined as the difference between the actual realized return on the Treasury index and the return under the market-implicit forecast. We can then decompose the effect of I, the external interest rate environment, in the following way:

$$I = E + U \qquad (7\text{--}3)$$

where

E = return on the default-free securities under the market-implicit scenario of no change in the forward rates
U = return attributable to the actual change in forward rates

We can interpret the component E as the expected return on a portfolio of default-free Treasury securities. The component U is then the unexpected part of the actual return on the Treasury index, due to the forward rate change. The sum I of these components is then the actual return on the Treasury index. We can attribute the difference between the actual portfolio return and the actual Treasury index return, C, to the management process.

In evaluating the management contribution C, consider the means by which the management process can affect the portfolio. Three principal management skills that have an effect on performance include maturity management, sector/quality management, and selection of the individual securities. A partitioning of the management contribution is as follows:

$$C = M + S + B \qquad (7\text{--}4)$$

where

M = return from maturity management
S = return from spread/quality management
B = return attributable to the selection of specific securities

As noted earlier, maturity management (which might more correctly be called duration management) is an important tool of a bond portfolio manager and one that typically has the largest impact on performance. The successful application of this skill is related to the ability of the manager to anticipate interest rate changes. Holding long duration portfolios during periods of decreasing interest rates and short duration portfolios during periods of rate increases will typically result in superior performance. Being short when rates decline or long when rates go up will have a negative impact on performance.

Sector and quality management allocates the portfolio among the alternative issuing sectors and quality groups of the bond market. There may be spread relationships among the individual sector/quality groups that the manager may be able to exploit. Having a portfolio concentrated in high-quality industrial issues, for instance, during a period when high-quality industrials generally perform better than other sectors, would increase the portfolio return. The ability to select the right issuing sector and quality group at the right time constitutes the sector/quality management skill.

Selectivity, or individual bond picking, is the skill of selecting specific securities within a given sector/quality group to enhance the portfolio return. Individual securities show specific returns over and above the average performance of their sector/quality group. While sector/quality management means selecting the right market segment, selectivity means concentrating on the bonds, within that segment, whose specific returns are the most advantageous. As with the other two management skills, selectivity is involved in the initial portfolio construction as well as in subsequent activities such as purchases, sales, or swaps within a sector/quality group.

The three skills of portfolio management discussed previously reflect timing of the managerial decisions. That means that timing is not a separate skill, but rather an aspect of each of the skills just identified. Timing the shift of the portfolio from short to long duration or vice versa is really an element of maturity management, rather than an independently exercised ability. Without timing, there would be no maturity management. Similarly, timing is an essential part of sector/quality management and a part of choosing the proper bonds within a given sector/quality group. To provide a meaningful analysis of the portfolio return, the timing aspect must be included in the calculation of the return components.

Measurement of Return Components

We can measure the return components by security repricing. Consider maturity management first. If all securities held during the evaluation period were Treasury issues and if each issue were consistently priced exactly on the term structure of default-free rates (so that there would be no specific returns on any security), the maturity management component M of the total return would be equal to the difference between the realized total return R and the effect I of the external environment. In other words, if the sector/quality effect and the selectivity effect were eliminated, the total management contribution can be attributed to maturity management. This means that we can reprice each security as if it were a Treasury issue priced from the term structure, measure the total return under such pricing, and subtract the external effect component I to obtain the effect of maturity management.

Practically, this is accomplished by estimating the term structure of default-free rates from the universe of Treasury issues as of each valuation date throughout the evaluation period. The default-free price of each security held on that date is then calculated as the present value of its payments discounted by the spot rates corresponding to the maturity of that payment. The total return over the evaluation period is then calculated using the default-free prices, but otherwise maintaining all actual activity in the portfolio, including all transactions, contributions and withdrawals, cash account changes, and the like. Finally, the actual Treasury index return over the evaluation period is subtracted to arrive at the maturity management component M.

To determine the spread/quality management component S of the total return, each security is priced as if it were exactly in line with its own sector/quality group (that is, with no specific returns), the total return under such prices is calculated, and the total of the external component I and the maturity management component M is subtracted.

One must be careful to determine the sector/quality prices correctly. It is not correct to base the sector/quality pricing on sector/quality indexes, since the differences in actual performance among various sector/quality indexes is primarily due to the different maturity composition of the market segments. For instance, the telephone issues would generally perform poorly during periods of increasing interest rates, not because they are telephones, but because they are longer than the bond market as a whole. Therefore, the following approach is recommended.

First, a meaningful classification of the bond market by sector/quality groups must be defined. Then the term structure of default-free rates from U.S. Treasury issues is estimated using the term structure analysis methodology. Next, for each valuation date, the default-free prices for all securities existing in the market at that date are calculated. The spreads, or yield premia, for each security are then calculated as the difference between the actual yield and yield determined from the default-free price. These yield premia are then averaged over all securities in the given sector/quality group to determine the average yield premium for the sector/quality group as of the given date. After all this is done, the sector/quality prices of the securities in the given portfolio can be calculated by determining their default-free prices from the term structure, calculating the yield, adding the appropriate average yield premium depending on the sector/quality of that security, and converting this yield back to price. When all securities in the portfolio have been priced according to their sector/quality group at each of the valuation dates, the total portfolio return with the sector/quality prices can be calculated. Again, the portfolio return with these prices is calculated including all actual purchases, sales, and swaps, contributions, and withdrawals. The sector/quality component S of the portfolio management is then obtained by subtracting the external effect component and the maturity management component from the return calculated on the sector/quality prices.

Finally, to determine the selectivity component of the management contribution, the actual prices, which reflect the specific returns on each security, are used. The selectivity component B is thus calculated by subtracting the total of all previously determined components from the actual total portfolio return.

In this way, we can partition the total portfolio return into five components as follows:

$$R = \underbrace{E + U}_{I} + \underbrace{M + S + B}_{C} \qquad (7\text{--}5)$$

These components are the effect of interest rate level (E), the effect of interest rate change (U), the maturity management (M), sector/quality management (S), and selectivity (B). The first component can also be interpreted as the expected return on default-free securities, and the second as the unexpected component of the actual return on the default-free Treasury market index. The first two components are the effect of external factors beyond the control of the portfolio manager, namely, the interest rate environment. Their sum is the actual return on the Treasury index. The last three components reflect factors within the control of the manager, that is, management skill. Together they add up to the total management contribution. The sum of all five components is the actual return on the portfolio.

An alternative way of looking at the composition of the total return, which will reflect the way these components are actually calculated, is to consider the cumulative totals. The first total, E is the expected return on a randomly selected portfolio of Treasury issues, calculated assuming no change in interest rates. The second total, $E + U$, is the actual return on a randomly selected portfolio of Treasury issues. The third total, $E + U + M$, is the return on the actual portfolio (including all activity) as if all securities were Treasury issues priced on the term structure (that is, no sector/quality effects and no specific returns). The fourth total, $E + U + M + S$, is the return on the actual portfolio as if all securities were priced according to their issuing sector and quality (that is, no specific returns). Finally, the fifth total, $E + U + M + S + B$, is the actual portfolio return. The decomposition of the total return into its components as specified in Equation 7–5 provides a meaningful and informative analysis of the portfolio performance.

Table 7-14
Bond Performance Analysis *(beginning date, March 31, 1983; ending date, June 30, 1983)*

	Portfolio Performance		Lehman Brothers Kuhn Loeb Government/ Corporate Index
	Evaluation Period Return (percent)	*Annualized Return (percent)*	*Evaluation Period Return (percent)*
Interest rate effect			
Expected	2.22%	9.02%	2.22%
Unexpected	−0.80	−3.29	−0.80
Subtotal	1.42	5.73	1.42
Management effect			
Maturity	0.02	0.08	−0.48
Sector/quality	0.36	1.47	0.69
Individual bonds	1.66	6.83	0.00
Subtotal	2.04	8.37	0.21
Total return	3.46%	14.11%	1.63%

Sources of return

Capital gains	0.81%
Interest income	2.64
Total return	3.46%

	3.32%
	10.78
	14.11%

Cash Account Balance ($000)

Month	Beginning Cash Balance	±	Contribution Withdrawal	−	Disbursement	+	Cash Account Adjustment	+	Cash Account Earnings	+	Interest Received	+	Principal Payments	+	Matured /Called	−	New Purchases	+	New Sales	=	Ending Cash Balance
4/83	$ 0.0		$ 0.0		0.0		0.0		2.1		82.0		134.1		0.0		0.0		0.0		218.2
5/83	218.2		0.0		0.0		0.0		13.2		252.7		38.6		0.0		0.0		1,028.6		1,551.3
6/83	1,551.3		5,004.8		0.0		0.0		5.1		1,046.4		30.9		650.0		7,767.3		0.0		521.2

Portfolio Market Value ($000)

Month	Beginning Portfolio Market Value	±	Contribution Withdrawal	−	Disbursement	+	Cash Account Adjustment	+	Cash Account Earnings	+	Interest Accrued	+	Capital Gains	=	Principal Payment Gains	=	Ending Portfolio Market Value	Total Monthly Return (percent)
4/83	$45,856.3		$ 0.0		0.0		0.0		2.1		402.7		1156.0		−9.0		$47,408.0	3.38%
5/83	47,408.0		0.0		0.0		0.0		13.2		405.0		−533.7		−1.8		47,290.6	−0.25
6/83	47,290.6		5,004.8		0.0		0.0		5.1		411.4		−256.8		−1.7		52,453.5	0.32

The effect of transaction costs is also included by this analysis. As a transaction is made, the cost is reflected in the price paid for a purchase and the price received for a sale. This in turn is captured in the return due to the selectivity component. Hence, excessive turnover of the portfolio would be reflected in the selectivity component of the portfolio.

After we have calculated components of return for the portfolio being analyzed, we can repeat the same return decomposition for a total bond market index such as the Lehman Government/Corporate Bond Index. The return components of the bond index provide benchmarks against which we can compare the return components of the portfolio.

Before presenting the illustration of the process for bond portfolio performance and analysis, a discussion of risk adjustments is in order. For equity portfolios, it is customary to calculate a risk-adjusted return, defined as the actual portfolio beta. Crude attempts at a similar adjustment for bond portfolios have been made by substituting the bond portfolio duration relative to an index for the beta of a stock portfolio. This is incorrect, since duration would measure the portfolio response only if interest rates always changed by parallel shifts of the forward rates.

It turns out that the correct adjustment for interest rate risk would actually be the maturity management component M as defined earlier. Similarly, the sector/quality component S would be an adjustment for the second source of risk in the bond market, namely, the default risk. If the investment policy of a fund constrains the manager as to the maturity composition and/or sector and quality composition of the portfolio, it may be appropriate to consider the maturity and/or the sector/quality return components risk adjustments. For instance, if both maturity and sector composition of the portfolio are specifically prescribed by policy, the risk-adjusted return is equal to the selectivity component B. In general, however, interpretation of the maturity and sector/quality components as risk adjustments would mean removing the principal sources of return from the observed performance.

Illustration

Tables 7–14 and 7–15 illustrate the bond portfolio analysis process. The evaluation period is the three-month period beginning March 31, 1983, and ending June 30, 1983. At the beginning of the period there were nine securities in the portfolio. These are shown in Table 7–15.

Table 7–14 shows the decomposition of the total portfolio return according to the four components described earlier. The analysis is for both the evaluation period and on an annualized basis. For comparative purposes, the last column shows a similar analysis for the Lehman Brothers Government/Corporate Index. Over the three month evaluation period the portfolio return was 3.46 percent compared to 1.63 percent for

Table 7–15
Individual Security Analysis (beginning date, March 31, 1983; ending date, June 30, 1983)

Initial Face Value ($000)	Issue	Initial Date	Last Date	Individual Security Performance								Annual Total Return (percent)
				Market Performance		Portfolio Management				Return Source		
				Market Expectation +	Rate Change	Maturity +	Sector /Quality +	Selectivity =	Total Return (percent)	Capital Gains +	Interest Income	
$ 5,000	American Telephone & Telegraph Co. 8.625% 2/1/7	3/31/83	6/30/83	2.22	−0.80	−1.01	0.70	−0.76	0.35%	−2.35	2.70	1.41%
1,000	Chrysler Corp. 10.350% 6/1/90	3/31/83	5/20/83	1.20	0.28	−0.00	0.01	6.15	7.64	6.13	1.50	61.67
5,000	Duke Power Co. 14.500% 8/1/12	3/31/83	6/30/83	2.22	−0.80	−0.99	1.32	13.47	15.22	11.71	3.51	65.76
3,427	Federal Home Loan Mortgage Corp. 12.450% 9/15/9	3/31/83	6/30/83	2.22	−0.80	0.06	0.0	4.51	5.99	2.78	3.21	24.78
650	First Bank System Inc. 8.750% 6/30/83	3/31/83	6/30/83	2.22	−0.80	0.86	0.0	0.06	2.34	0.20	2.14	9.52
4,405	Seaboard Coast Line Railroad Co. 7.750% 5/1/98	3/31/83	6/30/83	2.22	−0.80	−1.08	1.68	−0.35	1.67	−0.94	2.61	6.74
4,000	Stauffer Chemical Co. 8.125% 1/15/86	3/31/83	6/30/83	2.22	−0.80	0.29	0.27	0.06	2.05	−0.07	2.12	8.29
3,983	GNMA Pool 14.000% 3/15/11	3/31/83	6/30/83	2.22	−0.80	0.05	0.0	1.94	3.41	0.06	3.35	13.92
20,000	United States Treasury Notes 9.375% 12/31/84	3/31/83	6/30/83	2.22	−0.80	0.62	0.0	0.03	2.07	−0.25	2.32	8.41
6,905	General Telephone Co. California 14.125% 12/1/90	6/23/83	6/30/83	0.17	−0.09	−0.02	−0.35	−2.44	−2.73	−2.97	0.24	−102.81

Transactions

Date	Issue	Amount	Type of Transaction
6/23/83	General Telephone Co. California 14.125% 12/1/90	$6,905.00	Purchase

	Security Return −2.73%	Portfolio Return 0.07%	Marginal Effect of Transaction −2.80%

the index. This return can be decomposed into an interest rate effect of 1.42 percent and a management effect of 2.04 percent. The interest rate effect can be partitioned into the expected and unexpected returns, where the former is the market implicit expectation as of the beginning of the period (March 31, 1983). The unexpected return is simply the difference between the interest rate effect of 1.42 percent and the market implicit expectation of 2.22 percent. An analysis of the three management skills shows that 1.66 percent of the total portfolio return was attributable to individual security selection, clearly indicating that the manager excelled in this skill.

Table 7–14 also shows the sources of return in terms of the usual partitioning into capital gains and interest income. The two panels following the portfolio performance on Table 7–14 show the tracking of the cash account balance and the portfolio market value for each month of the evaluation period.

Individual security analysis in terms of the four components is shown in Table 7–15. The impact of the purchase of the General Telephone of California issue on June 23, 1983, is presented in the lower panel of Table 7–15. For the security evaluation period—June 23, 1983, to June 30, 1983—the security return was −2.73 percent. Over the same period, the portfolio return was .07 percent. Consequently, the acquisition of the issue had a marginal impact of −2.80 percent.

■ Summary

In this chapter we have explained several active management strategies and illustrated how they can be applied. The fixed income portfolio management process contains many elements and the portfolio manager must select from a menu of active strategies the manner in which active management will be pursued. The final strategy will consist of the portfolio manager's own strengths, fortified with complementary techniques and tools. The final result should be superior returns along with consistency of returns through risk control. As long as there is uncertainty associated with the judgments being used, then the strategies that we discussed in this chapter can assist portfolio managers in making the best investment decisions by increasing understanding and decreasing uncertainty. □

8
Futures and Options

With the advent of interest rate futures and options on both fixed income instruments and interest rate futures, active and offensive-minded bond portfolio risk management, in its broadest sense, assumes a new dimension. The portfolio manager and the individual investor can achieve new degrees of freedom. It is now possible to alter the market risk profile of a bond portfolio economically and quickly. These derivative contracts, as they are commonly known because they derive their value from the underlying security, now offer portfolio managers and individual investors risk and return patterns that were previously unavailable.

In this chapter, we will discuss these contracts and explain how they can be used in bond portfolio management. Whether the strategies that can be employed by using futures and options are permitted for a particular investment account may depend on client preference, applicable state statutory or regulatory provisions.

■ Futures

A futures contract is a firm legal agreement between a buyer (seller) and an established exchange or its clearing house in which the buyer (seller) agrees to take (make) delivery of *something* at a specified price at the end of a designated period of time. Prior to 1972, the *something* that the parties agreed to take or make delivery of was either traditional agricultural commodities (such as meat and livestock), imported foodstuffs (such as coffee, cocoa, and sugar), or industrial commodities. Collectively, such futures contracts are known as *commodity futures*.

Futures contracts based on a financial instrument or a financial index are known as *financial futures* and referred to by some as "pork bellies in pinstripes." It was not until 1972 that financial futures contracts were introduced. In that year, the International Monetary Market (IMM) of the Chicago Mercantile Exchange initiated trading in several foreign currencies. In October 1975, the Chicago Board of Trade (CBT) pioneered trading in a futures contract based on a fixed income instrument—Government National Mortgage Association certificates. Three months later the IMM began trading futures contracts based on 90-day Treasury bills. Other exchanges soon followed with other interest rate futures contracts.[1] In 1982, three futures contracts on broadly based common stock indexes made their debut.

At the time of this writing, only the CBT and IMM trade interest rate futures contracts. Futures contracts traded on the CBT are for the following cash market securities: Treasury bonds, 10-year Treasury notes, Government National Mortgage Association (GNMA or Ginnie Mae) certificates and GNMA II. Futures contracts for money market instruments are traded on the IMM for the following cash market instruments: 90-day Treasury bills, 90-day Certificates of Deposit (CDs), and Eurodollar Time Deposits.

Contract Specifications and Trading Mechanics

Figure 8–1 summarizes the contract specifications for the interest rate futures contracts traded at the time of this writing.

Trading unit. The size of the trading unit ranges from $100,000 for the Treasury bonds, 10-year notes and Ginnie Maes to $1,000,000 for the 90-day Treasury bills, 90-day CD, and Eurodollars.

Minimum price fluctuations. The exchanges specify a minimum price change (or tick) for each contract. For the three contracts traded on the IMM, the minimum price change is 1 basis point or $25 per contract, while for the CBT contracts, it is 1/32 of 1 percent of par or $31.25 per contract.

Daily price limit. There is a daily price limit imposed by the exchange on each contract. The daily price limit establishes the maximum

---

[1] A good number of these contracts failed. The failures include futures trading on the CBT of 90-day, A–1, P–1 commercial paper and futures contracts on Treasury bills and bonds introduced by the New York Futures Exchange in 1981. Plans for trading a futures contract on a municipal index are on the drawingboard. The architect of this contract is J. J. Kenny and Company, a New York broker in municipal bonds.

Figure 8–1
Contract Specifications of Interest Rate Futures *(as of July 25, 1984)*

Exchange:	Chicago Board of Trade	International Monetary Market
Contracts:	U.S. Treasury bonds Ten-year treasuries GNMA CDR GNMA II	90-day Treasury bills 90-day CDs Eurodollar time deposits
Trading unit:	$100,000	$1,000,000
Minimum price fluctuation:	$\frac{1}{32}$ of 1% = $31.25	.01(1 basis point) = $25
Daily price limits:	$^{64}/_{32}$(2 pts) = $2,000	T bil's: .60(60 basis points) = $1,500 CDs: .80(80 basis points) = $2,000 Eurodollar: 1.00(100 basis points) = $2,500
Margin requirements:		
Initial	$2,500*	$1,000
Maintenance	$2,000	$ 700
* $2,000 for hedgers.		

amount the price of the contract can change relative to the previous day's settlement price.

Margin requirements. An important consideration in determining whether to employ any of the strategies involving interest rate futures that will be discussed later in this chapter is the margin requirements. When a position is first taken in a futures contract, the investor must deposit a minimum dollar amount per contract as specified by the exchange. This amount is called the *initial margin.*[2] As the price of the futures contract fluctuates, the value of the investor's equity in the position changes. At the close of each trading day, an investor's position is "marked to market" so that any gain or loss from the position is reflected in the investor's equity account. *Maintenance margin* is the minimum level specified by the exchange by which an investor's equity position may fall as a result of an unfavorable price movement before the investor is required to deposit additional margin. The additional margin deposited is called *variation margin.* If there is excess margin, that amount may be withdrawn by the investor.

Although there are initial and maintenance margin requirements for buying securities on margin, the concept of margin differs for securities and futures. When securities are acquired on margin, the difference between

---

[2] Individual brokerage firms are free to set margin requirements above the minimum established by the exchange.

the price of the security and the initial margin is borrowed from the broker. The security purchased serves as collateral for the loan and interest is paid by the investor. For futures contracts, the initial margin, in effect, serves as "good faith" money indicating that the investor will satisfy the obligation of the contract. No money is borrowed by the investor.

Taking and liquidating a position. When an investor takes a position in the market by buying a futures contract, the investor is said to be taking a *long position*. If instead, the investor's opening position is the sale of a futures contract, the investor is said to be in a *short position*.

The investor has two choices to liquidate a position. To liquidate a position prior to the delivery date, the investor must take an offsetting position. For a long position this means selling an identical number of contracts; for a short position this means buying an identical number of contracts. The alternative is to wait until the delivery date. At that time the investor liquidates a long position by accepting delivery of the underlying fixed income instrument at the agreed upon price and liquidates a short position by delivering the fixed income instrument at the agreed upon price. It is rare for positions to be closed out by actual delivery. For example, in 1981, 5.6 million Treasury bill futures contracts were traded but delivery was made on only 5,183 contracts.

The role of the clearing corporation. When an investor takes a position in the market, there is another party who is taking the opposite position and agreeing to satisfy the terms set forth in the contract. But what if that party defaults on its obligations? Is the investor's only recourse to sue the defaulted party? If so, does that mean an investor must be concerned with the identity of the other party before taking a position in the futures market? Moreover, if the investor wants to liquidate a position before the final settlement date, must the investor do so only with that party?

Because of the *clearing corporation* associated with each exchange, the investor need not worry about the financial strength and integrity of the other party to the contract. Once an order is executed, the direct relationship between the two parties is severed. The clearing corporation interposes itself as the buyer for every sale and the seller for every purchase. Thus the investor is free to liquidate his position without involvement with the other party in the original contract, and without worry that the other party may default.

Deliverable grade for Treasury coupon securities. If a short wishes to deliver Treasury coupon securities, he has several acceptable Treasury issues from which to select. The acceptable delivery grade is determined by the exchange. For example, for the CBT's Treasury bond futures, the Treasury bond issue delivered must have at least 15 years to maturity from the date of delivery if not callable; if callable, the issue must not be callable for at least 15 years from the first day of the delivery month. For 10-year Treasury note futures, an issue is acceptable if the maturity is not less than 6.5 years and not greater than 10 years from the first day of the delivery month.

To make delivery equitable to both parties and to tie cash to futures prices, the CBT introduced *conversion factors* for determining the invoice price of each deliverable grade issue against a given futures contract. The standard selected by the exchange for determining the conversion factor is a hypothetical 8 percent coupon issue. For Treasury bonds, the hypothetical bond is based on a 20-year maturity. The invoice price is then determined using the following expression:

Invoice price
= Contract size × Futures contract settlement price × Conversion factor

For example, there were 17 eligible Treasury issues that could have been delivered by the short to settle the December 1982 T-bond futures contract that settled at 74–17.[3] The conversion factor for two of these issues, the 13 7/8s of 2011 and 7 5/8s of 2007, was 1.6155 and .9645, respectively. The invoice price, had these two issues been delivered by the short to settle one December 1982 T-bond futures contract, would have been:

Invoice price based on
delivery of 13 7/8s of 2011 = $100,000 × .7453125 × 1.6155
= $120,405

Invoice price based on
delivery of 7 5/8s of 2007 = $100,000 × .7453125 × .9645
= $71,885

The invoice price computed above is just for the principal. The long must also pay the short accrued interest on the bond delivered.

Since the short elects the issue to deliver, he or she will select the cheapest issue to deliver. The cost to deliver is the difference between the cost of purchasing the issue and the invoice price for the principal.[4] That is,

Cost to deliver = Cost of purchasing issue − Invoice price

Considering only the two issues whose invoice price we have computed, the cost of delivery, assuming a cash market offer price of 121–00 and 75–12 for the 13 7/8s of 2011 and 7 5/8s of 2007, respectively, would have been:

---

[3] T-bond futures are quoted in 32nds so 74–17 equals 74 17/32, or .7453125 of par value.

[4] This is equivalent to selecting the issue that would generate the greatest profit as measured by the invoice price for the principal minus the cost of purchasing the issue.

Cost to deliver
13 7/8s of 2011 = (1.21 × $100,000) − $120,405
= $595
Cost to deliver
7 5/8s of 2007 = (0.75375 × $100,000) − $71,885
= $3,490

The 13 7/8s is clearly the cheaper of the two issues to deliver.

Note that computation of the cost of delivery does not consider the accrued interest that the short must pay to acquire the issue. The reason is that the cost would be offset by the long when the issue is purchased from the short.

Commissions. Commissions are negotiable and vary with the size of the transaction.

Futures versus Forward Contract

A forward contract, just like a futures contract, is an agreement for the future delivery of *something* at a specified price at the end of a designated period of time. As we explained earlier, futures contracts are standardized agreements as to delivery date (or month) and delivery grade, and are traded on well-organized exchanges. A forward contract, on the other hand, is usually nonstandardized, and secondary markets are often nonexistent or extremely thin.

Although both futures and forward contracts require delivery, future contracts are not intended as delivery instruments. In fact, generally less than 2 percent of outstanding contracts are delivered. In contrast to futures contracts, forward contracts are intended for delivery. Usually less than 5 percent are not delivered.

Another difference is that futures contracts are marked to market at the end of each trading day while forward contracts are not. Consequently, there are interim cash flow effects with futures contracts as additional margin may be required as a result of adverse price movements or cash withdrawn as a result of favorable price movements. There are no interim cash flow effects with forward contracts because no variation margin is required.

Cash-Futures Price Relationship

To understand the cash-futures pricing relationship, some terminology must first be introduced. The *cost of financing* refers to the rate that must be paid on borrowed funds to acquire an asset, and it is equal to the short-term interest rate. The *net cost of financing,* or simply *net financing,* is the cost of financing less the yield that could be earned by holding the asset. That is,

Net financing cost (%) = Cost of financing (%) − Yield on asset (%)

The term *carry* refers to the net financing cost. When the cost of financing is greater than the yield on the asset, net financing cost is positive and carry is said to be negative.[5] When the net financing cost is negative, that is, the yield on the asset is greater than the cost of financing, carry is said to be positive.

The shape of the yield curve determines whether carry is positive or negative for the underlying security. When the yield curve is positive, that is, long rates are greater than short rates, then carry will be positive. Negative carry exists when the yield curve is inverted (negative yield curve environment), that is, when short rates exceed long rates.

Carry is the foundation for the pricing of interest rate futures. Using an arbitrage or equivalent portfolio approach, it can be demonstrated that the theoretical futures price is related to the cash or *spot* price (i.e., the price of the asset in the cash market) as follows:

Futures price = Cash price + Cash price × Net financing cost (%)

As can be seen from this relationship, if carry is negative so that the net financing cost is positive, interest rate futures should trade at a price that is greater than the cash price. That is, interest rate futures should trade at a premium relative to the cash price. When there is positive carry, so that the net financing cost is negative, interest rate futures should trade at a discount relative to the cash price.

Technically, the cash-futures relationship we have just described is for a forward contract, not a futures contract. As we explained earlier, there is a difference between forward and futures contracts in that futures contracts have cash flow consequences as the price of the futures contract changes. Cox, Ingersoll, and Ross have demonstrated that forward and futures prices need not be equal even in perfect markets if interest rates are stochastic.[6] However, empirical evidence suggests that forward and futures prices are essentially equal.[7] Moreover, Hanson and Kopprasch have sug-

---

[5] The term *negative carry* is used because it represents a cash outflow to the holder of the asset.

[6] John Cox, Jonathan Ingersoll, and Stephen Ross, "The Relation Between Forward Prices and Futures Prices," *Journal of Financial Economics*, December 1981, pp. 321–46; See also R. Jarrow and George Oldfield, "Forward Contracts and Futures Contracts," *Journal of Financial Economics*, December 1981, pp. 373–82; Kenneth French, "The Pricing of Futures and Forward Contracts," Ph.D. Diss., University of Rochester, 1982; S. F. Richard and M. Sundaresan, "A Continuous Time Equilibrium Model of Forward and Futures Prices in a Multigood Economy," *Journal of Financial Economics*, December 1981, pp. 347–72.

[7] Bradford Cornell and Marc R. Reinganum, "Forward and Futures Prices: Evidence from the Foreign Exchange Markets," *Journal of Finance*, December 1981, pp. 1035–45; Robert W. Kolb, Gerald D. Gay, and J. Jordan, "Are There Arbitrage Opportunities in the Treasury-Bond Futures Market?" *The Journal of Futures Markets*, Fall 1982, pp. 217–229. Richard J. Rendleman and Christopher E. Carabini, "The Efficiency of the Treasury Bill Futures Market," *Journal of Finance*, September 1979, pp. 895–914.

gested a procedure applicable to futures contracts on any underlying instrument that will allow a futures position to approximate a forward position if short-term interest rates are fixed.[8]

The spread between the cash price and futures price is called the *basis*. That is,[9]

$$\text{Basis} = \text{Cash price} - \text{Futures price}$$

The basis changes over time. As the futures contract approaches the delivery date, the futures price converges to the cash price and the basis approaches zero. Figure 8–2 summarizes the cash-futures price relationship.

Figure 8–2
Summary of Cash-Futures Price Relationship

Shape of Yield Curve	Net Financing Cost	Carry	Relationship between Cash and Futures Price
Positive	Negative	Positive	Cash price > Futures price
Negative	Positive	Negative	Futures price > Cash price
Flat	Zero	Zero	Cash price = Futures price

■ Options

An option is a contract in which the writer of the option grants the buyer of the option the right to purchase from or sell to the writer a designated instrument at a specified price within a specified period of time.[10] The writer, also referred to as the seller, grants this right to the buyer for a certain sum of money called the *option premium*. The price at which the instrument may be bought or sold is called the *exercise* or *strike price*. The date after which an option is void is called the *expiration date*. An *American option* may be exercised any time before the expiration date. A *European option,* on the other hand, may only be exercised at the expiration date.

When an option grants the buyer the right to purchase the designated instrument from the writer, it is called a *call option*. When the option buyer has the right to sell the designated instrument to the writer (seller), the option is called a *put option*.

An option on a futures contract gives the buyer the right to buy from or sell to the writer a designated futures contract at a designated price at any

---

[8] H. Nicholas Hanson and Robert W. Kopprasch, "Pricing of Stock Index Futures," chapter 6 in *Stock Index Futures*, ed. Frank J. Fabozzi and Gregory M. Kipnis (Homewood, Ill.: Dow Jones-Irwin, 1984).

[9] It should be noted, however, that in the commodities market, basis is usually defined as the futures price minus the cash price.

[10] When the designated instrument is a stock index, the buyer receives cash settlement.

time during the life of the option. If the option on a futures contract is a call option, the buyer has the right to purchase one designated futures contract at the exercise (strike) price. That is, the buyer has the right to acquire a long futures position in the designated futures contract at the exercise (strike) price. If the call option is exercised by the buyer, the writer (seller) acquires a short position. A put option on a futures contract grants the buyer the right to sell one designated futures contract to the writer at the exercise (strike) price. That is, the buyer has the right to acquire a short futures position in the designated futures contract at the exercise price. If the put option is exercised, the writer acquires a long position in the designated futures contract at the exercise price.

Notice that unlike a futures contract, the buyer of an option has the *right* but not the obligation to perform. It is the option seller (writer) that has the obligation to perform. Both the buyer and seller are obligated to perform in the case of a futures contract. In addition, in a futures contract, the buyer does not pay the seller to accept the obligation as in the case of an option where the buyer pays the seller the option premium.

Currently Traded Options

At the time of this writing, options on fixed income securities are traded on two exchanges—the American Stock Exchange and the Chicago Board Options Exchange.[11] The underlying fixed income securities for the options traded on these two exchanges are U.S. Treasury obligations. The Chicago Board of Trade is the only exchange that currently trades an option on an interest rate futures contract. The fixed income instrument underlying the interest rate futures contract is also a U.S. Treasury obligation. There are also over-the-counter options on Treasury notes and bonds, corporate bonds, mortgage-backed securities, and money market instruments. Investment banking firms act as principals as well as brokers for over-the-counter options.[12]

---

[11] Prior to the introduction of exchange-traded options on Treasury obligations, a few corporations and one municipality issued fixed income securities that granted the bondholder the right to purchase additional bonds. The three corporate issues are Continental Illinois (13⅝s, '85), Manufacturers Hanover (12¼s, '85) and Commercial Credit (14¼s, '85). The only two municipals were issued by the Municipal Assistance Corporation for the City of New York (10⅝s, '08 and 12¾s, '08). See Robert W. Kopprasch, "Contingent Takedown Options on Fixed Income Securities," Chapter 23 in *The Handbook of Fixed Income Securities*, ed. Frank J. Fabozzi and Irving M. Pollack (Homewood, Ill.: Dow Jones-Irwin, 1983). For Eurodollar and Yankee bonds that provide this option, see Tran Q. Hung and Karen A. Johnson, *Eurowarrants: The Potential for Capital Gains with Limited Risk* (New York: Salomon Brothers Inc., December 1981).

[12] For a further discussion of over-the-counter options, see Laurie S. Goodman, "Introduction to Debt Options" Chapter 1 in Frank J. Fabozzi (ed.) *Winning The Interest Rate Game: A Guide to Debt Options* (Chicago, Ill.: Probus Publishing, 1984).

Options on the Chicago Board Options Exchange. The underlying Treasury obligation for the options traded on the CBOE are particular U.S. Treasury bond issues. Options on several issues are traded concurrently. For example, at the time of this writing, three U.S. Treasury bond issues are the underlying security for separate option contracts—14s due November 2011, 12s due August 2013, and 10⅜s due November 2012.

Options on Treasury bonds are traded in two sizes—the large or standard contracts, and the small or mini contracts. The large or standard contracts involve $100,000 of principal of the underlying issue; the small or mini contracts involve $20,000 of principal of the underlying issue.

The exercise price for Treasury bond options is expressed as a percent of the issue's par value plus accrued interest. For example, an exercise price of 88 equals $88,000 (.88 × $100,000) plus accrued interest for a standard contract and $17,600 (.88 × $20,000) plus accrued interest for a mini contract. Although, for a given option contract, there is only one exercise price, there are option contracts available with different exercise prices. For example, at the time of this writing, there are three exercise prices (98, 100, and 102) available for calls that expire in March of 1984 for the larger contract in which the 12s of August 2013 are the underlying Treasury bond.

The option premium (price) for options on Treasury bonds are quoted in points and 32nds. Each point is equal to 1 percent of the principal value of the trading unit. Therefore, one point is $1,000 (.01 × $100,000) for a standard contract and $200 (.01 × $20,000) for a mini contract. One 32nd of a point is equal to $31.25 ($1,000/32) for a standard contract and $6.25 for a mini contract. The option premium is quoted in decimal form, where the value to the right of the decimal represents the number of 32nds. For example, a quote of 4.24 is equal to 4 points and 24 32nds. In dollars, the option premium would be $4,750 (4 × $1,000 + 24 × $31.25) for a standard contract and $950 (4 × $200 + 24 × $6.25) for a mini contract.

Options on the American Stock Exchange. Two types of options are traded on the American Stock Exchange—options on Treasury notes and options on 13-week Treasury bills.

Options on Treasury notes are for newly issued 10-year notes. The trading unit for each option is $100,000. A mini contract, as in the case of options on Treasury bonds, is not available. The exercise price and option premiums are expressed in the same manner as CBOE options on Treasury bonds.

Options on 13-week Treasury bills have a different structure than options on notes and bonds, due primarily to the conventions of the Treasury bill cash market. Unlike options on notes and bonds which are for a specific issue, the deliverable 13-week Treasury bill for this option changes from week to week throughout the life of any given option. The principal amount for each option is $1,000,000, reflecting the fact that this amount is a round lot in the Treasury bill cash market.

A distinctive feature of options on Treasury bills is the manner in which exercise prices are expressed and option premiums are quoted. Since Treasury bills are quoted on a discount basis in the cash market, the nominal exercise price of an option is found by subtracting the Treasury bill discount rate at which an option is exercisable from 100. For example, an option to buy or sell 13-week Treasury bills at a discount rate of 9.00 percent has a nominal exercise price of 91. However, the nominal exercise price does not reflect the actual dollar settlement price if an option is exercised. The adjusted exercise price in the case of settlement of an exercised option is the same as in the settlement in the cash market.[13]

Option premiums are quoted in basis points. For $1,000,000 of principal amount, one basis point converts into $25.[14] Consequently, a quote of .11 is equal to 11 basis points and an option premium of $275.

Options on the Chicago Board of Trade. The CBT option is an option on an interest rate futures contract rather than an option on a cash market Treasury obligation. The trading unit is one $100,000 principal value CBT U.S. Treasury bond futures contract of a specified month.

Upon exercise, the writer (seller) and buyer of a CBT option acquire a position in one Treasury bond futures contract at the exercise price. In the case of a call option, the buyer acquires a long futures position and the writer acquires a short futures position at the exercise price. For example, an exercise price of 64 for a CBT March call option means that if the buyer

---

[13] The procedure is as follows. First, obtain the annualized discount rate from the nominal exercise price by subtracting the latter from 100. Second, compute the actual discount rate for the Treasury bill by adjusting the annualized discount rate to reflect the maturity of the issue. This requires multiplying the annualized rate by a fraction. The numerator of the fraction is the exact number of days to maturity of the Treasury bill and the denominator is 360 days. In the case of 13-week Treasury bills, the numerator is 91 days and the fraction is 91/360. Third, determine the adjusted exercise price by subtracting the actual discount rate from 100. Finally, multiply the adjusted exercise price (expressed as a percent) by the trading unit of the option which is $1,000,000. To illustrate the settlement price if an option is exercised, suppose that the nominal exercise price of an option for a 13-week Treasury bill is 91. The annualized discount rate is then 9.00 percent (100 − 91). The actual discount rate is found by multiplying the annualized discount rate by 91/360. This results in an actual discount rate of 2.275 percent. Subtracting the actual discount rate of 2.275 percent from 100 gives an adjusted exercise price of 97.725 and a settlement price of $977,250 (.97725 × $1,000,000).

[14] For purposes of converting a basis point into dollar amounts it is implicitly assumed that the Treasury bill matures in 90 days. The price value of a basis point for a 90-day $1,000,000 Treasury bill is $25.

exercises the option, the writer (seller) acquires a short position in a CBT March Treasury bond futures contract at a price of 64 while the buyer acquires a long position at that price. For a put option, exercise by the buyer results in a short futures position for the buyer and a long futures position for the writer at the exercise price.

Option premiums are quoted in points and 64ths of a point. Since the CBT futures contract is for $100,000 of par value, each point is equal to $1,000 and one 64th is $15.625. A quote of 3–34 means 3 points and 34/64 which is equal to $3,531.25 (4 × $1,000 + 34 × $15.625).

The Option Premium (Price)

The cost to the buyer of an option is primarily a reflection of the option's *intrinsic* value and any premium over its intrinsic value.[15] Each is discussed below.

Intrinsic value. The intrinsic value of a call option is the difference between the current price of the underlying instrument and the exercise price. For example, if the exercise price for a call option is 78 and the current price of the designated instrument is 81, the intrinsic value is 3 (81 − 78). That is, if the option buyer exercised the option and simultaneously sold the underlying instrument, the option buyer would realize 81 from the short position, which would be covered by acquiring an offsetting long position at 78 through exercise of the option—thereby netting 3 points.

When a call option has intrinsic value, it is said to be "in the money." When the exercise price of a call option exceeds the current price of the underlying instrument, the call option is said to be "out of the money" and has no intrinsic value. An option for which the exercise price is equal to the current price of the underlying instrument is said to be "at the money."

For a put option, the intrinsic value is equal to the amount by which the current price of the underlying instrument is below the exercise price. For example, if the exercise price of a put option is 78 and the current price of the underlying instrument is 71, the intrinsic value is 7. When the put option has intrinsic value, the option is said to be in the money. A put option is out of the money when the current price of the underlying instrument exceeds the exercise price.

Premium over intrinsic value. The premium over intrinsic value is whatever amount buyers are willing to pay over and above any intrinsic value that the option may have. The option buyer hopes that at some

---

[15] Intrinsic value is sometimes referred to as *parity value*. The premium over intrinsic value is sometimes referred to as *time value*. Do not confuse the option premium, which is the price of the option, with the component of the option premium that represents the premium over the intrinsic value.

point prior to expiration, changes in the price of the underlying instrument will further increase the value of the rights conveyed by the option. For example, if the option premium (price) for a call option with an exercise price of 78 is 9 when the current price of the underlying instrument is 81, then the premium over intrinsic value of this option is 6 (9 − the intrinsic value of 3). If the current price of the underlying instrument is 72 instead of 81, then the premium over intrinsic value of this option is 9, since the option has no intrinsic value.

There are two ways in which an investor may realize the value of a position taken in the option. He may exercise the option giving him a position in the underlying instrument and simultaneously take an offsetting position in the cash market for the underlying instrument. For example, for our hypothetical call option with an exercise price of 78 and an option price of 9 and in which the current price of the underlying instrument is 81, the option buyer can exercise the option. This will give the option buyer a long position in the underlying instrument at 78. By simultaneously selling the underlying instrument for 81, the option holder will realize 3. Alternatively, the option buyer may sell the call option for 9. Obviously, the latter is the preferable alternative. Because the exercise of an option will cause the immediate loss of any premium over intrinsic value that the option has left (in this case 6), options are not likely to be exercised very often.[16] Furthermore, unlike the analogous exercise of an option on common stocks, which results in ownership of (or a short position in) a lasting asset, for an option on an interest rate futures contract, exercise results only in a futures position that is itself due to settle.

Factors that Affect the Option Premium[17]

The five factors that affect the option premium are (1) the current price of the underlying instrument relative to the exercise price, (2) the time remaining until the expiration of the option, (3) the anticipated volatility of the price of the underlying instrument, (4) the coupon (if any) of the underlying instrument, and (5) the level of short-term interest rates for borrowing and lending over the life of the option.[18]

---

[16] For a discussion of situations in which early exercise of exchange-traded fixed income options would be advantageous, see Robert W. Kopprasch, *Exchange-Traded Options on Fixed-Income Securities* (New York: Salomon Brothers Inc., February 1982), pp. 16–17.

[17] The results described in this section are discussed in greater depth in Mark Pitts, "An Introduction to the Pricing of Options on Debt Instruments," Chapter 3 in Fabozzi (ed.), *Winning the Interest Rate Game.*

[18] In the case of options on common stock and stock indexes, the cumulative dividends before expiration will affect the option premium because such distributions are not added to the exercise price if the option is exercised. However, in the case of exchange-traded options on fixed income securities, the accrued coupon interest is added to the exercise price. Consequently, accrued coupon interest will not affect the option premium for exchange-traded options on fixed income securities.

1. Current price of the underlying instrument relative to the exercise price. As we explained earlier, the current price of the underlying instrument relative to the exercise price determines whether the option has intrinsic value. But the relationship is also important for the premium over intrinsic value component of the option premium.

All other factors equal, an at-the-money option generally has the greatest premium over intrinsic value. For an in-the-money option in which the current price of the underlying instrument differs substantially from the exercise price, the premium over intrinsic value is small. One of the reasons is the reduced leverage provided by purchasing the option compared to directly acquiring a position in the underlying instrument. For a substantially out-of-the-money option, the premium over intrinsic value is generally small in spite of the substantial leverage afforded by purchasing the option. This is because there is a lower probability that it will be profitable to exercise the option.

2. Time remaining to the expiration of the option. An option is a "wasting asset." That is, after the expiration date the option has no value. All other factors equal, one would expect that the longer the time to expiration of the option, the greater the option premium. This is because, as the time to expiration decreases, less time remains for the price of the underlying instrument to change so as to compensate the option buyer for any premium over intrinsic value he has paid. Consequently, for American options, as the time remaining until expiration decreases, the option price approaches its intrinsic value.

3. Anticipated volatility of the underlying instrument. All other factors equal, the greater the anticipated volatility of the underlying instrument, the more an investor would be willing to pay for the option and the more an option writer would demand for it. This is because the greater the volatility, the greater the probability that the price of the underlying instrument will move in favor of the option buyer before expiration.

4. The coupon of the underlying instrument. Coupons tend to decrease the value of call options and increase the value of put options. Consequently, call options on fixed income instruments with a high coupon will be less desirable than for call options on lower coupon securities.

5. Level of short-term interest rates for borrowing and lending over the life of the option. Short-term interest rates reflect the cost of carrying a position in a particular underlying instrument or a call option on that underlying instrument. As short-term interest rates rise, the cost of carrying a nondebt instrument such as common stock will rise and the call will be more attractive relative to the underlying instrument. Consequently, for call options on common stock (and also stock indexes), as the level of short-term interest rates rise, the call option premium will increase. On the other hand, for debt instruments, any rise in short-term interest rates will have an adverse impact on the price of the debt instrument which will dominate the impact on carry. Consequently, for call options on debt instruments, a rise in short-term interest rates will cause option premiums to increase. Put options, however, will decrease in value as short-term interest rates rise.[19]

For options on futures contracts there is no carry. It can be shown that for European options on interest rate futures an increase in short-term interest rates will decrease the value of call options, as well as put options.[20]

We have limited our discussion to the factors that influence option prices. Evaluation of options is beyond the scope of this chapter, but any portfolio manager using options should try to have a thorough understanding of the principles of option evaluation. There is no reason why every portfolio manager should understand the mechanics of an option evaluation model or be prepared to develop detailed volatility estimates for the underlying instrument. A portfolio manager planning to employ options in a portfolio strategy should, however, understand that the principal decision variable in the process of option evaluation is the price volatility of the underlying instrument.[21] When planning to adopt the values furnished by vendors of a commercial option evaluation model, the portfolio manager should question how the volatility estimate is being used in the model and how it was developed.

Margin Requirements

There are no margin requirements for the buyer of an option once the premium has been paid in full. Because the premium is the maximum amount that the investor can lose no matter how adverse the price movement of the underlying instrument, there is no need for margin.

---

[19] See Pitts, "An Introduction to the Pricing of Options on Debt Instruments."

[20] Pitts, "An Introduction to the Pricing of Options on Debt Instruments."

[21] The most commonly used option evaluation model is that developed by Fischer Black and Myron Scholes, "The Pricing of Options and Corporate Liabilities," *Journal of Political Economy*, May–June 1973, pp. 637–54. For a discussion of various common stock option evaluation models, see Gary L. Gastineau, *The Stock Options Manual* (New York: McGraw-Hill, 1979), pp. 214–63. Option evaluation models for fixed income securities and interest rate futures are discussed in the following: Mark Pitts, "An Introduction to the Pricing of Options on Debt Instruments;" Albert Madansky, "Debt Options," presented to The Institute of Quantitative Research in Finance, Fall Seminar, 1982; and George Courtadon, "The Pricing of Options on Default-Free Bonds," paper presented at the Conference on Options Pricing Theory and Applications, sponsored by the Salomon Brothers Center for the Study of Financial Institutions, New York University, January 18–19, 1982.

On the other hand, because the writer (seller) of an option has agreed to accept all of the risk (and none of the reward) of the position in the underlying instrument, the writer (seller) is required to put up not only the margin required on the interest rate futures contract position if that is the underlying instrument, but, with certain exceptions, the option premium that he is paid for the option. In addition, as prices adversely affect the writer's position, the writer would be required to deposit additional margin on the increased premium as it was marked to market. An exception occurs when the option is out of the money, in which case the premium-plus-futures margin requirement is reduced, depending on the particular option.

Risk-Return Trade-Off for Basic Option Strategies

In this section we will illustrate the risk-return trade-off associated with the four basic option strategies—buying call options, buying put options, writing (selling) call options, and writing (selling) put options. We shall use options on interest rate futures in our illustrations because of the apparent greater popularity compared to options on cash market securities at the time of this writing. *In the illustrations, we shall assume that the option is held to expiration and not exercised early.*

Buying Call Options

The most straightforward option strategy for participating in an anticipated decrease in interest rates (i.e., upward movement of bond prices) is to buy a call option. The investor who buys a call option is said to be in a "long call" position.

To illustrate this strategy, assume the following hypothetical option premiums for three CBT December call options on the CBT Treasury bond futures contract:

Option	Option Premium
December 86 call option	6
December 88 call option	5
December 94 call option	3

Current price of the December futures contract: 88

Suppose the investor purchases the December 88 call for 5. The option premium is $5,000 (5 × $1,000). The option premium represents the maximum loss that the option buyer faces by buying a call. If the settlement price of the December CBT Treasury bond futures contract is 88 or less at expiration, the buyer of this call option will lose the entire option premium, $5,000. The investor will break even if the settlement price of the futures contract at expiration is 93 (the exercise price plus the premium). Any settlement price between 88 and 93 reduces the investor's loss to an amount less than the option premium. On the other hand, should the settlement price of the futures contract at expiration exceed 93, the option buyer will realize a profit of $1,000 for each point by which the settlement price exceeds 93.

Figure 8–3 graphically portrays the profit profile of an investor who buys the at-the-money December 88 CBT call option at 5. For comparative purposes, Figure 8–3 also shows the profit profile of an investor who buys a CBT December futures contract at 88. An investor who takes a long futures position will realize a $1,000 gain for each point by which the settlement price of the futures contract exceeds 88 and a $1,000 loss for each point by which the settlement price of the futures contract falls below 88. The unlimited return potential and limited risk position of the buyer of a call option versus the unlimited return and the substantial risk exposure of the long futures position can be seen from Figure 8–3.

The investor could have selected any one of the three hypothetical call options on the CBT December futures contract. The December 86 is in the money; the December 88 is at the money; and the December 94 is out of the money. Figure 8–4 portrays the profit profile for the December 86 call option at 6, the December 88 call option at 5, and the December 94 call option at 3. Because the premium paid for call options with high exercise prices will be lower than the premium paid for call options with low exercise prices, higher prices have both a higher potential return per investment (premium paid) and a smaller maximum dollar loss. Of course, higher exercise prices are also farther out of reach than lower exercise prices.

Buying Put Options

The most straightforward option strategy for benefiting from an anticipated increase in interest rates (i.e., decline in bond prices) is to buy a put option. The investor who purchases a put option is said to be in a "long put" position.

To illustrate this strategy, assume the following hypothetical option premium for a CBT December put option on the CBT's Treasury bond futures contract:

December 88 put option   Option premium: 5

Current price of the December futures contract: 88

Suppose an investor buys this at-the-money put option for a premium of

Figure 8–3
Profit Profile of a Long Call Option versus a Long
Futures Position

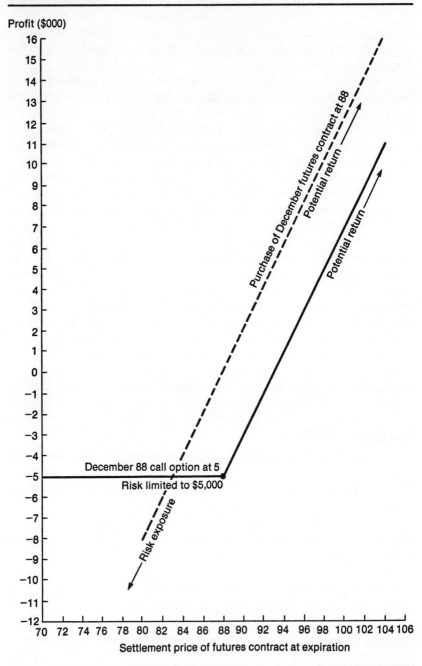

Profit ($000)

December 88 call option at 5
Risk limited to $5,000

Purchase of December futures contract at 88
Potential return
Potential return
Risk exposure

Settlement price of futures contract at expiration

Figure 8–4
Profit Profile for Three Long Call Positions

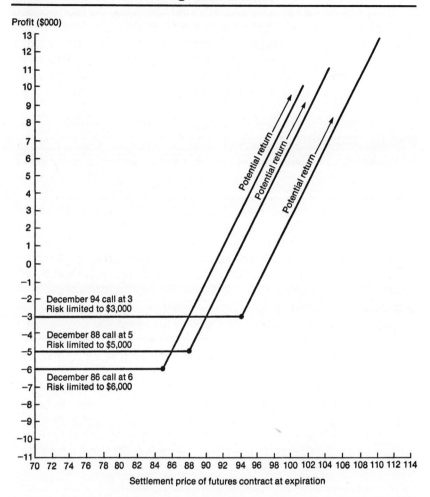

Profit ($000)

December 94 call at 3
Risk limited to $3,000

December 88 call at 5
Risk limited to $5,000

December 86 call at 6
Risk limited to $6,000

Settlement price of futures contract at expiration

$5,000 (5 × $1,000). Should the settlement price of the CBT December futures contract at expiration be greater than the exercise price of 88, the put option will expire worthless and the investor will lose the entire premium of $5,000. The investor will recover the premium but show no profit or loss if the settlement price of the futures contract is 83 (the exercise price of 88 minus the premium of 5). For any settlement price for the futures contract between 83 and 88 at expiration, the investor will reduce his loss below the premium of $5,000. The investor will realize a $1,000 profit for each point by which the settlement price of the futures contract at expiration is below the break-even price of 83.

The profit profile of the December 88 put option and the short position in a December futures contract are shown in Figure 8–5. Once again, it can be seen that the futures position offers a potential for substantial return but with substantial risk. As in the case of call options, there is limited risk for the buyer of a put; the return for the buyer is limited to the maximum price by which the underlying instrument can fall at expiration.

Writing (Selling) Call Options

An investor who believes that interest rates will advance or stay flat can, if his expectations are correct, realize income by writing (selling) a call option. A call writer is said to be in a "short call" position.

To illustrate this option strategy we shall use the three December call options on the CBT December futures contract used to illustrate the strategy of buying a call option.

The profit profile of the call writer is the mirror image of the profit profile of the call buyer. As in the case of a long futures and short futures position, we have a zero-sum game. That is, the profit position of the writer is of the same dollar magnitude but in the opposite direction of the buyer.

Figure 8–6 portrays the profit profile of the December 88 call option writer. The maximum profit that the call writer can realize is the amount of the premium, $5,000. As long as the settlement price of the futures contract is less than 93 (exercise price of 88 plus the premium of 5), the writer will realize a profit.

If the settlement price of the futures contract at expiration is greater than 93, the call writer will realize a $1,000 loss for each point above 93. Also shown in Figure 8–6 is the profit profile of a call buyer (long call position). Figure 8–7 graphically depicts the profit profile for the writer of a December 86, December 88, and December 94 call option.

Writing Put Options

An investor who believes that interest rates will decline or stay flat can, if his expectations are correct, realize income by writing (selling) a put option. A put writer is said to be in a "short put" position.

The December 88 put option will be used to illustrate the risk-return parameters of a put writer. It should be no surprise that the profit profile of the put writer is the mirror image of that of the buyer of a put option. What the put buyer gains (loses) the put seller loses (gains). The profit profile of the December 88 put option writer is depicted in Figure 8–8 along with the

Figure 8–5
Profit Profile of a Long Put versus a Short Futures Position

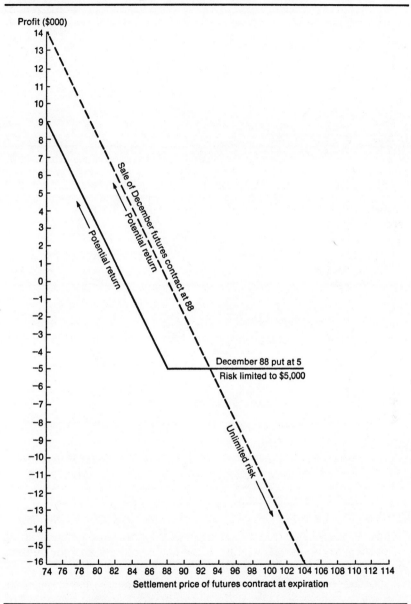

Figure 8–6
Profit Profile of a Short Call Position versus a Long Call Position

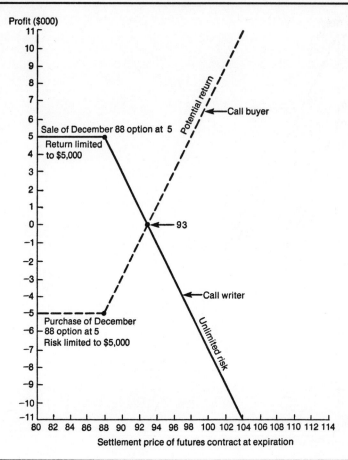

Profit ($000)

Sale of December 88 option at 5
Return limited to $5,000

93

Call buyer

Potential return

Call writer

Unlimited risk

Purchase of December 88 option at 5
Risk limited to $5,000

Settlement price of futures contract at expiration

long put position. The maximum profit that the option writer can realize is the amount of the premium. As long as the settlement price of the futures contract is greater than 83 (exercise price of 88 minus the premium of 5), the put writer will realize a profit. If the settlement price of the futures contract at expiration is 83, the put writer will break even. Any settlement price for the futures contract at expiration that is less than the break-even price will produce a $1,000 loss for each point below 83.

Figure 8–9 compares the profit profile for the writer of three different December put contracts. The assumed exercise prices are 84, 88, and 92 and the corresponding option premiums are 3, 5, and 7, respectively.

Figure 8–7
Profit Profile for Three Short Call Positions

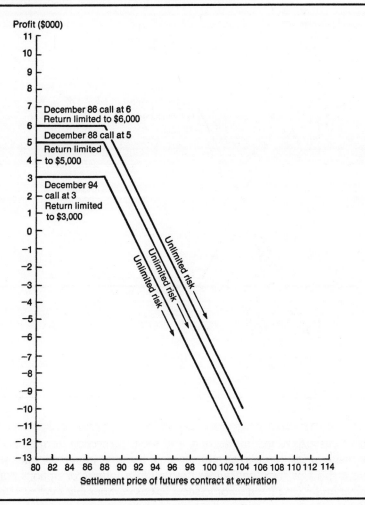

Profit ($000)

December 86 call at 6
Return limited to $6,000

December 88 call at 5
Return limited to $5,000

December 94 call at 3
Return limited to $3,000

Unlimited risk
Unlimited risk
Unlimited risk

Settlement price of futures contract at expiration

■ Bond Portfolio Applications

There are four ways in which futures and options may be used by a bond portfolio manager.

Hedging

The principle behind the hedging of a position in a fixed income security against adverse interest rate risk is quite simple. A bond portfolio manager

Figure 8–8
Profit Profile of a Short Put Position versus a Long Put Position

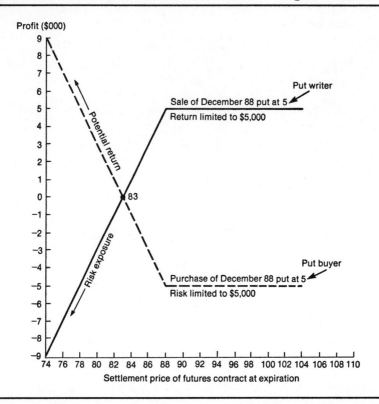

who owns a fixed income security and seeks protection from a decline in the value of his portfolio as a result of an increase in interest rates should take a short or short-equivalent position in a futures or options contract whose underlying fixed income security has comparable interest rate risk. On the other hand, a portfolio manager who wishes to protect against a future decrease in interest rates, should take a long or long-equivalent position in a futures or options contract whose underlying fixed income instrument has comparable interest rate risk. Such transactions will result in the market risk in one position being offset by the market risk in the other. When the fixed income security to be hedged has some of the risks in common with the fixed income security underlying the hedging instrument (futures or options contract) and some risks which are not common, a *cross-hedge* exists.

The key to hedging and cross-hedging is understanding how to deter-

Figure 8–9
Profit Profile for Three Short Put Positions

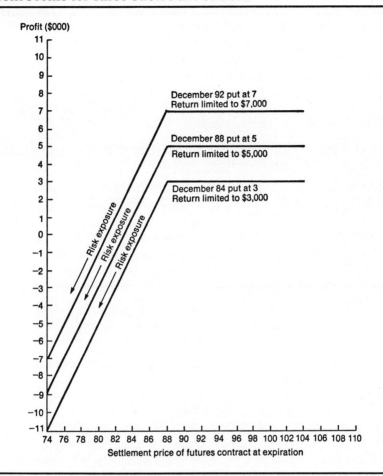

Settlement price of futures contract at expiration

mine the *bond risk equivalent* position. We will discuss how this is done after we illustrate the hedging strategies with both futures and options.

Immunization

In Chapter 6 we discussed immunization strategies. Basically, immunization involves constructing a portfolio of bonds so as to minimize the risk that the portfolio will not reach a target value regardless of how interest rates change. Our illustrations in that chapter restricted the universe of acceptable portfolio instruments to bonds. However, interest rate futures can be used to accomplish immunization. The advantage of using interest rate futures to immunize a portfolio is that the transaction costs, both initial and rebalancing, will be lower than for an immunized portfolio designed with only bonds. In addition, since during periods of high interest rates, the length of the immunization period is limited, interest rate futures can be used when an immunization period, greater than that possible with an all bonds approach, is sought. The disadvantage of using interest rate futures for immunization is that the immunization risk measure we presented in Chapter 6 will be inordinately large.

Increasing the Interest Rate Sensitivity of the Portfolio

When hedging, the portfolio manager attempts to eliminate or reduce the interest rate sensitivity of a portfolio. However, because the purchase of futures and call options results in a levered position, the interest rate sensitivity or duration of the portfolio will increase. A portfolio manager who expects interest rates to decline could increase the duration of the portfolio quickly and inexpensively by buying futures and/or buying call options rather than by swapping bonds with short durations for bonds with long durations.

Creating Alternative Investments

Futures and options can be used to create alternative synthetic investments that may offer enhanced returns. For example, by purchasing a Treasury obligation that is deliverable under a futures contract and selling that contract, a portfolio manager can effectively shorten the maturity of the Treasury obligation. The maturity of the synthetic short-term instrument is the delivery date of the futures contract. The redemption value of the synthetic short-term instrument is the futures price. Based on the maturity and redemption value of the synthetic short-term instrument, a return can be computed and compared to prevailing returns on short-term money market instruments of the same maturity to determine if there is a yield advantage after transaction costs for the synthetic short-term instrument.[22]

Call options offer several interesting strategies for creating alternative investments. For example, a portfolio manager can purchase a call as an alternative to investing in an equivalent par amount in the long-term sec-

---

[22] A simulation of how futures and options could have been used to create a synthetic short-term tax-exempt portfolio over the period January 1971 to September 1982 can be found in Gary L. Gastineau, "The Impact of Options and Financial Futures on Municipal Bond Portfolio Management," Chapter 35 in *The Municipal Bond Handbook: Volume I*, ed. Frank J. Fabozzi, Sylvan G. Feldstein, Irving M. Pollack, and Frank G. Zarb (Homewood, Ill.: Dow Jones-Irwin, 1983).

tor, using the excess funds to invest in short-term obligations. In our discussion of options, we explained how call options are beneficial when bond prices rise (i.e., interest rates fall). However, the synthetic investment created by this strategy generates a surprising result. This strategy actually provides an option on higher yields.[23]

■ Hedging with Interest Rate Futures

The most popular reason cited for using interest rate futures is the ability to hedge a cash market position. Hedging with futures involves the employment of a futures position as a temporary substitute for transactions to be made in the cash market at a later date. By hedging, the portfolio manager attempts to eliminate interest rate risk by trying to fix the price of a transaction to be made at a later date. If cash and futures prices move together, any loss (whether cash or futures) realized by the hedger from one position, will be offset by a profit on the other position.

In practice, hedging is not that simple. The amount of the loss and the profit from each position will not necessarily be identical. As we will explain, whether there is an overall profit or loss from a particular hedge will depend on the relationship between the cash price and the futures price when a hedge is placed and when it is lifted. Consequently, a hedger substitutes basis risk—the risk that the basis (cash minus futures price) will change—for price risk.

Some commodities do not have existing futures contracts. When a hedger assumes a futures position in a commodity different from that in which a cash position is held or will be held, the hedge, as we explained earlier, is a *cross hedge*. A hedger who seeks protection against potential adverse price movement for a commodity that does not have an existing futures contract will use a futures contract on an underlying commodity that he hopes will track the price of the commodity being hedged. For example, a party seeking to hedge against adverse price movements in okra will use a futures contract for some agricultural product rather than a futures contract on a precious metal such as gold or silver. Consequently, cross-hedging adds another dimension to basis risk. The future cash price of the commodity that is being hedged may not be tracked well by the commodity that is being used for the hedge.

Cross-hedging with futures, as well as options, is the name of the game in portfolio management. Other than the few interest rate futures contracts currently traded, there are no futures contracts for specific debt instruments and common stock shares. For example, suppose that a portfolio manager wants to hedge a position in a long-term corporate bond of a

---

[23] For an analysis of this strategy, see Kopprasch, *Exchange-Traded Options on Fixed-Income Securities*, pp. 10–14.

particular issuer against adverse price movements due to an increase in market yields. He would have to use an existing futures contract on long-term Treasury bonds or notes, since futures contracts on corporate bonds are not available. Because interest rates for all fixed income obligations frequently move in the same direction, the future cash price of the Treasury bond may track the future cash price of the corporate bond well.

The foregoing points will be made clearer in the illustrations presented here.

A *short hedge* is used by a hedger to protect against a decline in the future cash price of a commodity or financial instrument. To execute a short hedge, the hedger sells a futures contract (agrees to make delivery of the underlying commodity or financial instrument). Consequently, a short hedge is also known as a *sell hedge.* By establishing a short hedge, the hedger has fixed the future cash price and transferred the price risk of ownership to the buyer of the contract. Three examples of how a short hedge may be used are:

1. A corn farmer will sell his product in three months. The price of corn, like the price of any commodity, will fluctuate in the open market. The corn farmer wants to lock in a price today at which he can deliver his corn in three months.

2. A portfolio manager expects that interest rates will rise dramatically in the next three months and would like to liquidate the fixed income portion of the portfolio; however, because of tax and accounting consider-ations, as well as transaction costs in reestablishing the fixed income portfolio, the manager decides against liquidating.[24] A short hedge could be used as an alternative to liquidating the portfolio.

3. A pension fund manager knows that the beneficiaries of the fund must be paid a total of $3 million four months from now. This will necessitate liquidating a portion of the fund's bond portfolio. Should the value of the portfolio decline due to an increase in interest rates four months from now, then a larger portion of the portfolio must be liquidated. The pension fund manager would like to lock in the price of the bonds in the portfolio.

A *long hedge* is undertaken to protect against the purchase of a commodity or financial instrument in the cash market at some future time. In a long hedge, the hedger buys a futures contract (agrees to accept delivery of the underlying commodity or financial instrument). A long hedge is also known as a *buy hedge.* The following three examples are instances in which a party may use a long hedge:

1. A food processing company projects that in three months it must purchase 30,000 bushels of corn. The management of the company does not want to take a chance that the price of corn may increase by the time

---

[24] Another reason for not liquidating the portfolio is that the amount to be liquidated can have an adverse impact on the price in the cash market.

the company must make its acquisition. Management wants to lock in a price of corn today.

2. A bond portfolio manager knows that in two months $10 million of his portfolio will mature and must be reinvested. Prevailing interest rates are high but may decline substantially in two months when the funds are to be reinvested. The portfolio manager wants to lock in a reinvestment rate today.

3. A pension fund manager expects a substantial contribution from participants four months from now. The contributions will be invested in fixed income securities. The pension fund manager expects that interest rates will decline dramatically by the time the contributions are received. The pension fund manager therefore wants to lock in a yield today so that contributions can be invested at a yield that is expected to be higher than at the time when the contributions are to be received.

Hedging Illustrations

To explain hedging, we shall first present several numerical illustrations from the commodities area.

Suppose that a corn farmer expects to sell 30,000 bushels of corn three months from now. Assume further that the management of a food processing company plans to purchase 30,000 bushels of corn three months from now. Both the corn farmer and the management of the food processing company want to lock in a price today. That is, they want to eliminate the price risk associated with corn three months from now. The cash or spot price for corn is currently $2.75 per bushel. The futures price for corn is currently $3.20 per bushel. Each futures contract is for 5,000 bushels of corn.

Since the corn farmer seeks protection against a decline in the price of corn three months from now, he will place a short or sell hedge. That is, he will promise to make delivery of corn at the current futures price. The corn farmer will sell six futures contracts since each contract calls for the delivery of 5,000 bushels of corn.

The management of the food processing company seeks protection against an increase in the price of corn three months from now. Consequently, management will place a buy or long hedge. That is, it will agree to accept delivery of corn at the futures price. Since protection is sought against a price increase for 30,000 bushels of corn, six contracts are bought.

Let's look at what happens under various scenarios for the cash price and futures price of corn three months from now when the hedge is lifted.

Suppose that, when the hedge is lifted, the cash price declines to $2.00 and the futures price declines to $2.45. Notice what has happened to the basis under this scenario. At the time the hedge was placed, the basis is −$.45 ($2.75 − $3.20). When the hedge is lifted, the basis is still −$.45 ($2.00 − $2.45).

The corn farmer, at the time the hedge was placed, wanted to lock in a price of $2.75 per bushel of corn or $82,500 for 30,000 bushels. He sold six futures contracts at a price of $3.20 per bushel or $96,000 for 30,000 bushels. When the hedge is lifted, the value of the farmer's corn is $60,000 ($2.00 × 30,000). The corn farmer realizes a decline in the cash market in the value of his corn of $22,500. However, the futures price declines to $2.45 so that the cost to the corn farmer to liquidate his futures position is only $73,500 ($2.45 × 30,000). The corn farmer realizes a gain in the futures market of $22,500. The net result is that the gain in the futures market matches the loss in the cash market. Consequently, the corn farmer does not realize an overall gain or loss. When this occurs, the hedge is said to be a *perfect* or *textbook* hedge.

Because there was a decline in the cash price, the food processing company would realize a gain in the cash market of $22,500 but would realize a loss in the futures market of the same amount. Therefore, this buy or long hedge is also a *perfect* or *textbook* hedge.

This scenario illustrates two important points. First, for both participants there was no overall gain or loss. The reason for this result was that we assumed that the basis did not change when the hedge was lifted. Thus, if the basis does not change, a perfect hedge will be achieved. Second, notice that the management of the food processing company would have been better off if it had not hedged. The cost of corn would have been $22,500 less in the cash market three months later. This, however, should not be interpreted as a sign of poor planning by management. Management is not in the business of speculating on the price of corn in the future. Hedging is a standard practice to protect against an increase in the cost of doing business in the future.

Suppose that the cash price of corn when the hedge is lifted increases to $3.55 and that the futures price increases to $4.00. Notice that the basis is unchanged at −$.45. Since the basis is unchanged, the cash and futures price we have assumed in this scenario will produce a perfect hedge.

The corn farmer will gain in the cash market since the value of 30,000 bushels of corn is $106,500 ($3.55 × 30,000). This represents a $24,000 gain compared to the cash value at the time the hedge was placed. However, the corn farmer must liquidate his position in the futures market by buying six futures contracts at a total cost of $120,000 which is $24,000 more than when the contracts were sold. The loss in the futures market offsets the gain in the cash market and we have a perfect hedge. The food processing company would realize a gain in the futures market of $24,000 but would have to pay $24,000 more in the cash market to acquire 30,000 bushels of corn.

Notice that the management of the food processing company under this scenario saved $24,000 in the cost of corn by employing a hedge. The corn farmer, on the other hand, would have been better off if he had not used a hedging strategy and simply sold his product on the market three months later. However, it must be emphasized that the corn farmer, just like the management of the food processing company, employed a hedge to protect against unforeseen adverse price changes in the cash market.

In the previous two scenarios we have assumed that the basis does not change when the hedge is lifted. In the real world, the basis does, in fact, change between the time a hedge is placed and when it is lifted. Now we shall illustrate what happens when the basis changes.

Assume that the cash price of corn decreases to $2.00, just as in the first scenario; however, assume also that the futures price decreases to $2.70 rather than $2.45. The basis has now widened from −$.45 to −$.70 ($2.00 − $2.70). For the short (sell) hedge, the loss in the cash market of $22,500 is only partially offset by a $15,000 gain realized in the futures market. Consequently, the hedge resulted in an overall loss of $7,500.

There are two points to note here. First, if the corn farmer had not employed the hedge, the loss would have been $22,500 since the value of his 30,000 bushels of corn is $60,000 compared to $82,500 three months earlier. Although the hedge is not a perfect hedge because the basis widened, the loss of $7,500 is less than the loss of $22,500 if no hedge had been placed. This is what we meant earlier in the chapter when we said that hedging substitutes basis risk for price risk. Second, the management of the food processing company faces the same problem from an opposite perspective. An unexpected gain for either participant results in an unexpected loss of equal dollar value for the other. That is, the participants face a "zero-sum game." Consequently, the food processing company would realize an overall gain of $7,500 from its long (buy) hedge. This gain represents a gain of $22,500 in the cash market, and a realized loss of $15,000 in the futures market.

The results of this scenario demonstrate that when (a) the future price is greater than the cash price at the time the hedge is placed, (b) the cash price declines, and (c) the basis widens, then: *the short (sell) hedger will realize an overall loss from the hedge, and the long (buy) hedger will realize an overall gain from the hedge.*

Table 8–1 summarizes the impact of a change in the basis on the overall profit or loss of a hedge when the futures price is greater than the cash price at the time the hedge is placed.

Cross-Hedging

Not all commodities have a futures market. Consequently, if a hedger wants to protect against the price risk of a commodity in which a futures

Table 8–1
Summary of Basis Relationships for a Hedge

Price		Absolute Change in Basis	Overall Gain (+) or Loss (−) When at Time Hedge Is Placed Cash Price Is Less than Futures Price	
Cash	Futures		Short Hedge	Long Hedge
Decreases	Decreases by same amount	No change	0	0
Decreases	Decreases by a smaller amount	Widens	−	+
Decreases	Decreases by a greater amount	Narrows	+	−
Increases	Increases by same amount	No change	0	0
Increases	Increases by a smaller amount	Narrows	+	−
Increases	Increases by a greater amount	Widens	−	+

contract is not traded, the hedger may use a commodity that he believes has a close price relationship to the one he seeks to hedge. This adds another dimension of risk when hedging. The cash market price relationship between the commodity to be hedged and the commodity used to hedge may change.

Since hedging fixed income securities using interest rate futures frequently involves cross-hedging, we will first illustrate the key elements associated with a cross-hedge for a commodity.

Suppose that an okra farmer plans to sell 37,500 bushels of okra three months from now and that a food processing company plans to purchase the same amount of okra three months from now. Both parties want to hedge against price risk. However, okra futures contracts are not traded. Both parties believe that there is a close price relationship between okra and corn. Specifically, both parties believe that the cash price of okra will be 80 percent of the cash price of corn. The cash price of okra is currently $2.20 per bushel and the cash price of corn is currently $2.75 per bushel. The futures price of corn is currently $3.20 per bushel.

Let's examine various scenarios to see how effective the cross-hedge will be. In each scenario, the difference between the cash price of corn and the futures price of corn at the time the cross-hedge is placed and at the time it is lifted will be assumed to be unchanged at −$.45. This is done so that we may focus on the importance of the relationship between the two cash prices at the two points in time.

We must first determine how many corn futures contracts must be used in the cross-hedge. The cash value of 37,500 bushels of okra at the cash price of $2.20 per bushel is $82,500. To protect a value of $82,500 using corn futures with a current cash price of $2.75, the price of 30,000 bushels of corn ($82,500/$2.75) must be hedged. Since each corn futures contract involves 5,000 bushels, six corn futures contracts will be used.

Suppose that the cash price of okra and corn decrease to $1.60 and $2.00 per bushel, respectively, and the futures price of corn decreases to $2.45 per bushel. The relationship between the cash price for okra and corn assumed when the cross-hedge was placed holds at the time the cross-hedge is lifted. That is, the cash price of okra is 80 percent of the cash price of corn. The basis for the cash price of corn and the futures price of corn is still −$.45 at the time the cross-hedge is lifted.

The short cross-hedge produces a gain in the futures market of $22,500 and an exact offset loss in the cash market. The opposite occurs for the long cross-hedge. There is neither an overall gain nor a loss from the cross-hedge in this case. That is, we have a perfect cross-hedge. The same would occur if we assume that the cash price of both commodities increases by the same percentage and the basis does not change.

Suppose that the cash price of both commodities decreases but the cash price of okra falls by a greater percentage than the cash price of corn. For example, suppose that the cash price of okra falls to $1.30 per bushel while the cash price of corn falls to $2.00 per bushel. The futures price of corn falls to $2.45 so that the basis is not changed. The cash price of okra at the time the cross-hedge is lifted is 65 percent of the cash price of corn rather than 80 percent as assumed when the cross-hedge was constructed.

For the short cross-hedge the loss in the cash market exceeds the realized loss in the futures market by $11,200. For the long cross-hedge the opposite is true. There is an overall gain from the cross-hedge of $11,200. Had the cash price of okra fallen by less than the decline in the cash price of corn, the short cross-hedge would have produced an overall gain while the long cross-hedge would have generated an overall loss.

Hedging Bonds with Futures

To hedge a long or short position in a bond issue using interest rate futures it is necessary to determine the appropriate *bond risk equivalent* position. That is, the number of futures contracts that must be bought or sold per $100,000 par amount of the bond being hedged in order to equalize the dollar magnitude of the cash and futures market position must be estimated. This amount is referred to as the *hedge ratio*.

Several methods have been suggested to estimate the hedge ratio. One approach involves the following four steps:[25]

[25] Robert W. Kopprasch, *An Introduction to Financial Futures on Treasury Securities* (New York: Salomon Brothers Inc., December 1981), p. 13.

Step 1. Using regression analysis estimate the yield volatility of the bond issue to be hedged *relative* to the futures. The yield on the T-bond futures is derived from the price as if it were a 20-year bond with an 8 percent coupon. The regression to be estimated is:

yield on bond issue to be hedged = $a + b \times$ yield on T-bond futures

where a and b are the parameters to be estimated from time series data. The estimate of the slope, b, is the *relative yield volatility*.

Step 2. Determine the price volatility of both the bond issue to be hedged and the futures to equal yield changes at their current yield levels. Once again, the price volatility of the T-bond futures should be computed assuming a 20-year, 8 percent coupon bond.

Step 3. For the bond issue to be hedged, multiply its relative yield volatility, b, as found in step 1 by its price volatility as found in step 2. The result is the price volatility after accounting for relative yield volatility.

Step 4. Divide the quantity found in step 3 by the price volatility found for the T-bond futures in step 2. The result is the *hedge ratio*.

In step 1, the analysis could also be performed by estimating the relative yield volatility between the bond issue to be hedged and the cheapest deliverable issue at the time the hedge is placed. Using this approach, it would then be necessary to multiply the hedge ratio by the conversion factor for the cheapest deliverable issue in step 4. We shall illustrate this approach when we illustrate how to use options for hedging.

For example, suppose that in 1979 a bond portfolio manager sought to hedge a long position in the 10⅜s Treasury bonds maturing on November 15, 2009 and selling at 103.523 to yield 10 percent.[26] Using the December 1979 T-bond futures contract selling at 81.07, the hedge ratio is determined as follows:

Step 1. Regression analysis would suggest that the relative yield volatility, b, is 1.

Step 2. To determine the price volatility of both the 10⅜s of 2009 and the December 1979 T-bond futures contract to equal yield changes at their current yield levels, vary the yield up and down five basis points to determine the price change for 10 basis points:

Bond issue to be hedged: 10⅜s November 15, 2009
Yield: 10%
Price: 103.523

---

[26] This illustration is taken from Kopprasch, *An Introduction to Financial Futures*, pp. 13–14.

Price if yield decreases 5 basis points to 9.95% = 104.013
Price if yield increases 5 basis points to 10.05% = 103.038
Dollar price change for 10 basis point change   =   .975
Price volatility per basis point change   = $0.0975

T-bond futures contract: December 31, 1979 settlement
Yield based on 20-year, 8 percent coupon: 10%
Price: 81.07
Price if yield decreases 5 basis points to 9.95% = 81.466
Price if yield increases 5 basis points to 10.05% = 80.678
Dollar price change for 10 basis point change   =   .788
Price volatility per basis point change   = $0.0788

Step 3. Determine the price volatility of the 10⅜s after accounting for relative yield volatility by multiplying *b* as found in step 1 by the price volatility found in step 2. Since *b* is one and the price volatility per basis point change is $0.0975, price volatility after considering relative yield volatility is $0.0975.

Step 4. To find the hedge ratio, divide the price volatility found in step 3 by the price volatility for the T-bond futures found in step 2.

$$\text{Hedge ratio} = \frac{\$0.0975}{\$0.0788}$$
$$= 1.24$$

The hedge ratio of 1.24 means that 1.24 T-bond futures contracts would be sold per $100,000 par amount of the 10⅜s of 2009 to be hedged.

It is interesting to note that the conversion factor for the 10⅜s of 2009, if that issue had been used for delivery against the March 1980 T-bond futures contract, was 1.2675. The conversion factor in this case is not materially different from the hedge ratio computed above. When the relative yield volatility is 1 to 1, then the conversion factor can be used as the hedge ratio when hedging Treasury bonds.[27]

Figure 8–10 shows the effectiveness of hedging the 10⅜s of 2009 using T-bond futures over the period December 1979 to November 1981 using a hedge ratio of 1.25. The simulated results indicate that the hedging strategy would have been effective. While the value of the unhedged bond position ranged from 69.5 to 103.523, the value of the hedged position moved within a seven-point range despite the fact that the hedge ratio was not adjusted.

Although the foregoing illustration is for a hedge of Treasury bonds, the same principles apply for hedging corporate bonds. Figure 8–11 dem-

---

[27] The conversion factor can also be used to hedge a deliverable bond that will be held to settlement.

Figure 8–10
Treasury Bond Price Level: Hedged and Unhedged

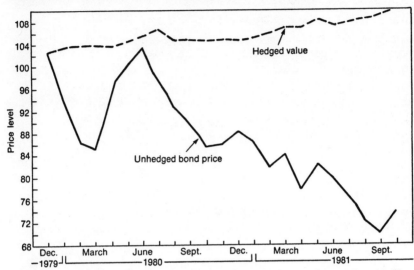

Source: Robert W. Kopprasch, *An Introduction to Financial Futures on Treasury Securities* (New York: Salomon Brothers Inc., December 1981), Figure 6.

Figure 8–11
Corporate Bond Price Level: Hedged and Unhedged

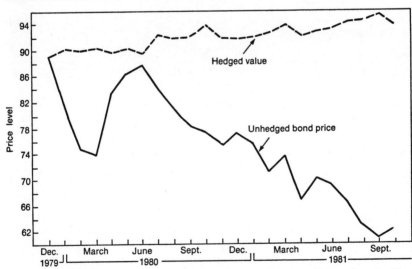

Source: Robert W. Kopprasch, *An Introduction to Financial Futures on Treasury Securities* (New York: Salomon Brothers Inc., December 1981), Figure 8.

onstrates the effectiveness of using T-bond futures to hedge a long position in 10% debentures rated AAA/Aaa for the period December 1979 to November 1981. The hedge ratio used for the entire period was 1.09. Despite the fact that the hedge ratio was not revised during the simulated period as it would be in an actual application, Figure 8–11 indicates that the hedged corporate bond portfolio remained stable while the unhedged corporate bond portfolio fluctuated substantially in value. It should be noted that Figure 8–11 does not indicate the margin flows over the period. The margin flows would have been substantial on several occasions—roughly $14,000 per contract in a two-month period. Therefore, provision must be made for margin variation when establishing a hedging strategy using futures.

■ Hedging with Options

When a portfolio manager uses interest rate futures to reduce downside risk, he sacrifices upside potential. Options on fixed income securities and options on interest rate futures also can be used to provide downside risk protection; however, the cost of this protection is known and leaves any remaining upside potential intact.

The purchase of put options provides protection against adverse interest rate movements. When interest rates are expected to rise and bond prices fall, the purchase of a put would be appropriate because it locks in a price (yield) at which a fixed income security (or an interest rate futures contract) can be sold. The locked-in price is the exercise price of the put. On the other hand, when rates are expected to fall and the portfolio manager seeks protection against such a situation, the purchase of a call option would be an appropriate strategy. This is because the buyer locks in the price (yield) at which he could purchase a fixed income security (or an interest rate futures contract). Once again, the locked-in price is the exercise price of the option. The cost of insuring a minimum price in the case of a put and a maximum price in the case of a call is the option premium.

Using Puts to Protect against a Rise in Interest Rates

The purchase of a put option can be used to protect against a rise in interest rates. Such a strategy is commonly referred to as a *protective put* strategy.

To illustrate this strategy, we shall consider the case of a put option on an interest rate futures contract. To simplify the illustration, assume the following. A portfolio manager has a long position in an interest rate futures contract that is currently selling at 90. A put option with an exercise price of 84 and *t* months to expiration is available on that particular futures contract. The option premium is 2. Table 8–2 shows the profit and loss at

Table 8–2
Illustration of a Protective Put Strategy to Protect against a Rise in Interest Rates

Assumptions:
Current price of futures = 90
Exercise price of put   = 84
Option premium   = 2

Settlement Price of Futures at Expiration Date	Profit or Loss from		
	Long Futures Position	Long Put Position	Combined Position (Protective Put)
106	16	−2	14
104	14	−2	12
102	12	−2	10
100	10	−2	8
98	8	−2	6
96	6	−2	4
94	4	−2	2
92	2	−2	0
90	0	−2	−2
88	−2	−2	−4
86	−4	−2	−6
84	−6	−2	−8
82	−8	0	−8
80	−10	2	−8
78	−12	4	−8
76	−14	6	−8

Profits and losses are computed as follows:
For long futures   = Settlement price − 90
For long put   = Max [0, (84 − settlement price)] − 2
For protective put = Long futures + long put

the expiration date of the put option for (1) a long position in the futures contract, (2) a long position in the put (i.e., purchase of the put), and (3) the protective put strategy (i.e., the combined position of the long futures and long put).

Notice from Table 8–2 that the maximum loss the portfolio manager is exposed to from this strategy is 8 points. This occurs when the settlement price of the futures contract at the expiration date is 84 or less. However, the upside potential is still intact. The upside potential mirrors that of the long futures position. The upside profit is simply reduced by 2, representing the cost of the option premium, for each settlement price.

There are two points worth noting about the protective put strategy. First, the maximum loss in this illustration is the difference between the current futures price and the exercise price (i.e., the amount by which this option is out of the money) plus the put premium. The portfolio manager usually has options with several exercise prices available and can thereby select the maximum loss that he is willing to accept. That is, the portfolio can determine the amount of the insurance he is willing to pay to protect against adverse interest rate movements. Second, notice from Figure 8–3 that the pattern of the profit profile of the protective put strategy is the same as that of the buyer of a call option. In fact, the protective put with an exercise price of 84 and a price of 2 has the same profit profile as that of the buyer of a call option with an exercise price of 84 and a price of 8.

Using Calls to Protect Against a Decline in Interest Rates

In our discussion of futures, we provided several scenarios in which a portfolio manager may find it desirable to protect against a drop in interest rates. A long call position (i.e., purchase of a call) can be used to provide protection in this case.

Once again, we shall use call options on interest rate futures to illustrate this strategy. The following are assumed in our illustration. A portfolio manager has a short position in an interest rate futures contract whose current price is 90. A call option with an exercise price of 94 and *t* months to expiration is available on that particular futures contract. The option premium is 4. Table 8–3 shows the profit and loss at the expiration date of the call option for (1) a short position in the futures contract, (2) a long position in the call (i.e., purchase of the call), and (3) the combined position of the short futures and long call.

The maximum loss that the portfolio manager is exposed to is 8 points. This occurs if the settlement price of the futures contract at the expiration date is 90 or greater. The upside potential remains intact, mirroring that of the short futures position. The upside profit is simply reduced by the cost of the option, 4 in our illustration, for each settlement price.

Notice that the pattern of the profit profile of the portfolio manager using this strategy is the same as that of a buyer of a put. In this case, the purchase of a put with an exercise price of 94 and a price of 8 will generate the same profit profile as the protective call strategy.

Cross-Hedging

In applying the two strategies just mentioned to hedge against adverse interest movements of a fixed income security that is not the underlying instrument of an options contract, it is necessary to create a cross-hedge. Constructing a cross-hedge requires that the portfolio manager (1) determine the appropriate exercise price and expiration date and (2) as in the case of hedging with futures, determine the appropriate bond risk equiva-

Table 8–3
Illustration of a Call Strategy to Protect against a Decline in Interest Rates

Assumptions:
Current price of futures = 90
Exercise price of call   = 94
Option premium   = 4

Settlement Price of Futures at Expiration Date	Profit or Loss from		
	Short Futures Position	Long Call Position	Combined Position
106	−16	8	−8
104	−14	6	−8
102	−12	4	−8
100	−10	2	−8
98	−8	0	−8
96	−6	−2	−8
94	−4	−4	−8
92	−2	−4	−6
90	0	−4	−4
88	2	−4	−2
86	4	−4	0
84	6	−4	2
82	8	−4	4
80	10	−4	6
78	12	−4	8
76	14	−4	10

Profits and losses are computed as follows:
For short futures   = 90 − settlement price
For long call   = Max [0, (settlement price − 94)] − 4
For combined position = Short futures + long call

lent position. As we explained earlier, the bond risk equivalent position is the number of contracts, in this case options, that must be bought or sold per $100,000 par amount of the bond being hedged in order to equalize the dollar magnitude of the cash and options market position. This amount we called the hedge ratio.

The first issue, the appropriate exercise price and expiration date, depends on the degree of protection the portfolio manager seeks. The cost of the protection is a function of the option premium which, in turn, depends on whether the option is in, at, or out of the money, and the time to expiration.

The four-step procedure employed to estimate the hedge ratio with futures can be used to estimate the hedge ratio when options are used. As we explained, there are two approaches that can be employed in step 1 of that procedure when options on futures are used for hedging. The first was to estimate the yield volatility of the bond issue to be hedged *relative* to the futures using regression analysis. The yield on the T-bond futures is derived from the price as if it were a 20-year bond with an 8 percent coupon. Alternatively, in step 1, an estimate of the relative yield volatility between the bond issue to be hedged and the cheapest deliverable issue at the time the hedge is placed can be estimated using regression analysis. It would then be necessary to multiply the hedge ratio by the conversion factor for the cheapest deliverable issue in step 4. We shall use the latter approach in our illustration of how to use options on futures for hedging.

To illustrate the protective put strategy for cross-hedging, let us assume the following:

1. A bond portfolio manager seeks to protect a long position in a long-term fixed income security, H, from a rise in interest rates.
2. The current price of H is 90.
3. The portfolio manager decides that he wants to lock in a price of 86. That is, a put option with the equivalent of an exercise price of 86 should be purchased. For purposes of this illustration, suppose that a price of 86 is equal to a yield to maturity of 13 percent.
4. The cheapest most deliverable bond for the T-bond futures contract is M. For purposes of this illustration, when the yield on M is 11.5 percent, the price of M is 135.
5. In step 1 of the four-step procedure to estimate the yield volatility of the bond to be hedged, H, *relative* to the cheapest deliverable bond, M, the result of the following regression:

$$\text{yield on bond } H = a + b \times \text{yield on bond } M$$

where b is the *relative yield volatility*, is:

$$\text{yield on bond } H = .10 + 1.12 \text{ yield on bond } M$$

6. At the current yield level, the price change of H for a one basis point change is \$.08 and the price change of M for a one basis point change is \$.10.
7. The conversion factor for M if it is delivered to settle a short position is 1.42.

The portfolio manager's mission is twofold. First, he must determine the exercise price of the put option on the futures contract that would be equivalent to an exercise price of 86 if there was a put option available on H. Second, he must determine the hedge ratio.

According to assumption 5, a yield of 13 percent for H is roughly equal to 11.5 percent for M. This is found by solving the following equation:

$$13\% = .10 + 1.12 \times (\text{yield on bond } M)$$

Assumption 4 states that when bond *M* yields 11.5 percent, its price is equal to 135. Since the conversion factor is assumed to be 1.42 (by assumption 7), the exercise price for the put option on the futures contract should be as close to 95 (135/1.42) as possible.

The determination of an exercise price of 95 for a put option on the T-bond futures that is roughly equivalent to an exercise price of 86 for a put option on *H*, if such an option were available, fulfills the first part of the twofold mission.

The second part of the mission, finding the hedge ratio, is accomplished by using the four-step procedure we explained in hedging with futures. These steps are described as follows:

Step 1. Assumption 5 gives us the estimate of *b*, the relative yield volatility, for step 1.

Step 2. The price volatility of both *H* and *M* to equal yield changes at their current yield levels must be determined. This is provided in assumption 6.

Step 3. Compute the price volatility after accounting for relative yield volatility by multiplying the relative yield volatility, *b*, as found in step 1 by *H*'s price volatility found in step 2. In our illustration it is:

$$1.12 \times \$.08 = \$.0896$$

Step 4. Divide the quantity found in step 3 by the price volatility for *M* found in step 2 and then multiply this quotient by the conversion factor.[28] The result is the hedge ratio. By assumptions 6 and 7, the hedge ratio is:

$$(\$.0896/\$.10) \times (1.42) = 1.27$$

The hedge ratio of 1.27 means that 1.27 put options on T-bond futures should be purchased per $100,000 of the *H* bond to be hedged.

■ *Conclusion*

In this chapter, we provide the fundamentals of futures and options that the bond portfolio manager should understand in order to use these contracts to control interest-rate risk. It seems to us appropriate to conclude this chapter with the following remark by Gary L. Gastineau, a recognized expert in options:[29]

---

[28] Recall that it is necessary to multiply by the conversion factor because in step 1 the cheapest deliverable bond is used in the regression analysis.

[29] Gary L. Gastineau, "Futures and Options on Fixed Income Securities: Their Role in Fixed Income Portfolio Management," Chapter 39 in *The Handbook of Fixed Income Securities*, ed. Frank J. Fabozzi and Irving M. Pollack (Homewood, Ill.: Dow Jones-Irwin, 1983), pp. 871–72.

Today's effective fixed income manager must understand duration, the nuances of credit-rating systems, bond portfolio immunization, the mathematics of bond yields, and much more. The manager who cannot adapt to new concepts and new techniques will be at a marketing and performance disadvantage. It seems safe to predict that in a few years the manager who does not understand risk-control and risk-adjusted enhancement with futures and options contracts will be obsolete. □

Appendix A: Mathematical Programming Techniques

Mathematical programming refers to a group of management science techniques that may be used to find optimal solutions to problems in which resources are to be allocated so as to attain a maximum or minimum value for an objective function subject to specified constraints. Linear programming, quadratic programming, integer programming, and dynamic programming are all examples of mathematical programming techniques.

Throughout this book, we have cited examples of a portfolio manager seeking to maximize or minimize an objective function subject to a set of constraints. The optimal solution to those problems was obtained by using primarily two mathematical programming techniques, linear programming or quadratic programming. In this appendix, we shall describe these two techniques.

■ The General Mathematical Programming Problem in Portfolio Management

In all mathematical programming problems in portfolio management, there are four steps that are followed. The first step is to define the variables about which a decision must be made. These variables are referred to as *decision variables*. The second step is to specify the objective that the portfolio manager seeks to optimize in mathematical terms. This mathematical expression is termed the *objective function*. The form of the objective function is what differentiates linear and quadratic programming. In the former models, the objective function is linear, while in the latter models it is quadratic. Immunization strategies and cash flow matching, both described in Chapter 6, are examples of portfolio management applications using linear programming. Examples of quadratic programming are the asset allocation problem described in Chapter 4, the methodology for tracking a bond index described in Chapter 5, and the variance/covariance approach for constructing an optimal bond portfolio described in Chapter 7. The objective function may be maximized in applications involving expected return or minimized in applications involving some measure of risk.

The third step is to establish the constraints under which the objective function is to be optimized. The final step is to solve the mathematical programming model. Computer programs to solve linear and quadratic programming problems with linear constraints can be purchased from commercial software vendors.

■ Linear Programming Formulation for Portfolio Management Problems

The general linear programming model in the context of portfolio management problems involving the maximization of expected portfolio return can be stated as follows.

Let

X_i = the proportion of the portfolio invested in security i
r_i = the expected return on security i
N = the number of potential securities
R_p = the expected return on the portfolio

The objective function is then:

$$R_p = r_1X_1 + r_2X_2 + \ldots + r_NX_N$$

In all applications, there will be a constraint restricting the total allocation of funds to be equal to one. That is,

$$X_1 + X_2 + \ldots + X_N = 1$$

Furthermore, if no short-selling is permitted, the following constraints must be imposed:

$$X_i \geq 0 \quad \text{for } i = 1, \ldots, N$$

The other constraints will vary from application to application. For example, there may be constraints imposed on the maximum or minimum concentration that may be allocated to a particular industry or quality sector.

In general, we can express these constraints as follows:

$$C_{1,1}X_1 + C_{1,2}X_2 + \ldots + C_{1,N}X_N \leq b_1$$

$$C_{2,1}X_1 + C_{2,2}X_2 + \ldots + C_{2,N}X_N \leq b_2$$

$$\vdots \qquad \vdots \qquad \qquad \vdots \qquad \vdots$$

$$C_{K,1}X_1 + C_{K,2}X_2 + \ldots + C_{K,N}X_N \leq b_K$$

where

b_j = the concentration limit for the jth constraint
$C_{j,i}$ = the constraint coefficient for security i with respect to the jth constraint
K = the number of constraints

For example, if constraint k is that the total allocated must equal one, then

$$C_{k,1} = C_{k,2} = \cdots = C_{k,N} = b_k = 1$$

If a maximum is imposed on the amount that may be allocated to a security, then the constraint coefficient for that security is one, all others are zero, and b_k is the maximum amount.

It is convenient to express the foregoing model in matrix notation. To do so, we shall use the following notation:

x = a column vector with the elements X_i
r = a column vector with the elements r_i
b = a column vector of constraints b_j
C = a matrix of constraint coefficient elements $C_{j,i}$

that is

$$C = \begin{bmatrix} C_{1,1} C_{1,2} \cdots C_{1,N} \\ C_{2,1} C_{2,2} \cdots C_{2,N} \\ \vdots \quad \vdots \qquad \vdots \\ C_{K,1} C_{K,2} \qquad C_{K,N} \end{bmatrix}$$

and letting a prime (') denote a matrix or vector transpose, the linear programming problem can be expressed as follows:

Maximize:

$$R_p = r'x$$

Subject to

$$Cx \leq b$$

■ Quadratic Programming Formulation for Portfolio Management Problems

The general quadratic programming model in the context of portfolio management problems involves the minimization of portfolio variance. This can be stated as follows.

Let

σ_i^2 = the variance of security i (or, in the case of the asset allocation model, the variance of asset class i)

$\sigma_{i,j}$ = the covariance between security i and security j

Σ = the variance/covariance matrix

σ_p^2 = the variance of the portfolio

Then the general quadratic programming problem can be expressed as:

Minimize:

$$\sigma_p^2 = x' \Sigma x$$

Subject to:

$$Cx \leq b$$

where one of the constraints is a minimum expected portfolio return, $\hat{R}_p$, to be well defined. That is,

$$\hat{R}_p \leq r_1 X_1 + r_2 X_2 + \cdots + r_N X_N$$

In the case of the asset allocation problem and the variance/covariance approach to bond portfolio optimization, it is necessary to generate an efficient frontier to obtain the optimal allocation of funds. This is accomplished by sequentially varying the minimum expected return and finding the minimum variance portfolio consistent with that return. In this way, the entire set of minimum variance portfolios may be traced out. The efficient frontier is then the positively sloped segment of the set of minimum variance portfolios including, of course, the global minimum variance portfolio itself.

Appendix B: Risk of Loss Analysis for Asset Allocation Model

In the process of locating points on the efficient frontier for the asset allocation model we described in Chapter 4, the standard deviation of the optimal portfolio at each point can also be obtained. These values form the basis for determining the probabilities of loss associated with these mixes. In this appendix we shall explain this process which we called *risk of loss analysis*.

If the optimal mixes associated with M values of R are called x_m (m = 1, 2, . . . , M), associated with R_m, the corresponding minimum standard deviations can be called σ_m. Using the matrix notation we adopted in Appendix A, these are related according to

$$R_m = r'x_m$$

and

$$\sigma_m = \sqrt{x_m'\Sigma x_m}$$

Thus R_m and σ_m represent the total expected return and total standard deviation, respectively, based on the individual components r and Σ given for a single time period.

The probability of not achieving the expected return level L with the constrained optimal portfolio with an expected return of R_m,

$$Q = Pr\{R \leq L|x_m\},$$

may now be determined.

This computation requires some assumption about the shape of the distribution of periodic returns R.

Assume that the periodic portfolio returns are lognormally distributed with mean R_m and variance σ_m so that the variable z given by

$$z = \ln(1 + R)$$

will be normally distributed with mean

$$\mu_{z_m} = \ln(1 + R_m)$$

and variance

$$\sigma_m = \ln \left[\frac{\sigma_m{}^2 + (R_m + 1)^2}{(R_m + 1)^2} \right]$$

Under this assumption, the probability of loss for this optimal mix (expected return R_m) with the loss threshold L may then be obtained as follows:

$$Q_m = Pr\{z_m \equiv \ln(1 + R) \leq \ln(1 + L)|x_m\}$$
$$= \frac{1}{2} + \frac{1}{2} erf \left[\frac{\ln(1 + L) - \mu_{z_m}}{\sqrt{2}\,\sigma_{z_m}} \right]$$

where "erf" is the error functional defined as

$$erf(x) = \int_0^x e^{-t^2} dt$$

The probability of loss over t time periods can be obtained using the random walk assumption discussed in Chapter 4. It will be

$$Q_m(t) = \frac{1}{2} + \frac{1}{2} erf \left[\frac{\ln(1 + L) - \mu_{z_m}{}^t}{\sqrt{2}t\,\sigma_{z_m}} \right]$$

which represents the probability of not achieving at least the total return L in t time periods using the optimal mix x_m, which has a total expected return R_m (or tR_m for t time periods) and standard deviation σ_m (or $\sigma_m\sqrt{t}$).

Appendix C: Multiple Scenario Extension for Asset Allocation Model

In Chapter 4, we described how the basic asset allocation model could be extended to multiple scenarios. In this appendix, we shall describe this approach.

Suppose the forecast of the course of future events is to be expressed in terms of N possible scenarios which are discrete or mutually exclusive and to each of which a probability of occurrence P_n, $n = 1, 2, \ldots, N$, is assigned. Suppose, in addition, that the joint distribution of asset returns under each of these possible scenarios is given by $f_n(z)$, where z is the vector of future returns of the J assets over the time period of the forecast. Just as in the case of a single scenario, the expected return of the nth scenario, $\hat{R}_n$, given its occurrence, will be

$$\hat{R}_n = E_n(R(z)) = \iint \ldots \int x'z f_n(z) dz_1 dz_2 \ldots dz_J$$
$$= x' E_n(z)$$

and its standard deviation will be

$$\hat{\sigma}^2{}_{R_n} = E_n[(R(z) - \hat{R}_n)^2]$$
$$= \iint \ldots \int (R_n(z) - R_n)^2 f_n(z) dz_1 dz_2 \ldots dz_J$$
$$= x' \Sigma_n x$$

where *x* is a column vector whose elements are the allocation of the portfolio to security i, and where Σ_n is the covariance matrix among the J assets given the occurrence of the nth scenario. Consider the unconditional distribution (i.e., without knowledge of which scenario will occur), which can be called the composite distribution and identified with the scenario subscript denoted by an asterisk (∗). Since the scenarios are assumed to be mutually exclusive, the composite joint distribution may be written merely as a superposition of the joint distributions of the individual scenarios:

$$f_*(z) = \sum_n P_n f_n(z)$$

This yields immediately the unconditional (or composite) expected return:

$$\hat{R}_* = \iint \ldots \int x'z \left[\sum_n f_n(z) \right] dz_1 dz_2 \ldots dz_J$$
$$= \sum_n P_n \hat{R}_n$$

The variance of the composite distribution requires slightly more effort but may be reduced to

$$\hat{\sigma}_*^2 = E[(R - R_*)^2]$$
$$= \iint \ldots \int \left(\sum_{j=1}^{J} x_j z_j - \hat{R}_* \right) \left(\sum_{k=1}^{J} x_k z_k - \hat{R}_* \right)$$
$$\times \left[\sum_n f_n(z) \right] dz_1 dz_2 \ldots dz_J$$
$$= \sum_n P_n \sum_{j=1}^{J} \sum_{k=1}^{J} x_j x_k \left[\text{cov}_n(z_j, z_k) - (\hat{z}_{jn} - \hat{z}_{j*})(\hat{z}_{kn} - \hat{z}_{k*}) \right]$$

where $\text{cov}_n(z_j, z_k)$ represents the conditional covariance between the assets j and k given the occurrence of scenario n. $\hat{z}_{jn}$ represents the mean return of the jth asset with the nth scenario, and $\hat{z}_{j*}$ is the mean return of the jth asset with the composite scenario, or

$$\hat{z}_{j*} = \sum_n P_n \hat{z}_{jn}$$

The quadratic form $\hat{\sigma}_*^2$ may now be minimized to obtain the constrained optimal mixes at each return level for the composite scenario just as for a single scenario.

The unconditional probability of loss may be readily estimated if the assumption that the distribution of total portfolio returns for each scenario is lognormal is again made. Since the scenarios are mutually exclusive, the distribution of portfolio returns will be the sum of the conditional distributions weighted by the probability of occurrence of each:

$$g_*(z) = \sum_n P_n g_n(z)$$

It follows immediately from the expressions derived for the individual scenarios that the probability of not achieving at least the total return L in t time periods using the optimal mix (for the composite scenario) x_{m*}, which has a total expected return $t\hat{R}_{*m}$ and standard deviation $\hat{\sigma}_{*m}\sqrt{t}$, will be

$$Q_{*m}(t) = \tfrac{1}{2} + \tfrac{1}{2} \sum_n P_n \text{erf} \left[\frac{\ln(1 + L) - \mu_{nz_m}t}{\sqrt{2t}\,\sigma_{nz_m}} \right]$$

where

$$\mu_{nz_m} = \ln(1 + \hat{R}_{nm})$$

and

$$\sigma_{nz_m} = \ln \left[\frac{\hat{\sigma}_{nm}^2 + (\hat{R}_{nm} + 1)^2}{(\hat{R}_{nm} + 1)^2} \right]$$

$\hat{R}_{nm}$ represents the portfolio expected return level for the nth scenario assumptions using the mth optimal mix for the composite portfolio and $\hat{\sigma}_{nm}$ the corresponding portfolio return standard deviation.

Appendix D: Term Structure Analysis*

Term structure of interest rates provides a characterization of interest rates as a function of maturity. As we demonstrated throughout this book, term structure analysis plays a prominent role in many fixed income management strategies. Specifically, we have shown how term structure analysis can be used to price fixed-income securities and thereby serve as a basis for the return enhancement passive strategy described in Chapter 5, the active management strategies described in Chapter 7, and portfolio performance evaluation described in Chapter 7.

The objective in empirical estimation of the term structure is to fit a spot rate curve (or any other equivalent description of the term structure, such as the discount function) that (1) fits the data sufficiently well and (2) is a sufficiently smooth function. The second requirement, being less quantifiable than the first, is less often stated. It is nevertheless at least as important as the first, particularly since it is possible to achieve an arbitrary good (or even perfect) fit if the empirical model is given enough degrees of

---

* This appendix is adapted from Oldrich A. Vasicek and H. Gifford Fong, "Term Structure Modeling Using Exponential Splines," *Journal of Finance*, May 1982, pp. 339–48.

freedom, with the consequence that the resulting term structure makes little sense.[1]

Several methodologies have been proposed to estimate the term structure of interest rates.[2] In this appendix, we shall describe the methodology suggested throughout this book. This approach can be termed an *exponential spline fitting.* The methodology described here has been applied to historical price data on U.S. Treasury securities with satisfactory results. The technique produces forward rates that are a smooth continuous function of time. The model has desirable asymptotic properties for long maturities, and exhibits both a sufficient flexibility to fit a wide variety of shapes of the term structure, and a sufficient robustness to produce stable forward rate curves. An adjustment for the effect of taxes and for call features on U.S. Treasury bonds is included in the model.

We will first provide a brief description of the basic concepts of the term structure, such as spot and forward rates, market-implicit forecasts, and the discount function. This will provide some background for understanding the term structure analysis model.

■ Concepts and Terms

The spot interest rate of a given maturity is defined as the yield on a pure discount bond of that maturity. The spot rates are the discount rates determining the present value of a unit payment at a given time in the future. Spot rates considered as a function of maturity are referred to as the *term structure of interest rates.*

Spot rates are not directly observable, since there are few pure discount bonds beyond maturities of one year. They have to be estimated from the yields on actual securities by means of a *term structure model.* Each actual coupon bond can be considered a package of discount bonds, namely one for each of the coupon payments and one for the principal payment. The price of such component discount bonds is equal to the amount of the payment discounted by the spot rate of the maturity corresponding to this payment. The price of the coupon bond is then the sum of the prices of these component discount bonds. The *yield to maturity* on a coupon bond is the internal rate return of the bond payments, or the discount rate that would equate the present value of the payments to the

---

[1] For a discussion of this point, see Terence C. Langetieg and Stephen J. Smoot, "An Appraisal of Alternative Spline Methodologies for Estimating the Term Structure of Interest Rates," working paper, University of Southern California, December 1981.

[2] Willard R. Carleton and Ian Cooper, "Estimation and Uses of the Term Structure of Interest Rates," *Journal of Finance*, September 1976, pp. 1067–83; J. Huston McCulloch, "Measuring the Term Structure of Interest Rates," *Journal of Business*, January 1971, pp. 19–31; and McCulloch, "The Tax Adjusted Yield Curve," *Journal of Finance*, June 1975, pp. 811–30.

bond price. It is seen that the yield is thus a mixture of spot rates of various maturities. In calculation of yield, each bond payment is discounted by the same rate, rather than by the spot rate corresponding to the maturity of that payment. Decomposing the actual yields on coupon bonds into the spot rates is the principal task of a term structure model.

Spot rates describe the term structure by specifying the current interest rate of any given maturity. The implications of the current spot rates for future rates can be described in terms of the *forward rates*. The forward rates are one-period future reinvestment rates, implied by the current term structure of spot rates.

Mathematically, if R_1, R_2, R_3 . . . are the current spot rates, the forward rate F_t for period t is given by the equation

$$1 + F_t = \frac{(1 + R_t)^t}{(1 + R_{t-1})^{t-1}} \qquad t = 1, 2, 3, \ldots \qquad (1)$$

This equation means that the forward rate for a given period in the future is the marginal rate of return from committing an investment in a discount bond for one more period. By definition, the forward rate for the first period is equal to the one period spot rate, $F_1 = R_1$.

The relationship of spot and forward rates described by Equation (1) can be stated in the following equivalent form:

$$(1 + R_t)^t = (1 + F_1)(1 + F_2) \ldots (1 + F_t) \qquad (2)$$

This equation shows that spot rates are obtained by compounding the forward rates over the term of the spot rate. Thus, the forward rate F_t can be interpreted as the interest rate over the period from $t - 1$ to t that is implicit in the current structure of spot rates.

Just as the forward rates are determined by the spot rates using Equation (1), the spot rates can be obtained from the forward rates by Equation (2). Thus, either the spot rates or the forward rates can be taken as alternative forms of describing the term structure. The choice depends on which of these two equivalent characterizations is more convenient for the given purpose. Spot rates describe interest rates over periods from the current date to a given future date. Forward rates describe interest rates over one-period intervals in the future.

There is a third way of characterizing the term structure, namely by means of the *discount function*. The discount function specifies the present value of a unit payment in the future. It is thus the price of a pure discount riskless bond of a given maturity. The discount function D_t is related to the spot rates by the equation

$$D_t = \frac{1}{(1 + R_t)^t} \qquad (3)$$

and to the forward rates by the equation

$$D_t = \frac{1}{(1 + F_1)(1 + F_2) \ldots (1 + F_t)} \tag{4}$$

The discount function D_t considered in continuous time t is a smooth curve decreasing from the starting value $D_0 = 1$ for $t = 0$ (since the value of one dollar now is one dollar) to zero for longer and longer maturities. It typically has an exponential shape.

While the discount function is usually more difficult to interpret as a description of the structure of interest rates than either the spot rates or the forward rates, it is useful in the *estimation* of the term structure from bond prices. The reason is that bond prices can be expressed in a very simple way in terms of the discount function, namely the sum of the payments multiplied by their present value. In terms of the spot or forward rates, bond prices are a more complicated (nonlinear) function of the values of the rates to be estimated.

The concept of forward rates is closely related to that of the *market-implicit forecasts*. The market-implicit forecast $M_{t,s}$ of a rate of maturity s as of a given future date t is the rate that would equate the total return from an investment at the spot rate R_t for t periods reinvested at the rate $M_{t,s}$ for additional s periods, with the straight investment for t + s periods at the current spot rate R_{t+s}. Mathematically, this can be written as follows:

$$(1 + R_t)^t (1 + M_{t,s})^s = (1 + R_{t+s})^{t+s} \tag{5}$$

The market-implicit forecasts can be viewed as a forecast of future spot rates by the aggregate of market participants. Suppose that the current one-year rate is 12 percent, and that there is a general agreement among investors that the one-year rate a year from now will be 13 percent. Then the current two-year spot rate will be 12.50 percent, since

$$(1 + .1250)^2 = (1 + .12)(1 + .13)$$

The two-year rate would be set in such a way that the two-year security has the same return as rolling over a one-year security for two years. There may not be such a general agreement as to the future rate, and in any case the forecast would not be directly observable. Knowing the current one-year and two-year spot rates, however, enables us to determine the future rate for the second year that would make the two-year bond equivalent in terms of total return to a roll-over of one-year bond. This rate is the market-implicit forecast.

The definition of the market-implicit forecasts as given by Equation (5) is perhaps more intuitive if stated in terms of the forward rates. It is given by the following equation:

$$(1 + M_{t,s})^s = (1 + F_{t+1})(1 + F_{t+2}) \ldots (1 + F_{t+s}) \tag{6}$$

Specifically, the market-implicit forecast of one-period rate is equal to the forward rate for that period,

$$M_{t,1} = F_t$$

It is seen from Equation (6) that the market-implicit forecast is obtained by compounding the forward rates over the period starting at the date of the forecasting horizon and extending for an interval corresponding to the term of the forecasted rate. In other words, the market-implicit forecast corresponds to the scenario of *no change in the forward rates*. The current spot rates then change by rolling along the forward rate series.

One last thing to mention about the market-implicit forecasts is that since it is a forecast of the future spot rates, we can also infer from it the corresponding forecast of yields, discount functions, and all other characterizations of the *future term structure*. The current and future term structures have the forward rates as the one common denominator, which makes the forward rates the basic building blocks of the structure of interest rates.

■ The Model

In specification of the model proposed for estimation of the term structure, we will use the following notation:

t = time to payment (measured in half years)

$D(t)$ = the discount function, that is, the present value of a unit payment due in time t

$R(t)$ = spot rate of maturity t, expressed as the continuously compounded semiannual rate. The spot rates are related to the discount function by the equation

$$D(t) = e^{-tR(t)}$$

$F(t)$ = continuously compounded instantaneous forward rate at time t. The forward rates are related to the spot rate by the equation

$$R(t) = \frac{-d}{dt} \log D(t)$$

n = number of bonds used in estimation of the term structure

T_k = time to maturity of the kth bond, measured in half years

C_k = the semi-annual coupon rate of the kth bond, expressed as a fraction of the par value

P_k = price of the kth bond, expressed as a fraction of the par value.

The basic model can be written in the following form:

$$P_k + A_k = D(T_k) + \sum_{j=1}^{L_k} C_k D(T_k - j + 1) - Q_k - W_k + \epsilon_k$$
$$k = 1, 2, \ldots, n \tag{7}$$

where

$$A_k = C_k(L_k - T_k)$$

is the accrued interest portion of the market value of the kth bond,

$$L_k = [T_k] + 1$$

is the number of coupon payments to be received, Q_k is the price discount attributed to the effect of taxes, W_k is the price discount due to call features, and ϵ_k is a residual error with $E(\epsilon_k) = 0$.

The model specified by Equation (7) is expressed in terms of the discount function, rather than the spot or forward rates. The reason for this specification is that the price of a given bond is linear in the discount function, while it is nonlinear in either the spot or forward rates. Once the discount function is estimated, the spot and forward rates can easily be calculated.

An integral part of the model specification is a characterization of the structure of the residuals. We will postulate that the model be *homoscedastic in yields*, rather than in prices. This means that the variance of the residual error on yields is the same for all bonds. The reason for this requirement is that a given price increment, say $1 per $100 face value, has a very different effect on a short bond than on a long bond. Obviously, an error term in price on a 3-month Treasury bill cannot have the same magnitude as that in price of a 20-year bond. It is, however, reasonable to assume that the magnitude of the error term would be the same for yields.

With this assumption, the residual variance in Equation (7) is given as

$$E(\epsilon_k^2) = \sigma^2 \omega_k, \qquad k = 1, 2, \ldots, n \tag{8}$$

where

$$\omega_k = \left(\frac{dP}{dY}\right)_k^2 \tag{9}$$

is the squared derivative of price with respect to yield for the kth bond, taken at the current value of yield. The derivative dP/dY can easily be evaluated from time to maturity, the coupon rate, and the present yield. In addition, we will assume that the residuals for different bonds are uncorrelated,

$$E(\epsilon_k \epsilon_\ell) = 0, \qquad \text{for } k \neq \ell$$

In specification of the effect of taxes, we will assume that the term Q_k is proportional to the current yield C_k/P_k on the bond,

$$Q_k = q \frac{C_k}{P_k} \left(\frac{dP}{dY}\right)_k, \qquad k = 1, 2, \ldots, n \qquad (10)$$

For the call effect, the simplest specification is to introduce a dummy variable I_k, equal to 1 for callable bonds and to 0 for noncallable bonds, and put

$$W_k = wI_k, \qquad k = 1, 2, \ldots, n \qquad (11)$$

Although more complicated specifications (such as those based on option pricing) are possible, Equation (11) seems to work well with Treasury bonds, which invariably have the same structure of calls five years prior to maturity at par.

We will now turn to the specification of the discount function $D(t)$. Earlier approaches fit the discount function by means of polynomial splines of the second or third order.[3] While splines constitute a very flexible family of curves, there are several drawbacks to their use in fitting discount functions. The discount function is principally of an exponential shape,

$$D(t) \sim e^{-\gamma t}, \qquad 0 \le t < \infty$$

Splines, being piecewise polynomials, are inherently ill suited to fit an exponential type curve. Polynomials have a different curvature from exponentials, and although a polynomial spline can be forced to be arbitrarily close to an exponential curve by choosing a sufficiently large number of knot points, the local fit is not good. A practical manifestation of this phenomenon is that a polynomial spline tends to "weave" around the exponential, resulting in highly unstable forward rates (which are the derivatives of the logarithm of the discount function). Another problem with polynomial splines is their undesirable asymptotic properties. Polynomial splines cannot be forced to tail off in an exponential form with increasing maturities.

It would be convenient if we can work with the logarithm $\log D(t)$ of the discount function, which is essentially a straight line and can be fitted very well with splines. Unfortunately, the model given by Equation (7) would then be nonlinear in the transformed function, which necessitates the use of complicated nonlinear estimation techniques.[4]

A way out of this dilemma is provided by the following approach. Instead of using a transform of the function $D(t)$, we can apply a transform to the *argument* of the function. Let α be some constant and put

$$t = -\frac{1}{\alpha} \log(1 - x), \qquad 0 \le x < 1 \qquad (12)$$

---

[3] See, for example, McCulloch, "Measuring Term Structure of Interest Rates;" and "An Estimate of the Liquidity Premium," *Journal of Political Economy*, February 1975, pp. 95–118.

[4] Langetieg and Smoot, "An Appraisal of Alternative Spline Methodologies."

Then G(x) defined by

$$D(t) = D\left(-\frac{1}{\alpha}\log(1-x)\right) \equiv G(x) \tag{13}$$

is a new function with the following properties: *(a)* G(x) is a decreasing function defined on the finite interval $0 \le x \le 1$ with $G(0) = 1, G(1) = 0$; *(b)* to the extent that D(t) is approximately exponential,

$$D(t) \sim e^{-\gamma t}, \qquad 0 \le t < \infty$$

the function G(x) is approximately a power function,

$$G(x) \sim (1-x)^{\gamma/\alpha} \qquad 0 \le x \le 1$$

(c) the model specified by Equation (7) is linear in G. Thus, we have replaced the function D(t) to be estimated by the approximate power function G(x) which can be very well fitted by polynomial splines, while preserving the linearity of the model. Moreover, desired asymptotic properties can easily be enforced.

If G(x) is polynomial with $G'(1) \ne 0$, then the parameter α constitutes the *limiting value of the forward rates,*

$$\lim_{t \to \infty} F(t) = \alpha$$

Indeed, in that case

$$G(x) = -G'(1)(1-x) + o(1-x)$$

and consequently

$$D(t) = -G'(1) e^{-\alpha t} + o(e^{-\alpha t})$$

as $t \to \infty$. Using polynomial splines to fit the function G(x) will thus assure the desired convergence of the forward rates. The limiting value α can be fitted to the data together with the other estimation parameters.

Let $g_i(x), 0 \le x \le 1, i = 1, 2, \ldots, m$ be a base of a polynomial spline space. Any spline in this space can be expressed as a linear combination of the base. If G(x) is fitted by a function from this space,

$$G(x) = \sum_{i=1}^{m} \beta_i g_i(x), \qquad 0 \le x \le 1 \tag{14}$$

the model of Equation (7) can be written as

$$P_k + A_k = \sum_{i=1}^{m} \beta_i \left(g_i(X_{k1}) + \sum_{j=1}^{L_k} C_k g_i(X_{kj})\right) - q\frac{C_k}{P_k}\left(\frac{dP}{dY}\right)_k - wI_k + \epsilon_k \tag{15}$$

$$E(\epsilon_k) = 0, \qquad E(\epsilon_k^2) = \sigma^2 w_k, \qquad E(\epsilon_k \epsilon_\ell) = 0 \text{ for } k \ne \ell$$

where

$$X_{kj} = 1 - e^{-\alpha(T_k-j+1)} \qquad j = 1, 2, \ldots, L_k$$

The model described by Equation (15) is used in the estimation of the term structure. It is linear in the parameters $\beta_1, \beta_2, \ldots, \beta_m, q, w$, with residual covariance matrix proportional to

$$\Omega = \begin{vmatrix} \omega_1 & & & & \\ & \omega_2 & & & \\ & & \cdot & & \\ & & & \cdot & \\ & & & & \cdot \\ & & & & & \omega_n \end{vmatrix}$$

If we write

$$U_k = P_k + A_k$$

$$Z_{ki} = g_i(X_{k1}) + \sum_{j=1}^{L_k} C_k g_i(X_{kj}), \qquad i = 1, 2, \ldots, m$$

$$Z_{k,m+1} = -\frac{C_k}{P_k}\left(\frac{dP}{dY}\right)_k$$

$$Z_{k,m+2} = -I_k$$

for $k = 1, 2, \ldots, n$, then the least-squares estimate of $\beta = (\beta_1, \beta_2, \ldots, \beta_m, q, w)'$ conditional on the value of α can be directly calculated by the generalized least-squares regression equation

$$\hat{\beta} = (Z'\Omega^{-1}Z)^{-1}Z'\Omega^{-1}U$$

where $U = (U_k)$, $Z = (Z_{ki})$. The sum of squares

$$S(\alpha) = U'\Omega^{-1}U - \hat{\beta}'Z'\Omega^{-1}U$$

is then a function of α only. We can then find the value of α that minimizes $S(\alpha)$ by use of numerical procedures, such as the three-point Newton minimization method.

Once the least-squares values of the regression coefficients $\beta_1, \beta_2, \ldots, \beta_m, q, w$ and the parameter α are determined, the fitted discount function is given by

$$\hat{D}(t) = \sum_{i=1}^{m} \hat{\beta}_i g_i(1 - e^{-\hat{\alpha}t}), \qquad t \geq 0 \qquad (16)$$

As for the spline space, cubic splines were selected as the lowest odd order with continuous derivatives. The boundary conditions are $G(0) = 1$, $G(1) = 0$. The base $(g_i(x))$ should be chosen to be reasonably close to orthogonal, in order that the regression matrix

$$Z'\Omega^{-1}Z$$

can be inverted with sufficient precision.

Although the model is fitted in its transformed version given by Equation (15), it may be illustrative to rewrite it in the original parameter t. In any interval between consecutive knot points, G(x) is a cubic polynomial, and therefore D(t) takes the form

$$D(t) = a_0 + a_1 e^{-\alpha t} + a_2 e^{-2\alpha t} + a_3 e^{-3\alpha t}$$

on each interval between knots. The function D(t) and its first and second derivatives are continuous at the knot points. This family of curves, used to fit the discount function, can be described as the *third order exponential splines.*

Since least-squares methods are highly sensitive to wrong data, a screening procedure should be used to identify and exclude outliers. Observations with residuals larger than four standard deviations should be excluded and the model fitted again. This procedure should be repeated until no more outliers are present.

Appendix E: Derivation of Risk Immunization Measures

In Chapter 6, we presented a measure of immunization risk against an *arbitrary interest rate change.* In this appendix, we shall derive the measure of immunization risk in the single-horizon and multiple liabilities cases. The risk measure represents the variance of the time to payments, and therefore the exposure of the portfolio to relative changes of rates of different maturities. The risk measure developed here is based on second-order conditions for the term structure change (first-order conditions define the duration).

Consider a portfolio at time $t_o = o$ immunized with respect to a given horizon H against parallel rate changes. Let the payments on the portfolio be $C_1, C_2, \ldots, C_m$, paid out at times $s_1, s_2, \ldots, s_m$, and denote by I_o the initial value of the investment,

$$I_o = \sum_{j=1}^{m} C_j P_o(s_j) \tag{1}$$

Here $P_o(t)$ is the discount function under the current interest rates. In terms of the instantaneous forward rates $i(t)$, $t \geq o$, the discount function can be written as

$$P_o(t) = \exp\left(-\int_o^t i(\tau) \, d\tau\right)$$

Suppose now that the forward rates change from $i(t)$ to $i'(t) = i(t) + \Delta i(t)$. The discount function then becomes

$$P_o'(t) = \exp\left(-\int_0^t i'(\tau)\, d\tau\right)$$

$$= P_o(t) \exp\left(-\int_0^t \Delta i(\tau)\, d\tau\right)$$

The change ΔI_H in the end-of-horizon value of the portfolio due to the change $\Delta i(t)$ in the forward rates is then obtained as

$$\Delta I_H = \sum_{j=1}^{m} C_j P_o'(s_j)/P_o'(H) - \sum_{j=1}^{m} C_j P_o(s_j)/P_o(H)$$

$$= \sum_{j=1}^{m} C_j \exp\left(\int_{s_j}^{H} \Delta i(\tau)\, d\tau\right) P_o(s_j)/P_o(H) - \sum_{j=1}^{m} C_j P_o(s_j)/P_o(H)$$

or

$$\Delta I_H = \sum_{j=1}^{m} f(s_j) C_j P_o(s_j)/P_o(H) - I_0/P_o(H) \tag{2}$$

where

$$f(t) = \exp\left(\int_t^H \Delta i(\tau)\, d\tau\right) \tag{3}$$

By expansion of $f(t)$ into Taylor series around the duration $D = H$ of the portfolio we have approximately

$$f(t) = -(t - H) \cdot \Delta i(H) - \tfrac{1}{2}(t - H)^2 \cdot \left(\frac{d(\Delta i)}{dt} - (\Delta i)^2\right)_{t=H} \tag{4}$$

After substitution for $f(t)$ into Equation (2), the change in the end-of-horizon investment value can be written as

$$\Delta I_H = -\Delta_S \cdot \sum_{j=1}^{m} (s_j - H)^2 C_j P_o(s_j)/P_o(H) \tag{5}$$

It follows that

$$\frac{\Delta I_H}{I_H} = -M^2 \Delta_S \tag{6}$$

where

$$M^2 = \sum_{j=1}^{m} (s_j - H)^2 C_j P_o(s_j)/I_0 \tag{7}$$

and

$$\Delta_S = \tfrac{1}{2}\left(\frac{d(\Delta_i)}{dt} - (\Delta i)^2\right)_{t=H} \tag{8}$$

Equation (7) is the risk immunization measure for the single horizon case.

Note that the term proportional to $\Delta i(H)$ in Equation (4) does not appear in the Equation (5) for the terminal value change. This is because the portfolio duration is equal to the horizon length H. Thus, any shift component of the rate change has no first order effect on immunized portfolios.

The quantity Δ_S can be interpreted as the change in the slope of the spot rates (the twist of the yield curve). Indeed, the change in the spot rates is related to the change in the instantaneous forward rates as follows:

$$\Delta R(t) = \frac{1}{t} \int_0^t \Delta i(\tau)\, d\tau$$

If the change in the forward rates is approximately linear,

$$i(t) = a + bt$$

the change in the spot rates is also linear with half the slope.

$$R(t) = a + \tfrac{1}{2}bt$$

We thus have approximately

$$\Delta\left(\frac{dR}{dt}\right) = \frac{d(\Delta R)}{dt} = \tfrac{1}{2}\frac{d(\Delta i)}{dt} = \Delta_S \tag{9}$$

the last approximation being justified by the negligible magnitude of $(\Delta i)^2$.

In the case of multiple liabilities, again let ΔI_H denote the change in the value of the investment at time $H = t_n$ (the date of the last liability), resulting from an arbitrary change $\Delta i(t)$ in the forward rates. After a derivation similar to that which led to Equation (2), the terminal value change can be written as

$$\Delta I_H = \sum_{j=1}^{m} f(s_j) C_j P_0(s_j)/P_0(H) - \sum_{i=1}^{n} f(t_i) A_i P_0(t_i)/P_0(H) \tag{10}$$

where $f(t)$ is again given by Equation (3). Expanding $f(t)$ into Taylor series around the portfolio duration D (which is now in general not equal to the horizon length H) and substituting into Equation (10) yields

$$\Delta I_H = -\Delta_S M^2 I_0/P_0(H) \tag{11}$$

where

$$M^2 = \sum_{j=1}^{m} (s_j - D)^2 C_j P_0(s_j)/I_0 - \sum_{i=1}^{n} (t_i - D)^2 A_i P_0(t_i)/I_0 \tag{12}$$

where D is the duration of the portfolio equal to the duration of the liability stream given by

$$D = \sum_{j=1}^{m} S_j C_j P_0(s_j)/I_0 = \sum_{i=1}^{n} t_i A_i P_0(t_i)/I_0$$

and

$$\Delta_S = \tfrac{1}{2} \exp \left(\int_D^H \Delta i(\tau) d\tau \right) \left(\frac{d(\Delta i)}{d\tau} - (\Delta i)^2 \right) t = D \qquad (13)$$

Equation (12) is the risk immunization measure for the multiple liabilities case and reduces to Equation (8) in the single horizon case. The approximate interpretation of Δ_S as the change in the slope of the yield curve is still appropriate.

Note that while the expansion of f(t) into finite Taylor series and the consequent results such as Equation (5) or (11) are approximations, Equations (2) and (10) are exact.

Index